Sin's Explosion–

Revival or Ruin

by Dr. Jack Van Impe

Jack Van Impe Ministries
P.O. Box J, Royal Oak, Michigan 48068
In Canada: Box 1717, Postal Station A
Windsor, Ontario, N9A 6Y1

ISBN 0-934803-65-X

Dedicated to my devoted wife, whose encouragement and love put iron in my spine so that I spoke out against every evil during my years of ministry; and to my parents—especially my father, who for years spent five hours daily on his knees praying that I would always "cry aloud and spare not in showing the people their transgressions."

This book is also dedicated to all ministers who call sin by its name and refuse to lower their standards, as multitudes of clergymen do today. Concerning such compromise, God says, *Woe unto them that call evil good, and good evil; that put darkness for light and light for darkness; that put bitter for sweet and sweet for bitter* (Isaiah 5:20).

Preacher, it is either black or white—never gray. There is no middle road. May this book help you as you continue to obey God by "reproving, rebuking, and exhorting" saint and sinner when it comes to the lofty standards God has set for one and all in His Holy Word.

Contents

Preface

Forty years ago, God called me to be a revivalist and an evangelist. During four decades my goal has always been to stir the saints and save the sinners. In 800 full-length crusades and more than 260 mass citywide endeavors with crowds totaling 10 million, I stayed on my knees until I felt the anointing of His Spirit.

As a result, the power of God fell in unbelievable ways even during my earliest years of Christian service. At times the power was so overwhelming that altar calls continued for up to four hours. Multitudes stayed and forgot about eating. The presence of the Lord meant more to them than food.

During those two-score years of evangelism, over 600,000 walked the proverbial sawdust trail to trust Jesus.

Today, my heart cries out for even greater exploits for Christ. A genuine, old-fashioned, Holy Spirit-empowered revival has not been witnessed in our land since 1857. Oh, we've had droplets of blessing, but nothing comparable to the revivals of the past where saloons were closed, where theatrical performances were abandoned, and where crime vanished.

Presently, in the midst of all our religiosity, sin has never been more rampant. Mass murder via abortion has taken the lives of millions. Sexual perversion is openly flaunted by homosexuals, bisexuals, and deviant heterosexuals in movies, television, books, and magazines. Furthermore, gay rights activists see to it that parades, promotional programs, and even homosexual churches are a part of every major city.

Crime is sweeping the nation at breakneck speed as 30 percent of the nation's households are victimized by serious crime every year. The U.S. Attorney General says that one in every 16 American families is brutalized by violent crimes such as murder, rape, and aggravated assault. The FBI index also paints a grim portrait: "A murder every 24 minutes; a forcible rape each seven minutes; a robbery every 68 seconds; and an aggravated assault each 51 seconds. The total figures show that a violent crime is committed every 27 seconds, a property crime every three seconds."

An even worse picture of the current scene in our nation is presented in the Doubleday book, *American Averages: Amazing Facts of Everyday Life* by Mike Feinsilber and William B. Mead. The authors report that on an average day in America: (1) 1,282 illegitimate babies are born; (2) 2,740 children run away from home; (3) 1,986 couples divorce; (4) 68,493 teenagers contract venereal disease; (5) 2,900 teenagers become pregnant; (6) 3,231 women have abortions; (7) people drink 90 million cans of beer; and (8) people smoke 1.6 billion cigarettes. I repeat—this is

8

each day, 365 days per year. Dear God, we need revival!

Religion is not the answer. Some of the biggest hate-mongers in the world are religious leaders. In Northern Ireland, the struggle is between the Protestant and Catholic religionists. In India, it is between Hindu and Moslem devotees. But worst of all, it's between Muslim brothers in Iran and Iraq who hate, plunder, pillage, and kill one another because they are of differing denominations (Sunni or Shiite) within Islam. Likewise, religion divides rather than unites us in America.

It is only when the Spirit of God controls the clergy and laity through revival that the dens of iniquity are closed and dregs of society are changed.

The number of atheists has swelled from three million in 1900 to 911 million TODAY. Could our bigoted religionists have contributed to this shocking figure because atheists saw no God in clergy or laity, including Christendom?

Here is another shocking figure: In 1988, the birth rate among Christians will total 78,000 daily while the conversion rate is 14,000. Revival could switch these figures as men become fired up for God and filled with the Spirit.

It takes godliness and holiness to win the lost. Revival must precede the redemption of sinners. In order to become holy, we must become aware of the glory and holiness of God. We must become nothing. Dr. Martyn Lloyd-Jones so convictingly describes this truth:

"During times of revival, there is this awe, this reverence, this holy fear, the consciousness of God in His majesty, His glory, His holiness, His utter purity. And that, as we have seen, leads inevitably to a deep and terrible sense of sin, and an awful feeling of guilt. It leads men and women to feel that they are vile and unclean and utterly unworthy and, above all, it leads them to realize their utter helplessness face-to-face with such a God. Or, like the publican depicted by our Lord in the parable, they are so conscious of all this that they cannot show their faces. They are far back near the door somewhere, beating their breasts and saying, 'God have mercy, on me, a sinner.' The holiness of God, their own utter sinfulness and wretchedness, their own unworthiness makes men realize they have never done anything good at all. Before they thought they had done a great deal, now they see that it is nothing—useless. Like Paul, they begin to talk about it as dung and filthy rags. In their utter helplessness and hopelessness they prostrate themselves and cast themselves upon the love and mercy and compassion of God."

How different Dr. Martyn Lloyd-Jones' views are compared to many of our modern self-esteem, "you-are-somebody" ministries today. No wonder revival is far from our shores.

The pertinent question before us is—how can we have revival? Revival does not occur just by reading the books about Martin Luther, John Wesley, George Whitefield, Charles Finney, D. L. Moody, or Billy Sunday. Nor does revival come by simply reading some of the quotes attributed to these men.

God is the source of these spiritual upsurges that have lifted the world to higher ground and given humanity new hope, strength, and courage. The supernatural is the explanation.

GOD CAN DO IT TODAY. Though sin permeates and inundates the land, God specializes in bringing sinners to himself when sin is rampant. D. M. Panton says, "It was the midnight hour of the Dark Ages that the revival we call the Reformation, breaking out in a monastery, convulsed Europe and changed the history of the world. It was when England was in the throes of demon power and the people sunk into the lowest depravity that the great Revival under Wesley happened. It was when America was invaded with French infidelity and the schools were given over to liberalism and licentiousness that God stepped into the crisis and brought on the Great Awakening."

Yes, God specializes in things thought impossible. He can do what no other can do, and do it when the people of God long for, desire, and are willing to pay the price for revival.

While the price is often days spent in fasting and prayer, and while the hours in the closet with God are often the source and origin of revival, it is equally true that God has used preachers, pulpiteers, and power-packed proclaimers of the gospel to see revival through to its glowing results.

Romans 10:14 declares, *How shall they hear without a preacher?* This is God's way of accomplishing His purposes upon earth. In studying multiplied volumes on the subject of revival, I noticed repeatedly that God uses men—preachers of righteousness.

Skevington Wood mentioned the powerful preaching of both John and Charles Wesley, while Clare G. Weakly stated that Methodism was the direct outcome of their persuasive proclamations.

Numerous historians inform us that George Whitefield was undoubtedly the supreme open-air preacher of all time, whose voice was so powerful that he could be heard for five miles without amplification.

D. W. Bebbington tells us that Spurgeon quickly gained fame for his directness in preaching, which seemed to some to border on irreverence. But the power of his sermons led to multitudes being saved.

Billy Sunday, according to William Warren Street, "stormed up and down the country during the first two decades of the twentieth century, gaining headlines wherever he went. His denunciations of alcohol and saloons played a conspicuous part in his evangelism, and undoubtedly his influence had much to do in making America dry."

This same story about God's revivalist preachers is constantly told in the books dealing with the revivals and revivalists of history.

In fairness, it must be noted that their presentations of truth do not equal the pablum often fed to congregations today. Spineless proclamations that stand for nothing, do nothing. These giants of God acted upon the command of the Holy Spirit who, through Paul, said in 2 Timothy 4:2, *Preach the word; be instant in season, out of season; reprove, rebuke, exhort with all longsuffering and doctrine.*

This kind of preaching, under the unction and filling of the Spirit, produces results. So, preacher, don't just fill time, fill heads and hearts with the thunderings of Sinai against sin and then the truth of grace that liberates the convicted, contrite sinner as he comes to the cross, for *where sin abounded, grace did much more abound* (Romans 5:20).

Because of the abundance of books covering the history of revival and revivalists, and because of being a revivalist-evangelist, I felt that I should do what revivalists do to change lives—and that is to preach. This book, then, contains a total of thirty sermons the Spirit of God has burned into my heart. Each one is preceded by quotes from scores of books on revival. I pray that such God-inspired statements, along with the preaching of the Word, may cause revival fires to burn at least within individual hearts.

Chapter 1

America, We Love You

John the Baptist did well to evade prison for six months. He and Elijah would not last six weeks in the streets of a modern city. They would be cast into a prison or mental home for judging sin and not muting their message.

—Leonard Ravenhill

Paul was not merely a citywide preacher but a citywide shaker.

—Leonard Ravenhill

Why were the false prophets so popular? Well, is it not obvious, their message was this: they said, "Peace, peace," when there was no peace.

—Martyn Lloyd-Jones

Mere preachers may help anybody and hurt nobody; but prophets will stir everybody and madden somebody. The preacher may go with the crowd; the prophet goes against it. A man freed, fired, and filled with God will be branded unpatriotic because he speaks against his nation's sins; unkind because his tongue is a two-edged sword; unbalanced because the weight of preaching opinion is against him. The preacher will be heralded; the prophet hounded.

—Leonard Ravenhill

Many of us in the "Deeper Life" bracket are hunting mice—while lions devour the land.

—Leonard Ravenhill

Revival is that which changes the moral climate of a community.

—A. W. Tozer

Revival is imperative, for the sluice gates of hell have opened on this degenerate generation.

—Leonard Ravenhill

Multitudes came together...The scene was new and passing strange. It baffled description. Many, very many, fell down as men slain in battle, and continued for hours together in an apparently breathless and motionless state, sometimes for a few moments reviving and exhibiting symptoms of life by a deep groan or piercing shriek, or a prayer for mercy fervently uttered.

—Fischer, Reviving Revivals, pp. 165,166

America cannot fall—because she is already fallen! She cannot go into slavery—because her people are fettered at the moment in chains of self-forged, self-chosen moral anarchy. Here are millions, diseased morally, with no longing for healing. Here are men paying for shadows at the price of their immortal souls, men who not only reject the Substance, but who openly sneer at and caricature it.

—Leonard Ravenhill

Evan Roberts was a young man consumed with compassion over a world with no one to weep for it.

—*Pratney*

Arnold Toynbee said, "The only thing we learn from history is that we don't learn from history." Let's not make that mistake.

—Martyn Lloyd-Jones

Righteousness exalteth a nation: but sin is a reproach to any people.

—*Proverbs 14:34*

"My country, 'tis of thee, Sweet land of liberty, Of thee I sing…Long may our land be bright, With freedom's holy light; Protect us by Thy might, Great God, our King."

I love America—the greatest nation on the face of the earth. She has always been a bulwark of liberty and freedom for all, and I pray that this may always be true of my homeland.

My parents left Belgium for "the land of the free and the home of the brave" in 1929, the year of "The Great Depression." During the next 48 months, they experienced extreme deprivation and heartache, eking out a mere existence. Nevertheless, America— even in her worst hour of economic crisis—allowed

Sin's Explosion

Oscar and Louise Van Impe to enjoy a higher standard of living than they had ever known.

Mom and Dad speak with great pride of the glorious day when they became naturalized citizens of the United States of America. The experience has lived in their memories for a lifetime. As their son, I continually thank God for having been born in the land of their dreams.

Yes, the Van Impe family honestly, sincerely, loudly, and dogmatically wants the world to know that we love America! Our feelings can be best expressed by quoting a portion of an editorial which appeared in an issue of *Christianity Today* magazine:

I am American and I am patriotic. I am not a blind patriot, for I am an evangelical whose patriotism is formed by the Bible and tempered by biblical realism. When I fly over New York harbor, I scan the horizon for the lady of liberty. Tears roll down my cheeks and a lump rises in my throat. Without apology, I salute the flag, and pledge my allegiance to my country. I identify with Nathan Hale and regret that I have only one life to give for my country. I pay my taxes [and] vote at (almost) every opportunity. I want to be a good citizen and a loyal American for Christ's sake.

I love America, and I am thankful for this country. Thankful for what? I am thankful that I live in a land: where pilgrim fathers first set foot on these shores in search of freedom to worship God according to the dictates of their conscience; where founding fathers believed that human freedom was worth fighting for; where statesmen first formed a union to preserve those liberties and recognized that all true and legitimate governments are constituted for the welfare of the people; where citizens valued education and dotted this land with schools from kindergarten to university; where leaders risked the existence of this Union to extend its liberty to all races; where courts have gradually implemented these rights to make the law a reality; where women are not slaves, but are honored and protected as persons to whom all rights as full persons must be granted; where we are free to worship God as we choose, and our constitution guarantees that no alien religion or irreligion will be forced upon us in public schools; where one may freely choose his life's work, and jobs are relatively well paid; where one can be a conscientious objector; where we imprint "In God We Trust" on our coins, appoint chaplains, and pray for our congressmen; where educational opportunities are available to all, and higher education to most; where we can vote out of office those who stand for what we deem wrong; where policemen are generally on my side and who consider it their main duty to protect me.

I am an American and proud of my country. I love my country, but because I love it, I seek to improve it; and to improve it, I must judge it. But to weigh and to judge and to seek to improve are not incompatible with patriotism and love of country. Rather, they are expressions of highest love—informed, intelligent, sacrificial love—

biblical love, that is. And so, as a biblically informed patriot, I love America, I honor and, under God, I serve America. God willing, under appropriate circumstances, I might even dare to die for this country.

In Defense of the Flag

"An incident occurred a few years ago on the campus of San Diego State University where a riotous crowd had gathered. Their objective was to take down and destroy the American flag. They were screaming and threatening vengeance on the U.S. government, and menacing any who opposed them.

"A navy veteran who was on his way to a class, saw the riotous crowd. He was a man who had seen service aboard an aircraft carrier in Vietnam. As he weighed 250 pounds, he had undergone tryouts with two national football leagues.

"He calmly walked to the flagpole, took the flag and raised it to the top and then stood there alone for three-and-a-half hours, defying the crowd and defending the flag.

"He said, 'I was born under that flag; I fought under that flag and I am going to college because of what it stands for!'

"Now that veteran not only has the satisfaction of knowing that he defended the flag and that for which it stands, but he was rewarded with the highest award of the Freedoms Foundation. He received the George Washington award and a $5,000 check!"

This article blessed me immensely. I am tired of the punks who do nothing but criticize our nation as they live and loaf off of checks provided by the government. Anyone who believes life to be more enjoyable, worthwhile, and rewarding in a socialistic nation should carefully consider the following report.

Russian Prisoner Update

"The number of Evangelicals being held in Soviet prisons and concentration camps has risen to hundreds, Soviet authorities are bent on destroying the Church of Jesus Christ. They attack believers, interrogate children, raid homes, tear down prayer tents, disrupt services, imprison pastors, confiscate printing equipment, isolate Christian prisoners from their families, and put Christians in psychiatric hospitals.

"Three imprisoned pastors are seriously ill. They were each sentenced to five years hard labor for actively preaching the gospel and evangelizing children and young people.

"Solitary confinement is used to punish prisoners. It is a small, cold cell, often underground, no windows, stone walls and floors. The prisoner is barefoot and stripped to his underwear. Food rations are meager: watery soup and a piece of bread once every other day. Confinement lasts usually 10-15 days. Afterward, the prisoner is so weak physically that he can barely stand. Nevertheless, he is forced to return to work immediately.

"Life in a concentration camp is cruel. Sometimes camp officials order prisoners to beat other prisoners. The beatings are terrible. Even when the prisoner loses consciousness they still keep beating him."

Sin's Explosion

Presently, we hear a lot of griping about our nation. Still, I have personally visited and ministered in 50 nations of the world. Believe me when I say that there is no place like home! Even in this hour of deep economic distress, we are wealthy in comparison to the thousands I saw sleeping in the streets of Cairo, Egypt. That would be the only bed most of them would ever know.

Again, when you and I complain about a few meatless days as we attempt to balance our household budget, we need to remember the millions—yea, approximately one *billion*—who go to bed hungry night after night, wishing for just a handful of rice. This is the picture internationally as millions of laborers receive less than $100 annually in wages. (I often chuckle as I watch the television reports concerning "hungry Americans" because most of the chronic complainers are in the 220-pound category!)

We have been so blessed individually that we seldom stop to thank God for the great nation which has made it possible—America. *U.S. News & World Report* states, "Even in recession and with millions unemployed, the U.S. economy remains unrivaled in the world for its output of goods and services."

No other nation on earth even comes close to the USA in productivity. In fact, just 25 eastern states virtually equal the output of the Soviet Union. California exceeds Africa and Pennsylvania equals Australia in economic power. In one year the United States produces $2.6 trillion in goods and services versus $9.6 trillion for the remainder of the world.

Why has God so blessed America? I believe the answer is that this nation has been basically good, under God.

America's Goodness and Godliness

In Deuteronomy 11:26-28, God says, *Behold, I set before you this day a blessing and a curse; A blessing, if ye obey the commandments of the Lord your God, which I command you this day: And a curse, if ye will not obey the commandments of the Lord your God, but turn aside out of the way which I command you this day, to go after other gods, which ye have not known.*

For decades, pulpits thundered the truth of this text, making and keeping America "one nation, under God." This is what Alexis de Tocqueville witnessed as he traveled throughout our nation. He said, "I sought for the greatness and genius of America in her commodious harbors and her ample rivers, and it was not there.

"I sought for the greatness and genius of America in her fertile fields and boundless forests, and it was not there.

"I sought for the greatness and genius of America in her public school system and her institutions of learning, and it was not there.

"Not until I went into the churches of America and heard her PULPITS aflame with righteousness did I understand the secret of her genius and power.

Sin's Explosion

"America is great because America is good, and if America ever ceases to be good, America will cease to be great."

Yes, our greatness came into being because our foundations and roots were anchored in God and the Bible. For example, the Mayflower Compact, signed November 11, 1620, began, "In the name of God, Amen. We, whose names are underwritten...have undertaken, for the glory of God, the advancement of the Christian faith." Again, the final sentence of the Declaration of Independence contains a declaration upon Almighty God. George Washington, in his first inaugural address, given on April 30, 1789, directed supplications to God for His continued blessings upon the formation of our new government.

America's educational system used the McGuffey Reader for nearly 100 years. This series was loaded with the Word of God. In fact, one story in every four was a biblical narration. Some of the lessons with religious instructions were: "The Hour of Prayer," "Religions, the Only Basis of Society," "Control Your Temper," "The Bible and the Best of Classics," "The Baptism," "The Folly of Intoxication," and "Beware of the First Drink."

Today, through the influence of one loud-mouthed atheist, the Bible has been virtually eliminated from the curriculum of the American educational system. The result? Righteousness has been replaced by debasing and debauching trash—and God has been replaced by Karl Marx!

U.S. News & World Report stated, "A small but determined band of radical teachers is giving college students a different view of history, sociology, political science, and economics. Their target: the American capitalistic system. What do the radicals believe? A majority share the belief that the views of Karl Marx are increasingly applicable to modern life."

If these radicals are correct, it is only because a growing proportion of modern society is beginning to live and act as Mary did. (See chapter 11.)

America's Defilement

By replacing righteousness with trash, and God with Marx, the predicted results are becoming evident. *The Detroit News* recently reported that 10 public schools in that city are "near a state of anarchy." When revolutionaries with Ph.D. degrees teach revolution, revolutionary anarchists are created! Look at the mess humanistic educators have spawned since God has been dethroned in America. Our nation has never been in such a state of degradation and hopelessness. Truly, America is laden with iniquity. The pollution inundating the land centers around:

1. Drunkenness, culturally identified as "alcoholism." Ten million inebriates drink themselves into insensibility on a continual basis while millions more spend *billions* on booze annually.

2. Drug addiction, which mars and scars another 10 million in our nation.

3. Tobacco, which pollutes both lungs and land to the tune of *$10 billion* per year.

4. Gambling, which robs needy millions through governmentally controlled lotteries and mafia-dominated casinos in the amount of *$60 billion* each year.

5. Prostitution and pimping, which spreads disease and shame to nine million Americans every 12 months—and costs $25 to $100 per act.

6. Homosexuality, which seeks to arrogantly, egotistically, blatantly, and publicly boast about its perverted members.

7. Smut peddling, which spreads sexual filth via magazine racks throughout the nation. This satanically inspired garbage is found everywhere—including the corner grocery store! Christians should rise up in arms, boycott establishments loaded with soul-destroying adulterous materials, and patronize the businesses of decent Americans.

8. Immoral lepers, who also plague the nation. As a result, millions are carrying illegitimate babies. Thousands of the victims are 11 to 13 years of age. It appears that high school sex education courses have stimulated rather than educated our children. Young man, young woman, mom and dad, beware—*They that plow iniquity, and sow wickedness, reap the same* (Job 4:8).

9. Abortion, which is the murder of the unwanted babies produced by the immoral lepers. This sin has reached epidemic proportions—claiming 15 million innocent lives since 1973!

10. Euthanasia or "mercy killing," which is also being openly advocated. In fact, Drs. Watson and Crick, the famous Nobel prize-winning discoverers of the DNA molecule, have both recommended the practice. Dr. Crick advocates compulsory death for all at the age 80. *This is the ultimate deed of a depraved society, created by human beings who have decided to play God.*

11. Murder. This age-old sin, born of a wanton disrespect for human life, currently stalks every area of the country, claiming 50,000 victims annually.

12. Robbing and looting, which flood America on a daily basis as one segment of society plunders and pillages the lifetime accumulations of others.

Facing the Facts

I believe that the motion picture and television industries have played a major role in glorifying and thus spreading the decadence described in the preceding paragraphs. In fact, *U.S. News & World Report* quotes David E. Silber, professor of psychology at George Washington University, who states, "There is a lot of evidence to suggest that some people model their behavior on what they observe." Likewise, Roger Ebbert of the *Chicago Sun Times* says, "Recent violent acts in our city have been attributed to the inspiration provided by movies. God save the kids of this generation from the dreams they are storing away."

Ultimately, however, the blame for the present condition of our nation must come to rest at the feet of the individual citizen—particularly the Christian. God has invested him with the responsibility of maintaining the never-ending battle against the world, the flesh, and the devil (see 1 John 2:15-17).

Mortan A. Hill, president of Morality in Media and a member of the Presidential Commission on Obscenity and Pornography, believes that the influence of secular humanism in America has duped the public into believing that it has to accept everything with no right of dissent. He states that millions of Americans have also accepted the philosophy that there is no right or wrong. "We already have federal, state, and local laws making it a crime to traffic in obscenity," says Mr. Hill, "but the public does not care enough to demand law enforcement."

The Road Back to Godliness and Greatness

No nation can continue indefinitely under such sinful circumstances. The Bible says, *Righteousness exalteth a nation: but sin is a reproach to any people* (Proverbs 14:34). Sin can only produce disaster, both for individuals and nations alike. This is why Psalm 9:17 declares, *The wicked shall be turned into hell, and all the nations that forget God.*

The solution? Second Chronicles 7:14: *If my people, which are called by my name, shall humble themselves, and pray, and seek my face, and turn from their wicked ways; then will I hear from heaven, and will forgive their sin, and will heal their land.*

I pray that every Christian reading this message will here and now accept his God-given responsibility to help return America to the godliness and greatness she has known in the past. If we do not, all that we have accomplished through 212 years of "liberty and justice for all" will soon be only history! Yes, Alexis de Tocqueville, you were right. If America ever ceases to be good, she will cease to be great.

As you read the chapters which follow, you will realize that unless a God-sent revival occurs, there is little hope for survival.

Chapter 2

The Devil Made Me Do It

Revivals are dangerous. They are fatal to the kingdom of darkness.

—Pratney

It is not our care, endeavor, or desire to proselyte any from one congregation or society to another. We would not move a finger to do this, even to make 10 thousand such proselytes. Our desire is to proselyte from darkness to light, from Satan to Christ, from the power of Satan unto God. Our one aim is to proselyte sinners to repentance, the servants of the devil to serve the living and true God.

—*Charles Wesley*

The church wardens forbade my preaching and demanded my local license. I said nothing but that I heard them. They were very abusive and said, "You all have the spirit of the devil," mentioning Whitefield, Stonehouse, and me by name.

—Charles Wesley

Sin's Explosion

Then followed not faith but a fearfully increased asceticism, with Whitefield wearing a patched gown, dirty shoes, eating the worst food, "whole days and weeks...spent lying prostrate on the ground...bidding Satan depart from me in the name of Jesus...begging for freedom from those proud hellish thoughts that used to crowd in upon and distract my soul."

—Whitefield, Journals

Lord, even demons are subject unto us in Thy name.

—The Seventy

Should all the hosts of death
And powers of hell unknown
Put their most dreadful forms
Of rage or malice on,
I shall be safe; for Christ displays
SUPERIOR POWER and guardian grace.

—Isaac Watts

Look at Paul in Corinth (Acts 19). Seven men were attempting to use a religious formula over a Gadara-type victim. But slinging theological terms at devil-possessed men is as ineffective as snowballing Gibraltar in the hope of removing it. One man, demon-controlled, was an easy match for these seven silly sycophants.

—Leonard Ravenhill

Christianity is the only religion in the world where a man's God comes and lives inside of him. Paul no longer wrestled with flesh (neither his own nor any other man's); he wrestled "against principalities, against powers, against the rulers of the darkness of this world." Does that shed any light on why this demon said, "And Paul I know?" Paul had been wrestling against the demon powers. (In these modern days this art of binding and loosing that Paul knew is almost forgotten or else ignored.) On the last lap of his earthly pilgrimage, he declared, "I have fought a good fight." Demons could have said amen to that statement for they suffered more from Paul than Paul suffered from them. Yes, Paul was known in hell.

—*Leonard Ravenhill*

Be sober, be vigilant; because your adversary the devil, as a roaring lion, walketh about, seeking whom he may devour.

—*1 Peter 5:8*

In this message we will study the source of sin.

First Timothy 4:1 states, *Now the Spirit speaketh expressly, that in the latter times some shall depart from the faith, giving heed to seducing spirits, and doctrines of devils.* Thus, the Bible pictures the last days as a period of time given over to the reign of demonic spirits.

During the 7-year period of time known as the Tribulation, all the world will turn to devil worship. One of the reasons God will bombard the earth with judgment during the Tribulation Hour is that mankind will have accepted a new religion—one which honors Satan and his army of demons. *Yet* [men] *repented not of the works of their hands, that they should not worship devils* (Revelation 9:20).

Sin's Explosion

Notice that the noun is plural, and therefore means "demons." The two Greek words are *diabolus* and *demonia*. *Diabolus* is the one devil—Satan—and *demonia* means "a plurality of demons." Thus, men will make evil spirits gods in the last days. Already we see the dawning of this frightening era.

The Coming Antichrist

Mankind's increasing infatuation with the spirit world will lead to the appearance of the Antichrist, or world dictator, who will rule over all nations during the Tribulation Hour. Since he comes to power through an international peace plan (see Daniel 9:27), the world will honor him as the substitute for Christ. We should note that the word *antichrist* does not always mean "against Christ." It can also mean "in place of," or "a substitute for the true Christ."

As a result of the Antichrist's peace plan, earth's citizens will respect him. However, they will not realize that Satan has chosen to enter the body of this individual in order that he may hold full sway over them. Second Thessalonians 2:3,4, describes this devil-possessed monarch: *And that man of sin* [shall] *be revealed, the son of perdition; Who opposeth and exalteth himself above all that is called God, or that is worshipped; so that he as God sitteth in the temple of God, shewing himself that he is God.* Verses 8-10 state, *And then shall that Wicked be revealed...whose coming is after the working of Satan with all power and signs and lying wonders, and with all deceivableness of unrighteousness in them that perish.*

The Antichrist will be able to proclaim himself as God because the evil spirit of Satan energizing his body allows him the power to work "signs and lying wonders." The present-day fanatical rush toward demon-inspired activities and the rash of mental cultic groups which leave minds open to the invasion of seducing spirits is but the prelude to that which will soon occur when Satan's personal power dominates the world.

The devil and his malicious demons have long exercised their power to work signs and wonders, causing millions of humans to reject the truth of God's Word and the Lord Jesus Christ. Witchcraft, sorcery, ouija boards, clairvoyants, palm readers, fortune-tellers, tarot cards, numerology, tea leaf readers, crystal gazing, white magic, telepathy, seances, and the perpetrators of astrological charts are either one of two things (and I am giving them the benefit of the doubt): (1) fakes who put on a good show, (2) human beings energized by the demonic forces of the spirit world. A Christian should have nothing to do with the occult in any way, shape, or form! By doing so, he opens himself to demon-inspired influence and the judgment of God.

Deuteronomy 18:10-12 states, *There shall not be found among you any one that...useth divination* [fortune-telling], *or an observer of times* [astrological charts and horoscopes], *or an enchanter* [magicians having to do with real magic backed by evil spirits as opposed to "the hand is quicker than the eye" form], *or a witch, or a charmer, or a consultor with familiar spirits* [mediums possessed with a spirit or guide—even under the guise of religion, such as spiritualism which is really spiritism], *or a wizard* [a clairvoyant or psychic], *or a necromancer* [a medium who consults with the dead]. ***For all that do these things are an abomination unto the Lord*** (emphasis mine). Bishop Pike forgot to read these verses prior to departing on the venture which led to his death.

Leviticus 19:26 warns, *Ye shall not...use enchantment, nor observe times.* Away with those astrological charts and horoscopes! Obey God. *Regard not them that have familiar spirits, neither seek after wizards* [clairvoyants and psychics], *to be defiled by them: I am the Lord your God* (vs. 31).

Who said it? God did! Forget your parapsychology, ESP, and all the other forms of mind conditioning. Give your life to Jesus and let Him take care of your future! He came that all men might have an abundant life (see John 10:10) and has promised never to leave or forsake those who put their trust in Him (see Hebrews 13:5). [But] *the soul that turneth after such as have familiar spirits, and after wizards, to go a whoring after them, I will even set my face against that soul, and will cut him off from among his people* (Leviticus 20:6). God said it, not me. I cannot and will not change God's message against these unbiblical, unholy practices!

In 1 Chronicles 10:13, we find that King Saul of Israel *died for his transgression which he committed against the Lord, even against the word of the Lord, which he kept not...*[What was the horrible sin for which he died?]...*for asking counsel of one that had a familiar spirit, to enquire of it.* Yes, Saul went to a demon-possessed fortune-teller to peer into his future.

Christian, this is a dangerous business! Unsaved man, woman, boy, or girl, dealing with the spirit world and purchasing all the garbage sold in the occult stores can only bring you into league with the devil and his vile, malicious spirits who will delight in wreaking havoc and misery in your life! Heed the admonition of the great Prophet Isaiah, *And when they shall say unto you, Seek unto them that have familiar spirits, and unto wizards that peep, and that mutter: should not a people seek unto their God?* (Isaiah 8:19). The answer for all—Christian and the unbeliever alike—is to turn to the Almighty, not demon-controlled humans.

The reason I am speaking out so boldly is that the world in which we live is full of Satan's victims who "innocently" started out with a ouija board which spelled out weird words and frightening messages. Demon influence found its beginning with this seemingly harmless fascination, but now holds these individuals in its terrifying grasp. Additional millions are tampering with their precious God-given minds through the use of drugs and Oriental meditation cults. Little do they realize that they are exposing themselves to demons who will give them a false peace through calm, easy, lighthearted feelings and "new" religious experiences. Witness Timothy Leary for example. Many claim that while under the influence of LSD they were brought "closer to God."

What these individuals do not know is that Satan— the slimy serpent, that great dragon, the archdemon and devil—is the god of this world (see 2 Corinthians 4:4). He is able to appear "as an angel of light" and give one the greatest religious, goose-pimpled feeling he has ever experienced. However, it is but the religion of the pit which caters only to the flesh. Don't depend on feelings which demons produce. Rely strictly on God's program of faith: [For] *without faith it is impossible to please him* (Hebrews 11:6).

Demons and Their Power

Because of the supernatural characteristics and powers possessed by demons, one immediately becomes vulnerable when he toys with Satan and his hosts—even when doing so "in fun" or "out of curiosity." Beware!

Lucifer, the prince of the fallen angels or demons, and his co-workers have basically the same characteristics.

First, they are personalities, not mere influences alone (see Mark 1:25). They also possess intelligence (see Matthew 12:44,45) and speak. The unclean spirit speaking through the man he possessed in Mark 1:24 cried out, *Let us alone; what have we to do with thee, thou Jesus of Nazareth?*

A similar situation occurred while I was preaching in Sioux City, Iowa. During the message, a woman stood to her feet and cried, "Lies, lies, lies!" Normally, she would not have done this as she was a very timid person. She stated that she didn't know what had possessed her.

In a San Bernardino, California meeting, a young man went completely berserk and began crying out all kinds of evil statements. I immediately realized that a demon was in him.

Likewise, as my father began closing a service in Ann Arbor, Michigan, one of the deacons of a fundamental church stood to his feet and said, "Cut out the invitation. We don't want invitations here." Later, the deacon came to Dad with tears in his eyes and said, "That wasn't me. I don't know what happened."

Not only can demons influence people, they can actually use the vocal cords of human beings. In fact, the Hebrew Old Testament word *egastromuthos* means "a ventriloquist demon."

Demons also possess the ability to deceive. Revelation 12:9 states that Satan deceives the entire world. In addition, demons can afflict one physically. In 2 Corinthians 12:7, Paul states, *There was given to me a thorn in the flesh, the messenger of Satan to buffet me.* They also have the power to bind multitudes with a spirit of infirmity (see Luke 13:11). Demons also hinder (see 1 Thessalonians 2:18) and lie (John 8:44 says that Satan is the father of all lies).

One important function of the demons' work is to get Christians to believe lies. How often Christian workers believe the gossip of church members concerning the pastor or other believers. In such cases, the demon is not only behind the lie, but behind the wicked mind which readily accepts it. Don't believe the carnal tales emanating from the lips of some church members. First Timothy 5:19 warns, *Against an elder receive not an accusation, but before two or three witnesses.* Again I say, do not let demon influence ruin your church just because one member accepts the lie a satanic spirit has placed in his mind. *Submit yourselves therefore to God. Resist the devil, and he will flee from you* (James 4:7).

Sin's Explosion

Demons also sap the strength of Christians, or in modern English, they "put them through the mill" via trials and tribulations (see Luke 22:31,32). Then, too, they work through the minds of human beings to create periods of depression, self-torture, and even suicide. Read Mark 5 carefully. The man of Gadara was possessed by demons that caused him to run through the local graveyard naked, cut himself with stones, and live in constant torment (vss. 2-5).

Defeating Demons

Now that we fully realize the awesome powers demons possess, let's talk about those things they CAN'T do. We begin by discovering that Satan and his henchmen can't make one do anything his mind rejects. Flip Wilson had it wrong when he said, "The devil made me do it," for God's Word says, *Every man is tempted, when he is drawn away of his own lust, and enticed* (James 1:14). Knowing this, Satan's hell-bound cohorts plant thoughts of stealing, vow breaking, swearing, coveting, revenge, deceit, seduction, jealousy, slander, gossip, greed, hording, anger, discouragement, drinking, drugs, fornication, adultery, orgies, and even sickness in the human mind. The flesh reacts through the mind-gate or mental processes and BANG—the individual caught unprepared or unawares responds by committing the demon-inspired act. However, if one resists the devil and his workers of iniquity through a mind given over to pure thinking, victory begins immediately.

Perhaps someone reading this message is sick—not because of a virus or other natural cause, but as a result of living in obedience to the thoughts placed in his mind by this mafia of the spirit world. Because he constantly thinks he is sick, he is! He has been trapped by responding to the power of suggestion. If one "is what he eats," surely one can also "become what he thinks." One can actually live an entire life of misery just by listening to and believing in the wrong advice. When the Lord Jesus Christ was tempted by Satan in Matthew 4, His response was quick and to the point—*Get thee hence, Satan* (vs. 10). Try it, and realize the difference!

If one continues heeding the advice of an evil spirit, that spirit will bring in reinforcements and soon possess him (see Matthew 12:44,45). As a result, he may be led into further depravity, perhaps even becoming a murderer. What? That's right. Jesus said in John 8:44, [Satan] *was a murderer from the beginning.* Whom did he murder? Although he didn't perform the act personally, he placed the desire in Cain's heart to murder his brother, Abel (see Genesis 4:8). Likewise, Satan's buck privates are capable of invading minds to induce thoughts of murder and suicide.

In Matthew 17:15, a man came to Jesus saying, *Lord, have mercy on my son: for he is lunatick, and sore vexed: for ofttimes he falleth into the fire, and oft into the water.* In other words, this man's son had tried to commit suicide by throwing himself into the fire and through attempted drowning. What was the Saviour's answer? Did He advise the man to wait another 1,900 years until Dr. Sigmund Freud began a movement which would produce psychologists and psychiatrists? No! *And Jesus rebuked the devil; and he departed out of him: and the child was cured from that very hour* (vs. 18).

Praise God, *(The weapons of* [the Christian's] *warfare are not carnal* [of this world], *but mighty through God to the pulling down of strong holds;) Casting down imaginations, and every high thing that exalteth itself against the knowledge of God, and bringing into captivity every thought to the obedience of Christ* (2 Corinthians 10:4,5).

In closing this message, let's consider these additional questions: Were Jerusalem, Capernaum, and the cities of Samaria and Galilee filled with mentally depressed people? Were they just overworked and overtaxed physically? Were they all suffering from nervous frustration and exhaustion? A million times no! Granted, a great deal of that which takes place in one's life is the result of his running at a rapid pace without ever taking time to slow down. Still we preachers do a great service for the devil when we promote psychiatry and psychology as the answer to every problem and ill of mankind.

Remember—the same demons who ran rampant in Christ's day are as alive and active today as they were then. Demons do not die. Thus, Satan and his evil army remain as powerful and determined as ever. Their purpose and their methodology have not changed. Oh, how we need to resist the devil in this twentieth century!

Too many believers think that the battle is finished, and fail to heed the admonition of 1 Peter 5:8, *Be sober, be vigilant; because your adversary the devil, as a roaring lion, walketh about, seeking whom he may devour.*

Yes, this present world system is literally filled with wicked spirits—and no unconverted, unsaved, irreligious psychiatrist will ever be able to exorcise a demon! I have met many psychiatrists who appear to need psychiatric treatment themselves. Most of them are unsaved men following the program of a wicked Freud who probably could have used a good old-fashioned dose of exorcism in his own life. Thank God for every Christian psychiatrist and psychologist who recognizes problems resulting from demonic powers and then helps his patient both physically and spiritually.

As a final note, may I emphasize that only the unsaved can be demon possessed. Christians can only be influenced mentally. Still, it is important to realize that the results can become overwhelming.

What is the answer? To the unsaved, I say, "Please, come to Jesus today." When one receives Christ as personal Saviour, the Holy Spirit comes to dwell within his body and the new convert becomes a partaker of the divine nature (see 2 Peter 1:4). The Holy Spirit and a demon cannot dwell within the same body. There is no room for both, and any demon or demons present will be forced to flee. That's why 1 John 4:4 says, *Ye are of God, little children* [newborn Christian], *and have overcome them* [Satan and his evil spirits]*: because greater is he that is in you, than he that is in the world.*

Oh, unbeliever, you have suffered long enough. Believe the message of Christ's cross and His blood shed for the forgiveness of your every sin. Trust Him as your Saviour and Deliverer.

Sin's Explosion

To those Christians who find themselves influenced through thought patterns and suggestions, I say, "Resist the devil in your thought life, calling upon the name of the Lord Jesus Christ." James 4:7 states, *Submit yourselves therefore to God. Resist the devil, and he will flee from you.* Psalms 19:14 and 139:23,24 are also good verses to memorize.

Finally, brethren, whatsoever things are true, whatsoever things are honest, whatsoever things are just, whatsoever things are pure, whatsoever things are lovely, whatsoever things are of good report; if there be any virtue, and if there be any praise, think on these things (Philippians 4:8). Let's get on our knees. Let's get into God's Word. Therein lies victory and therein lies deliverance and revival. Without victory and revival, the sins discussed in the following chapters will continue to permeate the lives of millions as satanic forces continue to enslave the masses.

Chapter 3

Pornography, the Eyegate to Perversion

Preachers who do not have the courage or the conviction or the devotion to preach hard against sin, rationalize and excuse their failure.

—John R. Rice

Every preacher should PREACH against sin because he must be against sin.

—John R. Rice

There are preachers who are hobbyists, preachers who have gone off on a tangent, who preach "believe," but do not preach "repent." They preach only one side of the truth. They preach a mutilated Bible, a one-sided gospel, an emasculated message.

—John R. Rice

A revivalist was likely to be drastic, radical, possibly at times violent, and the curious crowd that gathered to watch him work soon branded him as extreme, fanatical, negative. And in a sense they were right. He was single-

minded, severe, fearless, and these were the qualities the circumstances demanded.

—*A. W. Tozer*

A baptism of holiness, a demonstration of godly living is the crying need of our day.

—**Duncan Campbell**

The work of regeneration; the Holy Spirit of God doing a work down in the very depths of the personality, and putting there a new principle of life, something absolutely new, so that there is the "new man." Now that, always, is a doctrine that comes out in every period of revival and of reawakening.

—*A. W. Tozer*

This overwhelming sense of God bringing deep conviction of sin is perhaps the outstanding feature of true revival.

—**Pratney**

Dearly beloved, I beseech you as strangers and pilgrims, abstain from fleshly lusts, which war against the soul.

—*1 Peter 2:11*

The epitaph of the twentieth century may be, "They gained their rights except the right to live." This was my opening statement on the nationwide special, entitled "The AIDS Cover-Up."

Furthermore, I stated, "The Statue of Liberty may become the most expensive tombstone in history between 1993 and 1997." Why? *U.S. News & World Report* stated, "If there is not a cure for AIDS within the next thirteen years, tens of millions will die."

History may record the event as follows, "Here lies the greatest civilization ever developed upon this earth. This civilization died not as a result of external crumbling of the character of its people. The phenomenon was more in the nature of suicide than murder. The people had become so luxury-loving and soft that they would not exert themselves to protect their bodies or their country.

"Here lies the nation that abandoned the faith of its fathers, who had made it great, for the cynical skepticism and atheism of its enemies. Here lies the nation that died from loss of faith in God, loss of pride and confidence in itself, and loss of will to defend itself against both its internal problems and external enemies.

"Here lies a people who abandoned their priceless heritage of patriotism, religious faith, and truth for socialism, sex, and drugs.

"Here lies the United States."

On the Precipice of Disaster

Don't misunderstand me. I love my country. And while I love America, I know that our nation is on the precipice of disaster. I agree with Rev. Del Fehsenfeld Jr. who states, "In 212 years, the United States grew from infancy to greatness. And in the last 25 years, the nation has begun to slide toward destruction." What went wrong? Rev. Fehsenfeld tells us:

Sin's Explosion

"God honors and blesses those nations and people who honor and obey Him. First Samuel 2:30 says, *Them that honour me I will honour, and they that despise me shall be lightly esteemed.*

"*Righteousness exalteth a nation: but sin is a reproach to any people*, states Proverbs 14:34. Psalm 33:12 reads, *Blessed is the nation whose God is the Lord.* Proverbs 29:2 declares, *When the righteous are in authority, the people rejoice: but when the wicked beareth rule, the people mourn.*

"Under all of the cosmetic laughing on our television screens, the American people in this hour are mourning and grieving—with a divorce rate now reaching 55 percent, pornography a $2-billion-a-year industry in the United States, and marijuana production/sales one of the top three corporations in receipts last year. In the United States of America, the people are mourning and grieving because they are no longer experiencing the beauty and the refreshing of the presence of God. They have forsaken God's commandments and have forgotten the God of the Bible.

"God has promised ultimate destruction, disaster, and judgment on any people or nation who forgets Him. When the people refuse to obey His commandments and honor Him, according to Psalm 9:17, *The wicked shall be turned into hell, and all the nations that forget God.* God told the Israelites that if they ever forgot the Lord their God and followed other gods (which America has done in pursuing the gods of sex, money, and humanism), they would surely be judged (see Deuteronomy 11:28). Years later, when Israel turned away from God, this indeed came true.

The Eyegate to Perversion

"God also places nations under captivity when they decay morally and become spiritually confused and politically corrupt.

"God lifts up and tears down nations at His own good pleasure for His own purposes. The key is the heart response of the people toward Him. God destroyed Sodom and Gomorrah, but He set Israel free. Why? Israel repented. Sodom and Gomorrah did not."

I agree totally with Rev. Fehsenfeld's scriptural conclusions.

The Root of Sexual Immorality

Furthermore, may I at this point show you clearly, plainly, and conclusively just what sins are dragging America down to destruction, devastation, disease, and death? We begin with the sin that leads to every immoral and indecent act ever committed—namely, pornography. As we deal with this abomination, please notice that pornography is one of the signs pointing to Christ's soon return.

Jesus said in Matthew 24:37, *But as the days of Noe* [Noah] *were, so shall also the coming of the Son of man be.* In order to comprehend what Christ meant in this text, one must consider Genesis 6:1, 2, and 5, *And it came to pass, when men began to multiply on the face of the earth, and daughters were born unto them, that the sons of God saw the daughters of men that they were fair; and they took them wives of all which they chose. And God saw that the wickedness of man was great in the earth, and that every imagination of the thoughts of his heart was only evil continually.*

What was the root of the sexual problems in Noah's day? Simply stated, "Lustful eyes!" You see, sin begins in the eye of the beholder. That's why God says, *Whosoever looketh on a woman to lust after her hath committed adultery with her already in his heart* (Matthew 5:28). Second Peter 2:14 declares, [They have] *eyes full of adultery, and that cannot cease from sin.* A look often leads to lust and *when lust hath conceived, it bringeth forth sin: and sin, when it is finished, bringeth forth death* (James 1:15). This is why 1 John 2:15-17 warns, *Love not the world, neither the things that are in the world. If any man love the world, the love of the Father is not in him. For all that is in the world, the lust of the flesh, and the lust of the eyes, and the pride of life, is not of the Father, but is of the world. And the world passeth away, and the lust thereof: but he that doeth the will of God abideth for ever.*

Because of the damage lust does to one's body and soul, Christians are to abstain from fleshly lusts which war against the soul (see 1 Peter 2:11). We are to walk in the Spirit and not fulfill the lusts of the flesh (see Galatians 5:16). Obviously, then, Christians should battle pornographic filth with all the vim, vigor, vitality, and strength they have—for it is dehumanizing and soul-destroying!

A Soldier in Christ's Army

Since morality is the essence of God's Ten Commandments, as well as the entire teaching of the Holy

Bible, Christians should be crusaders in the battle against the world, the flesh, and the devil. Paul cries out in Ephesians 6:11, *Put on the whole armour of God, that ye may be able to stand against the wiles of the devil.* How sad to see many pornographic bookstores within a few doors of gospel-preaching churches! Does Rev. Milquetoast do anything about it? No! He wants peace with the world—an armistice with iniquity! This is contrary to the Almighty God who, in Isaiah 58:1, demands that His servants, *Cry aloud, spare not, lift up thy voice like a trumpet, and shew my people their transgressions.*

Yes, ministers are to preach the Word (not just little soothing nuggets of truth, but the condemnatory passages as well!) that reproves, rebukes, and exhorts (see 2 Timothy 4:2). However, many clergymen do not have enough backbone to take a chiropractic adjustment, and therefore never speak out against sin, debauchery, depravity, and the dens of pornography that inundate their communities. They are at peace with the world and it matters not that little 3- to 12-year-old girls are seduced, abused, and destroyed.

Preacher, deacon, church leader—get a glimpse of the abominable pornography currently flooding America via newsstands and the theater. Then get a vision of what you as a soldier in Christ's army should do. I say with the songwriter, "Onward Christian soldiers, Marching as to war. With the cross of Jesus, Going on before. Christ, the Royal Master, Leads against the foe, Onward, then, ye soldiers, See His banner flow." Oh, make a decision today to march against the hosts of hell!

The Results of Pornography

Next let's look at the results of pornography via magazines and movies. Because the "lust of the eyes" was rampant in Noah's day, we discover that *all flesh had corrupted his way upon the earth* (Genesis 6:12). Soon their sexual escapades caused judgment to fall from heaven in the form of a flood. Has God changed? No! Soon Jesus Christ will return and then the most horrendous period of judgment the nations have ever known will inundate the world. However, even before that hour arrives, sin is being punished. God says, "They that plow iniquity and sow wickedness reap the same."

Today, 30 million Americans are being judged—not by a flood but by a vile, loathsome disease, called herpes simplex II. The total may reach 50 million in the near future, and once one has herpes, they have it for life. *Time* magazine said, "The herpes plague is altering sexual rites in America, changing courtship patterns, sending thousands of sufferers spinning into months of depression and self-exile, and delivering a numbing blow to the one-night stand!" They concluded that herpes may be ushering a reluctant, grudging chastity back into fashion. It is painful, indeed, for worldlings to have to admit that Bible-believing Christians may have been right, after all, about the dangers and the wages of sin!

A New York therapist states, "People are beginning to realize that romance is what relationships are all about. They're disillusioned with free sex and terrified of getting herpes and having it forever!" Prostitutes brag about how many men they have infected. In Atlantic City, one harlot laughs as she exclaims, "I bet me and my sister must have given herpes to a thousand guys!" The person who picks up the disease from an unholy relationship suddenly finds himself blasted with two disasters—the revealing of his unfaithfulness and a lifelong disease as a memento of the event.

John Leo in the same *Time* magazine article writes, "Many people who contract herpes go through stages similar to those of mourning for the death of a loved one—shock, emotional numbing, isolation and loneliness, sometimes serious depression and impotence."

Recently, on the medicine page of *Newsweek* magazine, doctors told of "the misery of herpes," calling it a "virus of love," an insidious VD that feels like a soldering iron against the skin. They describe the sores, blisters, fever, muscle aches, and swollen lymph glands.

The editor of *Time* magazine writes, "On rare occasions, herpes in the tri-geminal ganglia will journey to the brain, where it causes a generally fatal form of encephalitis. Or, in about a half-million cases per year, it will journey to the eye and can seriously damage vision if left untreated. Or it may travel to the spinal cord causing a mild form of meningitis."

Well, sin always has its payday. The wages may be delayed, but are always paid—either in this life or in the life to come. Is it any wonder that God says in Numbers 32:23, *Be sure your sin will find you out*?

Presently, everyone is alarmed. Women are furiously spraying their bathrooms with Lysol. Others are lecturing their husbands on the virtues of chastity. Men are frantically trying to find a way of explaining why they are blighted with sores and fever. Wild suggestions fill the air; none of them curing herpes. People are trying seaweed applications, earwax, snake venom, baking soda, bleach, yogurt, and carburetor fluid in an effort to kill the germ. Yet, the bug lives on! A Washington doctor states, "Everything from the full moon to poultices has met with failure."

The Threat of AIDS

Until now, herpes was our most frightening disease. However, herpes is nothing compared to AIDS. In the near future, America and the entire world will face the greatest plague in history as millions upon millions die. The World Health Organization predicts that 100 million will be infected with the AIDS virus by 1991. They add that if it begins its deadly spread throughout the Orient and South America, the number infected may reach 150 million within *48 months*. In America alone, there will be 15 million victims. When the carnage and chaos occurs in horrifying rapidity by 1997, the Statue of Liberty may become the most expensive tombstone in history.

World leaders are stunned. One stated, "Thirty-five years from now, in 2020, the last human could be expiring on this earth from AIDS."

It looks like the Tribulation Hour is just around the corner. There is no doubt in my mind that the AIDS epidemic may fulfill the prophecy of Revelation 16:10,11, *And the fifth angel poured out his vial upon the seat of the beast; and his kingdom was full of darkness; and they gnawed their tongues for pain, and blasphemed the God of heaven because of their pains and their sores.*

The plague has already begun. Mankind is already crying out, *The thing which I greatly feared is come upon me* (Job 3:25), and *My skin is broken, and become loathesome* (Job 7:5).

And worst of all, 2 Chronicles 36:16 states, *The wrath of the Lord arose against his people, till there was no remedy.* It's here. How astonishing to hear doctors say, "You have AIDS and there is NO REMEDY."

I believe that AIDS could be the final plague mentioned in Revelation 6:8. However, since the explanation is a complete discussion in itself, I ask you to study chapter six carefully.

I personally believe that this description of lust, lewdness, and licentiousness indicates that Christ's return to judge the world is near. Why? Revelation 9:21 describes earth's inhabitants prior to Christ's appearance or return to earth. When He comes, debauchery reigns as the immoral refuse to repent "of their fornication" (or continuous episodes of adultery and perversion). The sign is with us! Jesus *is* coming soon!

Chapter 4

Hollywood's Barnyard Morals

Revival is a divine attack on society.

—Pratney

*The true prophet came, and he searched, and he probed,
and he condemned, and he rebuked.*

—*Leonard Ravenhill*

Preach the word; be instant in season, out of season;
reprove, rebuke, exhort with all longsuffering and doctrine.

For the time will come when they will not endure
sound doctrine; but after their own lusts shall they
heap to themselves teachers, having itching ears.

—2 Timothy 4:2,3

*Holiness-teaching contradicted by unholy living is the
bane of this hour! "A holy minister is an awful weapon in
the hands of God."*

—*Robert Murray McCheyne*

Sin's Explosion

Dr. R. A. Torrey preached against the dance, preached against the theater, preached against the lodges. Dr. Torrey preached a literal hell, a place of eternal punishment for Christ-rejecting sinners. Oh, the revival that swept around the world under the marvelous preaching of this great Bible teacher-evangelist, R. A. Torrey!

—John R. Rice

The whole blame for the present international degeneration and corruption lies at the door of the Church! It is no longer a thorn in the side of the world.

—*Leonard Ravenhill*

Many times great numbers of persons in a community will be clothed with this power, when the very atmosphere of the whole place seems to be charged with the life of God. Strangers coming into it and passing through the place will be instantly smitten with conviction of sin and in many instances converted to Christ.

—Wallis, In the Day of Thy Power, pp. 71

Cry aloud, spare not, lift up thy voice like a trumpet, and shew my people their transgression, and the house of Jacob their sins.

—*Isaiah 58:1*

Love not the world, neither the things that are in the world. If any man love the world, the love of the Father is not in him. For all that is in the world, the lust of the flesh, and the lust of the eyes, and the pride of life, is not of the Father, but is of the world. And the world passeth away, and the lust thereof: but he that doeth the will of God abideth for ever.

—*1 John 2:15-17*

The return of the Lord Jesus Christ is imminent. Every sign Christ gave regarding His return to this earth is already in progress. Let's consider a few of these outstanding predictions found in Matthew 24:37. Jesus said, *But as the days of Noe were, so shall also the coming of the Son of man be.*

In order to comprehend what Christ meant in this text, one must consider Genesis 6:1-11, where the Noahic period of history is described. Here one finds the following words:

And it came to pass, when men began to multiply on the face of the earth, and daughters were born unto them, that the sons of God saw the daughters of men that they were fair; and they took them wives of all which they chose. And the Lord said, My spirit shall not always strive with man, for that he also is flesh: yet his days shall be an hundred and twenty years. There were giants in the earth in those days; and also after that, when the sons of God came in unto the daughters of men, and they bare children to them, the same became mighty men which were of old, men of renown.

And God saw that the wickedness of man was great in the earth, and that every imagination of the thoughts of his heart was only evil continually. And it repented the Lord that he had made man on the earth, and it grieved him at his heart. And the Lord said, I will destroy man whom I have created from the face of the earth; both man, and beast, and the creeping thing, and the fowls of the air; for it repenteth me that I have made them. But Noah found grace in the eyes of the Lord.

These are the generations of Noah: Noah was a just man and perfect in his generations, and Noah walked with God. And Noah begat three sons, Shem, Ham, and Japheth. The earth also was corrupt before God, and the earth was filled with violence.

What a sordid story! Is it any wonder God rained judgment down upon the antediluvian society? They took wives of all which they chose because every imagination of the thoughts of their hearts was evil continually. The result—they corrupted the entire world of their day and made it an extremely violent place to live. But wait. Before we condemn them, let's look at ourselves. We are as bad, or worse, than they ever were. The sins that dominated their society then permeate ours today as well.

Sin in Noah's Day

First, they chose wives (plural). One woman was not enough for them. They married, divorced, married, divorced and kept score. As wicked as they were, they probably never had as many mates, concubines, or adulterous affairs as some of our Hollywood stars. These adulterers set the stage, play the role, and brainwash the public into glorifying immorality. Love them and leave them is their hue and cry. God help us.

Is it right? NO! Jesus set standards that will never be abrogated. He said in Matthew 19:4-9, *Have ye not read, that he which made them at the beginning made them male and female, and said, For this cause shall a man leave father and mother, and shall cleave to his wife: and they twain shall be one flesh? Wherefore they are no more twain, but one flesh. What therefore God hath joined together, let not man put asunder.*

They say unto him, Why did Moses then command to give a writing of divorcement, and to put her away? He saith unto them, Moses because of the hardness of your hearts suffered you to put away your wives: but from the beginning it was not so. And I say unto you, Whosoever shall put away his wife, except it be for fornication [a prolonged, practiced period of adultery], *and shall marry another, committeth adultery: and whoso marrieth her which is put away doth commit adultery.*

What caused all this immorality? The people of Noah's day entertained mental impurities from morning to night. Yes, every imagination of the thoughts of their hearts was evil continually. This sin leads to adultery, homosexuality, and every practiced abomination that tears down marriages. The lust of the eyes leads to further debaucheries. This is why pornography—whether in print or on the screen—leads humans astray. This is why the Christian conscience should be incensed over the filthiness permeating America and should cry out against the trash of this world. Lust through magazines and movies destroys marriages, lives, homes, and nations. It also sends men into eternity lost forever.

Jesus said, *Whosoever looketh upon a woman to lust after her hath committed adultery with her already in his heart* (Matthew 5:28). Sin begins in the eye of the beholder. God says they have eyes full of adultery that cannot cease from sin (see 2 Peter 2:14). This look leads to lust and, *when lust hath conceived, it bringeth forth sin: and sin, when it is finished, bringeth forth death* (James 1:15).

This is why 1 John 2:15-17 warns, *Love not the world, neither the things that are in the world. If any man love the world, the love of the Father is not in him. For all that is in the world, the lust of the flesh, and the lust of the eyes, and the pride of life, is not of the Father, but is of the world. And the world passeth away, and the lust thereof: but he that doeth the will of God abideth forever.*

Obviously, then, Christians should battle pornographic filth with all the vim, vigor, vitality, and strength they have, for it is dehumanizing and soul-destroying. Recently, a massive demonstration against pornography occurred. Five national organizations enlisted the names of several million Americans in support of "Pornography and Obscenity Awareness Week." They called upon Americans to become aware of pornography in their local communities and fight it. The group, disgusted with crime and corruption which lustful filth produces, hoped to make a dent in battling the sleazy purveyors of smut.

Sin in Our Day

Allan C. Brownfeld, in an article entitled "It Is Time to End This National Disgrace," states:

"Slowly, Americans have come to learn of one of the nation's fastest growing industries: child pornography. Recent congressional hearings have shown that the absence of specific federal legislation is permitting the mushrooming of an unsavory commerce that exploits an estimated 500,000 or more children, as young as two or three years of age. The problem, as the Congress has recently learned, is staggering. Los Angeles police estimate that adults sexually exploited over 30,000 children under 17 last year photographing many of them in the sex act. In Houston, police arrested Roy Ames after finding a warehouse full of pornography, including 15,000 color slides of boys in homosexual acts. In congressional testimony, the Odyssey Institute of New York noted that the Crossroads Store in New York's Times Square carried *Lollitots*, a magazine showing girls 8-14, and *Moppits*, displaying little ones aged 3-12 nude and involved. They also saw a film depicting children violently deflowered on their communion day at the feet of a "freshly crucified" priest representing Jesus. Another film pictured an alleged father engaging in sex with his 4-year-old daughter. Nineteen films involved children and sixteen involved incest."

Dr. Jensen-Gerber, founder of Odyssey Institute, states that such inappropriate sexuality is "highly destructive" to children. It leads them to join the deviant population of drug addicts, prostitutes, criminals and pre-adult parents. This degradation of children scars them for life. It must stop, and soon! Unfortunately, the penalties for the production and distribution of child pornography are minor—no more than mere wrist slapping. In fact, only six states have laws prohibiting obscene performances by minors. Now, over 100 Congressmen are pressing for stiff remedial legislation. The proposed plan would make the sexual abuse of children a felony punishable by 20 years in prison or a $50,000 fine or both. Those opposing these laws—"civil libertarians"—cry out that child pornography is protected under free speech.

These lust-ridden leeches are the vermin of society. Their consciences are warped and defiled. Ephesians 4:19 describes them, *Who being past feeling have given themselves over unto lasciviousness, to work all uncleanness* [immorality and impurity] *with greediness*.

Is there any hope? Yes! If the laws of the land cannot stop them, the holy laws of God, meted out at the Judgment Day, will. Then they will pay for every little child they ruined. Romans 1:18 states, *For the wrath of God is revealed from heaven against all ungodliness and unrighteousness of men, who hold the truth in unrighteousness*. They are worthy of death (see Ephesians 4:32) and this includes the second death which is the Lake of Fire (see Revelation 21:8). Do not fear. God will deal with these sinners.

Meanwhile, are we to sit back and do nothing? I like what William A. Stanmeyer said, "Some say, 'The best way to deal with pornography is to let it run its course. People will eventually get bored with it.' This is somewhat like saying the best way to deal with the filth in Lake Erie is to let Lake Erie fill up till it can't take any more. Why should parents have to let their children's moral environment get so corrupt that by comparison Sodom and Gomorrah resemble a Trappist monastery? The salient issue is: May we draw a legal line somewhere? Or must we draw no lines? Must we tolerate everything, no matter how depraved—how sick? The public's answer is: We will draw a line, because we have the right to rear decent children in a decent society; and children or not, decent adults also have a right to a decent society."

This fight for morality should be directed against the purveyors of smut at every level, including television. Today's movie and television presentations emanate an obnoxious odor. Ellen Farley sums it up correctly by saying, "A new film distribution company under the name, 'Meat Cleaver Massacre,' produces movies that feature sex and violence together. I am not as concerned over an individual producer or director who is violently oriented as I am over the millions of movie goers who storm the box offices to see such degrading rubbish. Sick minds fill our nation. Is it any wonder we have so many brutal murders? Many of them are reenactments of former TV shows. Is it any wonder that sane Americans are nauseated? Joseph Papp, founder and producer of the New York Shakespeare Festival, says, 'TV violence is enough to turn one's stomach. The films being made for TV are horrifying and frightening. The kind of body violence seen on TV each night is an assault on one's senses.'"

Steve Allen, actor and comedian, states, "TV has gotten too dirty. Much of the television is what I call junk food for the mind. I don't see any hope in lifting the quality of commercial television. The people who run the networks are perfectly intelligent people— responsible citizens. However, they run junk to keep the ratings high. The sad thing is that by the time one graduates from high school he has watched 15,000 hours of trash in comparison to 12,000 hours of study in the classroom."

Sin's Explosion

A Yale University psychiatrist, Dr. Robert Abramovitz, said, "Kids learn aggression from TV. Anyone who has been brainwashed 15,000 hours via television by the age of 18 has learned aggression, profanity, and filthiness." Remember, the eyegate is the greatest method of teaching the human race. Vulgarities, profanities, and sexual promiscuities committed and reenacted before one's eyes imbed themselves in one's mind. It is a means of indoctrination. One becomes what he eats physically and becomes what he sees mentally."

George Rogers, a Chicago Broadcasting executive, recently said, "The day of filth has arrived. Every other record I receive has cursing in it. The majority of TV shows have cursing in them...Have we sunk so low that we have sold our children to the dogs in order to make a dollar? Do our children have to hear 'damn' and 'hell' and worse in their homes from morning to night? Do they have to watch nudity, such as 'Born Innocent' (a recently repeated, made-for-TV movie), in which a girl is raped with a broom handle?" Why?

Thank God for Gene Rogers who takes a better stand than thousands of our ministers who never speak out—who never raise their voices against sin. We should because "soap opera" episodes, namely, "As the World Turns," feature one illicit affair after another. The result? Marriages break up, adultery flourishes, and the viewers, church members included, feel that is is all right to be immoral—after all, everyone is doing it. The situation is so deplorable that even Ingrid Bergman, now deceased, who could not qualify for an "Emmy" in morality, said, "I find this skin game nauseating. Love is more than walking around naked, copulating. It's an emotion one should be able to convey without going into the crudest details and filthiest language."

A Harvest of Wickedness

This bombardment of continual wickedness, implanting filth in the individual minds of Americans, is presently reaping the harvest, sexually. Patricia McCormack says in a UPI release, "Unmarried sex is rampant among girls 15-19. Most of these girls had their first act of intercourse in their boyfriend's home. Homes are preferred over cars, motels, or hotels. Homes have refrigerators, radios, and hi-fi's. It is also cheaper."

The National Alliance Concerned with School-Age Parents also released this recent report, "Among 15-year-olds, one girl out of every four has had intercourse and 10 percent of all 13-year-olds have had sex." The culprit is pornography in magazines, movies, and on TV. We become what we see. How ridiculous in the light of the facts to mourn over the moral problems of, and crimes being committed by, children, yet let them receive training by the hour in front of "the god with the glass face."

Millions of children have parents who allow them to watch anything. Hundreds of thousands of children have their own sets. If people are so vile that they must feed on moral garbage, let them go to smoke-filled dens and wallow in slime, but in the name of decency and sanity, why allow it to be piped into the living room via TV for hours daily to children?

Sin's Explosion

To Christians I say, *Ye that love the Lord, hate evil* (Psalm 97:10). *Have no fellowship with the unfruitful works of darkness, but rather reprove them. For it is a shame even to speak of those things which are done of them in secret* (Ephesians 5:11,12). *Whatsoever things are true, whatsoever things are honest, whatsoever things just, whatsoever things are pure, whatsoever things are lovely, whatsoever things are of good report...think on these things* (Philippians 4:8). Yes, *turn away* [your] *eyes from beholding vanity* (Psalm 119:37). Be like David, the psalmist, who said, *I will set no wicked thing before mine eyes* (Psalm 101:3). Remember, *the world passeth away and the lusts thereof, but he that doeth the will of God abideth forever*.

The present craze of immorality, impurity, and iniquity indicates that Jesus Christ is coming soon. The Saviour said in Matthew 24:37, *But as the days of Noe were, so shall also the coming of the Son of man be*. It's happening! We are at the bottom of the pit. The situation could not get worse. The hour is late, the time short. Christ may come at any moment.

While we await His return, pray for a revival that will place additional millions into the body of Christ.

Chapter 5

Rock-and-Roll Your Way to Filthiness

Since this message contains such a voluminous number of quotes already, let me simply state that the only good association that rock-and-roll has to genuine Christianity is that a believer's faith is founded in and on Christ Jesus the Rock and his name is on the roll, the Book of Life.

—Dr. Jack Van Impe

Be filled with the Spirit; Speaking to yourselves in psalms and hymns and spiritual songs, singing and making melody in your heart to the Lord.

—*Ephesians 5:18,19*

I was one of the first revivalists to speak out against the vile rock music of our day. The following is a portion of my conversion story taken from my record album, entitled "From Night Clubs to Christ." These facts I proclaimed bombastically throughout America in the sixties and seventies. At that time, I was lambasted in newspapers, on radio, and over TV as a simpleton, a lunatic, and every other degrading term worldly pagans could concoct.

Threats to physically abuse me always followed my exposé of rock music. Here is what I said 15-20 years ago.

I maintain that the music of Herman's Hermits, the Beatles, and all these rock groups is garbage! Now wait a minute! I have an article by Herman himself, who says, "Our music is rubbish, but it's making us millionaires." Thank you, Herman.

Dr. Vernon Zybell, one of the leading nerve specialists, went to see the Beatles. He said, "I'm not a religious man, but if you asked me to describe what I saw, I would say demon possession."

Rock-and-Roll, A Communist's Goal

Friends, I believe rock music is more dangerous than alcohol, LSD, heroin, or anything else you can name. I am going to state some facts which will literally startle you. Point no. 25 of the communist's goals is "to corrupt American young people through movies and music." I have all the evidence in my files. Don't say, "I can't agree with you." Look up the information for yourself. It is in the *Congressional Record*!

Hans Eisler, one of the founders of the International Music Bureau, a communist organizational movement, states, "Communist music becomes heavy artillery in our battle for America." Sidney Finklestein, spokesman for the communist conspiracy, says a major goal is to destroy America with the jungle beat.

Drs. J. A. Barr and William Bryan, leading Canadian hypnosis specialists, write, "The music of the jungle, where it is used to incite warriors to such a frenzy that by night-time their neighbors are cooking in the pot, is the same music presently inciting our youth. This music will definitely bring on hypnosis in 29 minutes of time."

The beat can hypnotize a young man or woman within 29 minutes! You say, "I don't believe it!" Then tell me why millions of girls had illegitimate babies or abortions last year and millions more had to get married! Students are now living on college campuses from coast to coast without marriage contracts and every sex standard is being broken. Explain it!

Pete Seeger and Woody Guthrie brought over "Chamber" and other communist label records in the beginning. Now American companies have picked up "the beat" for money-making purposes. The communists don't care because their goal was only to get it introduced to corrupt and destroy our youth.

Today, years later, the corruption has happened. The filthy, sexual innuendoes of rock lyrics have produced liberated sexual deviants whose orgies have produced a plague of venereal diseases—26 at last count—including herpes and AIDS that will soon destroy millions by 2000 A.D. But wait, it's not over. It's getting worse. Let me quote what rock stars and others are saying and singing today. My predictions of 15-20 years ago have come to pass.

Circus Magazine declared that "no matter what anyone tells you, drugs will always be a part of the rock scene." Chris Stein, the lead guitarist for Blondie, says, "Everybody takes it for granted that rock-

and-roll is synonymous with sex." Says Andrew Oldham, the manager for the Rolling Stones, "Rock is sex. You have to hit teenagers in the face with it." Jesse Jackson states, "Rock music is pornography."

"Dirty Mind" is a song recorded by Prince. Listen to its filth: "Whenever I'm around you, babe, I get a dirty mind."

In a study conducted by Dr. Patricia Shuller, popular music with sexual lyrics was played for several hours to girls between the ages of 12 and 21. Without exception, every one of them was so nervous and aroused by the music that the ability to rationalize clearly and make moral judgments was totally lost. Sadly enough, those girls that had the least control over their response to the music were all between the ages of 12 and 14.

Paul Stanley of the group KISS told a reporter, "We've been getting a lot of letters from 15- and 16-year-old girls with nude Polaroid snapshots of themselves. That's amazing! That's great! There's nothing like knowing you're helping the youth of America."

Donna Summer, often referred to as "the first lady of lust," had a chartbreaker disco hit titled "Love to Love You Baby" in which she simulated 22 orgasms during the 17-minute number (*The Pied Piper of Rock Music* by Dennis Corle).

David Lee Roth of Van Halen told a reporter, "I've managed to live out 100 percent of my sexual fantasies with pretty women on the road." He says, "Whatever your vice, whatever your sexual ideals...whatever somebody else can't do in his 9-to-5 job, I can do in rock-and-roll...I'm in this job to exercise my sexual fantasies."

The depth of rock's perversion is well illustrated in the lyrics of "Get My Rocks Off" by Dr. Hook:

Sometimes I dream of chicks
 To bring me everlasting joys.
Sometimes I dream of animals,
 Sometimes I dream of boys.

"Shoot to Thrill" is a number from the album, "Back in Black" by the group AC-DC. The singer says he gets his thrill from shooting the girls after his sexual encounters.

Just like an eagle I get under your skin,
 Just like a bomb that's ready to blow,
Cause just like an eagle I got everything that all
 You women need to know.
I'm gonna break you down, yeah, down, down, down,
 So don't you fool around.
I'm gonna pull in, pull out, pull the trigger.
Shoot to thrill, play to kill—
 I've got my gun and I'm ready and I fire it well.
Shoot to thrill, play to kill—
 I can't get enough, I just can't get my fill.
I'll shoot to thrill. I'm ready to kill.
 Yeah, pull the trigger.

David Lee Roth of Van Halen made this shocking statement during a recent interview with *Record* magazine, "Rape and pillage play an important part in rock-and-roll."

Alice Cooper delves into the topic of necrophilia, which seems to be one of his favorites, and states, "Necrophilia is an erotic attraction to dead bodies."

I love the dead before they're cold,

Sin's Explosion

Their bluing flesh for me to hold.
They mourn, mourn your silly grave
But I have other uses for you, darling.

Ted Nugent compares his performances with sexual release as well. "I used to rape (an audience), now I like to use a little foreplay." Mick Jagger also describes his music as "raw sex" and drew an analogy between his act and that of a striptease dancer.

Jefferson Starship reports, "We are the forces of anarchy and confusion." Irwin Silber, from the *Marxist Writer*, says, "The great strength of rock-and-roll lies in its beat...it is a music which is basically sexual, un-Puritan...and a threat to established patterns and values."

The Blasphemy of Rock

Rock music stars are also blasphemous—read on.

The Dead Kennedys sing "Religious Vomit." One of their albums pictures Christ hanging on a cross made of a dollar bill, with a computer readout above reading "666."

Rock stars have made some shocking statements about Christ and Christianity. Bob Dylan suggests that God is probably a woman. Gene Simmons of KISS says, "If God is such hot stuff, why is He afraid to have other gods before Him?" Mick Jagger of the Rolling Stones declared, "If Jesus had been indicted in a modern court, He would have been examined by a doctor, found to be obsessed by a delusion, declared incompetent and incapable of pleading His case, and sent to an asylum." Jimi Hendrix was known to say, "I think religion is just a bunch of _____."

Beatle Ringo Starr announced, "We are not anti-Christ...just anti-Christian. Jesus is dead."

Grace Slick of Jefferson Airplane/Starship bore an illegitimate child which she named god, with a small "g." She said, "We've got to be humble about this." Homosexual performer Wayne County has been quoted, "If Jesus Christ came back again and took me for a beer, I'd never change. I mean, He was one of the strange boys himself."

Rock also promotes demonism and the occult.

David Bowie in *Rolling Stone Magazine* said, "Rock-and-roll has always been the devil's music. It could well bring about a very evil feeling in the West."

Little Richard was one of the earliest rock performers, who later professed Christianity. He told reporters, "Some rock groups stand in a circle and drink blood; others pray to the devil. Rock-and-roll hypnotizes us and controls our senses."

Ginger Baker, drummer for Creem, told a reporter, "It happens to us quite often—it feels as though I'm not playing my instrument, something else is playing it—and that same thing is playing all three of our instruments. That's what I mean when I say it's frightening sometimes."

Pink Floyd recorded a song concerning Satan as the god they worship.

> The Lord is my shepherd, I shall not want.
> He makes me down to lie.
> Through pastures green he leadeth me
> The silent waters by.
> With bright knives he releaseth my soul.

He maketh me to hang on hooks in high places,
He converteth me to lamb cutlets.
For lo, he hath great power and great hunger...

Van Halen has recorded songs with titles such as "Running With the Devil," "Sinners Swing," and "On Fire." Steve Hackett, who is guitarist for Genesis, recorded a solo album, "Voyage of the Acolyte," with songs based on his musical interpretation of the Tarot cards. Heart's song, "Devil's Delight," speaks of a "dirty daughter demon that screams and dances through the night." Santana had hits entitled "Evil Ways" and "Black Magic Woman" as well as their album, "Abraxas," named after a very powerful demon in the world of witchcraft. Queen's Freddy Mercury says, "On stage I'm a devil," and they do a number entitled, "Bohemian Rhapsody," which says, "Beelezebub has a demon set aside for me."

Black Sabbath may be the originators of "Satan rock." They have been known to hold black masses before concerts complete with a nude on an altar sprinkled with chicken blood.

According to *American Photographer* magazine, the letters that make up KISS stand for "Kids In Satan's Service." Gene Simmons has been known to make such shocking statements as, "I've always wondered what human flesh tasted like. I've always wanted to be a cannibal."

Alice Cooper has publicly claimed to be the reincarnation of a seventeenth century witch and says, "I'm an entertainer, not a musician." He often "entertains" his audience by choking chickens, chopping up baby dolls and spilling blood across the stage, and throwing watermelons at cripples. Among his other strange fascinations, he revealed his eternal aim on his album, "Alice Cooper Goes to Hell." The cover pictures him walking down a white staircase and the last few steps are glowing red.

"Iron Maiden—Forged in the Fires of Hell" is an excerpt from the material promoting this group's album, "The Number of the Beast—666." The group calls themselves, "The masters of molten metal madness," and admits that during the recording of this album there were "a lot of strange things going on." This album cover portrays the musician in the control of the devil, and hell being filled with people. Some of the lyrics say:

Woe to you, of death and see...
For the devil sends the beast with wrath;
  'Cause he knows the time is short.
Let him who has understanding
  Reckon the number of the beast;
For it is a human number,
  It's the number six hundred and sixty-six.
Satan's work is done!
666 the number of the beast!
Sacrifice is going on tonight!

Another of their biggest songs, "Highway to Hell," included these lyrics:
Ain't nothin' I'd rather do
  Going down for the last time.
My friends are gonna be there too.
I'm on a highway to hell, a highway to hell.
Hey, Satan, I paid my dues
  Playing in a 'rockin' band.

Sin's Explosion

Hey, Momma, look at me,
   I'm on my way to the Promised Land.
I'm on the highway to hell,
I'm on the highway to hell, don't stop me.

The consensus of rock stars, then, is that: "Rock music is sex" (Andrew Oldham, Rolling Stones). "Rock-and-roll is devastating to the mind" (Little Richard). "Rock-and-roll is a part of a communist plot to take over America" (Jerry Rubin, communist revolutionary). "All rock is revolutionary...celebrating freedom and sexuality" (*Time* magazine).

Rock-and-roll has always been the devil's music, so can there be any such thing as "Christian rock-and-roll"?

The *Albuquerque Journal* stated, "...hard rock is making its way into Christian music. Groups with long hair, loud music, and colored lights are growing in popularity with youth by putting the sounds of the early seventies behind religious lyrics...KLYT-FM is a non-commercial radio station which plays Christian rock 24 hours a day in the Albuquerque area. Much of the music played on the station is of a harder style than music played on popular rock stations."

As I was preparing my message on rock music, God providentially provided me with a message by David Wilkerson on Christian rock. My heart was stirred as this great, godly man spoke out on the evils of Christian rock to his own Pentecostal brothers. Read his words carefully and weep with him.

● ● ● ● ● ●

Last night I attended a Christian music festival. I

will never forget what I saw, and I can truly say it was a heartbreaking experience. Since leaving the concert I have been weeping for hours, groaning in the Spirit, feeling the wrath of a holy God burning against what I saw.

I went to the festival because the "star performer" featured last night had been in my office just hours before, crying, telling me how much he loved Jesus, how sincere he was, how he wanted to learn more about holiness. He told me my written messages convicted him. His words sounded right—his attitude seemed humble. At his request I went to hear him and his group because he assured me I would not be offended.

I went last night with an open heart, full of love and compassion—for him, for all Christian musicians, and especially for the 3,000 or so young people attending the festival.

There was an inner tug at my heart making me ill at ease. I reasoned, "If Satan is camouflaged in this somehow, if there is a leaven of evil—it will be revealed. Satan always reveals himself in one way or another."

Suddenly the singer yelled in the microphone, "JESUS IS COMING—HE IS GOING TO CRACK THE SKIES—GET READY!" The song was entitled, "CRACK THE SKIES." Suddenly smoke was billowing out of smoke machines, the pounding beat was turned up to a frenzied pitch, eerie lights began flashing, the musicians stood like phantoms rising from a murky swamp. It was ghostly, weird, strange—and the crowd went wild—they seemed to love it. At the same festival, a wild spiked-hair group had entertained—with painted faces, prancing about like homosexual peacocks.

At first, I couldn't believe what I was seeing on stage. I said out loud, "This can't be happening at a Christian festival—they can't do this to my Jesus! These people can't be this blind—the leaders of this youth ministry can't be so undiscerning! Oh, God—what has happened to your church that its leaders, its people, can't see the evil of the abominations?"

Suddenly I was on the ground, on my back, weeping and sobbing, and groaning in the Spirit. I sat up and took another look at the stage. I WAS HORRIFIED BY WHAT I SAW IN THE SPIRIT. I SAW DEMONIC IMAGES RISING FROM THAT STAGE! I HEARD SATAN LAUGHING! Laughing at all the blind parents—the blind shepherds—the blind youth—the backslidden church! It was an overt manifestation of Satan—worse than anything I've ever seen on the streets of New York.

I stood to my feet, literally shaking with the fear of God—consumed with a sense of His holy wrath against such wickedness. I rushed into the crowd crying at the top of my voice—ICHABOD! (The glory of the Lord has departed!) ICHABOD! I ran through the crowd, pushing aside chairs, weeping, shouting at the top of my voice, "Ichabod—this is satanic! Stop! God is grieved!" I was mostly ignored and I think most thought I was a crazy lunatic. I doubt anybody knew who I was—the musicians could not hear me, and the crowd was too tight to allow me near the stage. I wanted to get to a microphone and cry like an Elijah—"THIS IS VOMIT ON THE TABLE OF THE LORD! WHO ARE YOUR TEACHERS,

THAT YOU COULD BE SO BLIND, SO WORLDLY, SO DECEIVED? WHAT KIND OF BLASPHEMY IS THIS?"

I will not shut up on this matter! I will not be silent while multitudes of our Christian youth are being deceived by smooth-talking wolves in sheep's clothing! True love demands that the truth be told.

What hurt my spirit the most, and what is so hard for me to understand, is that this particular group, and many others, attend Pentecostal churches. The musician I refer to told me he gave up drugs, drinking, evil sex, and rock-and-roll performing when he got saved. He cut his long, feminine hair, he quit dressing like an exhibitionist and began to change all his ways. It was a pastor who encouraged him to "quit looking square and use rock-and-roll to reach the kids." A teacher, in his sixties, travels on occasion with them, teaching them and encouraging them in their evil methods. According to their teacher, rock-and-roll is going to be the "normal music in all Pentecostal and evangelical churches."

It's now the middle of the night and I can't sleep! I can't stop weeping inside. I am shut in with God in my study diligently asking Him to show me what is happening, because hours ago I saw a few thousand young Christians, with uplifted hands, thinking it was Jesus, when it was most assuredly the devil. HAS THE CHURCH—OR WHAT MAN CALLS THE CHURCH—SO BACKSLIDDEN THAT THERE IS NO MORE DISCERNMENT WHATSOEVER? Has God given up on some who are set on bringing devilish practices into the realm of worship?

NOW I WONDER—WHO DARES TEACH SUCH A JESUS—a Jesus who winks at deception? How blatantly they are mislearning Jesus Christ! WHAT JESUS ARE THEY PREACHING?

That is what Paul said in his letter to the Ephesians. He was warning them not to walk as some do *in the vanity* [pride] *of their mind* (Ephesians 4:17). He was warned of those who learned Christ in a perverted way, because their understanding was darkened. They were cut off *from the life of God through the ignorance that is in them, because of the blindness of their heart* (Ephesians 4:18).

Some teacher, some shepherd, had MISTAUGHT JESUS CHRIST to them. The Christ they learned was not the Christ of God, the Lord of holiness, the Master of purity. While they speak so sweetly of Jesus, and weep when they mention the name, and tell of a hunger to walk in the ways of Christ—Paul said of them, they are *PAST FEELING* [and] *HAVE GIVEN THEMSELVES OVER UNTO LASCIVIOUS-NESS* [lustfulness], *TO WORK ALL UNCLEANNESS WITH GREEDINESS* (Ephesians 4:19).

That is what I saw last night at the music festival— a group of musicians who were pied pipers, leading many young people right into the arms of Satan with their smooth words about Jesus, about celebrating forgiveness—then with an energy of flesh and carnal greediness hard to fathom—they put their stamp of approval on paganism right out of the devil's treasury. They were saying, by their music and their worldly ghastly performance—that Jesus and the garbage of this world are compatible. They wore two masks— one of sincere followers of Christ, the other of performing clowns. With their faces lifted up to God, they cursed Him by their blasphemous mockery. Isaiah prophesied of such, *They shall...curse their king and their God, and look upward* (Isaiah 8:21). What they preach and practice are two different gospels.

They are deceived, and consequently they are deceivers themselves. They have MISLEARNED CHRIST! They have been duped, manipulated, and cheated! They should have had a pastor or teacher with enough Holy Ghost discernment, with enough devotion to the true and holy Lord—to WARN THEM, TO SHOW THEM that God does not put up with holding on to the old man and the old carnal ways. Why didn't their shepherds discern that these boys were walking in ignorance and spiritual blindness, not understanding the true demands of Christ? Why wasn't their greed dealt with—not so much for money and fame, but a greed that would not let go of the very thing that once led them into drugs and emptiness. It's all coming out now—that these groups are falling on all sides, going back to the secular crowd, back to cocaine, back to groupies—playing the part of hypocrites and gospel phonies. Their shepherds are so easily conned, because they are blind in every way. Paul said it right, *For it is a shame even to speak of those things which are done of them in secret* (Ephesians 5:12). The very music they perform drives them back to darkness.

Now—it's probably too late! They have rejected the reproof of prophets and watchmen who really preach the truth! They are like those Paul warns about, who have become so lost in spiritual ignorance and blindness, they are past feeling conviction. They are confirmed in their worldly ways! They are so blind they believe they are honoring Christ and blessing multitudes of youth the church "can't reach."

I blame their smooth talking, sin-soft shepherds. Those same shepherds must one day stand before Christ's judgment seat and answer—not only for the musicians under their care—but for all the Christian young people they in turn have hurt and destroyed. Without flinching, I declare that cowardly ministers, those who want to be loved and honored rather than rejected for preaching truth, are driving this generation into deep spiritual darkness.

We would not be facing a generation of backslidden, pleasure-loving, worldly minded youth in our churches—IF WE HAD MORE HOLY, BOLD PREACHERS AND EVANGELISTS WHO COULD TEACH AND PREACH THE TRUTH OF CHRIST WITH PURITY AND AUTHORITY.

I am not accusing all preachers and teachers— thank God for the few who still do not cower to the crowd or compromise for the sake of numbers and success. Maybe the youth won't listen to those of us who cry out against their lusting after the world—but when the judgments accelerate—they will turn to the preachers of holiness for a sure word from God.

There is filth in Zion, and strangers have been exalted in the house of God—by blind, compromised, and undiscerning Christian leaders. They are calling evil good, and the counsel of a righteous God is lightly esteemed. Hearts are hardening, ears are closing, eyes are being shut—because pride and flesh and ungodly entertainment is grieving the Holy Spirit out of His temple.

Isaiah warned, *Their root shall be as rottenness... because they have cast away the law of the Lord of hosts, and despised the word of the Holy One of Israel. Therefore is the anger of the Lord kindled against his people* (Isaiah 5:24,25).

Hell must be ecstatic at the spectacle of ministers not just abdicating to the immoral music standards of the young—but actually promoting what only demons should be promoting. Who brings these worldly bent groups into the church for concerts? Who encourages the youth to embrace the music of devils? Who ridicules evangelists and prophets and watchmen who cry out against it? Who puts it on radio and TV and who promotes the concerts and festivals that are now degenerating into SATANIC SHOWCASES? It is the pastors, youth ministers, Christian radio and TV station owners and managers. They will all live to see the wicked harvest of their soft gospel and compromise—as their very own children fall away to the spirit of this age.

All spiritual work that is tainted with the least bit of darkness, God calls UNFRUITFUL WORKS! This refutes the big lie of the devil being promoted by the pushers of "new wave" music which argues, "But it can't be of the devil. Look at all the kids getting saved! Listen to their wonderful testimonies. They really reach the youth—many are getting saved. They speak in a way the kids understand—they glorify Christ in their speech."

God never has judged a work by results. No one is more successful in holding converts than the Muslims. The Jehovah Witnesses claim to be winning multitudes to Christ.

God judges everything by LIGHT! That means, by how godly, how Christ-like it is—by how clear, how pure, how transparent it is. He repudiates and spits out of His mouth all that has even a part of darkness connected with it. John saw the Holy City descending out of heaven from God, having the glory of God. That is a holy people, a bride adorned and prepared for the Bridegroom. Its main characteristic is this: *Her light was like unto a stone most precious, even like a jasper stone, clear as crystal* (Revelation 21:11).

Whatever is of God is CLEAR AS CRYSTAL! It is holiness so pure, it is translucent as a pure jasper stone. Those who are numbered in this holy Zion, this New Jerusalem coming down from God—have all STEPPED OUT INTO THE LIGHT. There is no darkness in them at all—they hate darkness—they reprove it wherever it appears. The enemy has come into religious circles to destroy what is pure and clear by introducing a pagan element that creates a shadow or film. If Satan can inject the slightest degree of error, or evil leaven, he knows the Holy Spirit will draw back because of grieving. That is why no mixture—no shadow of dark paganism must be permitted in Christ's church.

Also, the Bible speaks of EVERY SEED YIELDING AFTER ITS OWN KIND (see Genesis 1:12). An evil seed produces evil fruit, often not recognized until maturity. The rock-and-roll "prophets" of this generation are yielding a seed that will one day bring forth a fruit that will wither and die. Jude makes that very clear, [These feed] *themselves without...water, carried about of winds; trees WHOSE FRUIT WITH-ERETH, without fruit, twice dead, plucked up by the roots* (Jude 12).

What of the good sounding testimonies, the sincere and convincing sermonettes? Paul has the answer. *Now I beseech you, brethren, mark them which cause divisions and offenses contrary to the doctrine which ye have learned; and avoid them. For they that are such serve not our Lord Jesus Christ, but their own belly; and by good words and fair speeches deceive the hearts of the simple* (Romans 16:17,18).

Oh, how God's people need discernment. Great deceptions abound everywhere, not only regarding the rock and punk music of the young, but also in regard to new forms of worship and praise being promoted. Some of it is born of the Holy Spirit, but much is born of the flesh—and only those who walk in the light know the difference.

Thank God for those in the camp who worship in Spirit and in truth—who lift clean hands and who have pure hearts—who come before His holiness with a broken heart and a contrite spirit. If they are walking in holiness, trembling at God's Word, repentant and free from the bondage of sin—it is a glorious and acceptable offering unto the Lord. God does inhabit the praises of His people—but only if those people are walking in practical righteousness.

There is the shout of the overcomer and the shout of the idolater—and we had better know the difference. The Lord commanded Moses to *Go, get thee down;*

for thy people, which thou broughtest out of the land of Egypt, have corrupted themselves: They have turned aside quickly out of the way which I commanded them: they have made a molten calf, and have worshipped it (Exodus 32:7,8).

As Moses and Joshua approached the camp of Israel, *Joshua heard the noise of the people as they shouted* (vs. 17). But it was not the shout of those who had overcome the enemy. The true shepherd, Moses, having come fresh from the very presence of God's holiness—could easily discern that the GREAT SHOUT coming from the Lord's chosen people was not pure. Something was terribly wrong—it did not ring of the holiness of God.

Moses said, *It is not the voice of them that shout for mastery, neither is it the voice of them that cry for being overcome: but the noise of them that sing do I hear* (Exodus 32:18).

That's all it was, MEANINGLESS, SHALLOW NOISE—but an abomination in the ears of a holy God. They had no right to sing; their hearts were lusting after an idol. Their hearts were given to pleasure and fun. They stood before a golden calf—and in the name of the Lord offered burnt offerings. The people *sat down to eat and to drink, and rose up to play* (Exodus 32:6).

I receive many letters from Christians whom I know have come through the school of Christ. They have come through much suffering and spiritual warfare to a place in God where nothing else matters but knowing Him in fullness. They were driven by such deep hunger for God, they began to thirst for Christ as *the hart that panteth after the water*. They tell me how out of place they feel in these great assemblies where the shout in the camp goes forth. It all looks good, and on the surface sounds good. But they can't enter in, because they discern something is basically wrong. They can't even explain it—the Spirit of God within them will not let them partake of it. They discern some kind of unspeakable darkness—something subtle, yet ominous about all the flesh that accompanies the singing and shouting. It is almost too professional, too put on, too carnal. They leave, thinking to themselves, "Is it me—is there something wrong with me? Am I too judgmental? Why am I not comfortable amidst all this singing and shouting?"

Those who have STEPPED OUT INTO THE LIGHT can easily discern the shadow of darkness. They will not be fooled by false shouting, false worship, or false praying.

True Zion saints REJOICE WITH TREMBLING! (See Psalm 2:11.) They know that gladness belongs only to *the upright in heart* (Psalm 97:11). They can sing when the Spirit moves them, but with David they can say, *Zion heard, and was glad; and the daughters of Judah REJOICED BECAUSE OF THY JUDGMENTS, O LORD* (Psalm 97:8). Zion saints, *GIVE THANKS* [TO THE LORD] *AT THE REMEMBRANCE OF HIS HOLINESS* (Psalm 97:12).

No punk or rock or phony shouting and praising for those walking in the light. They praise Him for both His goodness and because they tremble at His great and terrible name.

The Lord is great in Zion; and he is high above all the people...Let the people tremble...Let them

Sin's Explosion

PRAISE THY GREAT AND TERRIBLE NAME; FOR IT IS HOLY (Psalm 99:1-3).

Chapter 6

AIDS Will Kill You

We need a revival that will stop the flood tides of sin, the lawlessness, and ungodliness that is literally swamping our nation and the world.

—Joe Henry Hankins

A revival is something like a revolution. It is apt to be wonderfully catching.

—*Pratney*

Such are the prophets. They are never expected, never announced, never introduced—they just arrive. They are sent, and sealed, and sensational. John the Baptist "did no miracles"—that is, no rivers of derelict humanity swept down on him for his healing touch. But he raised a spiritually dead nation!

—Leonard Ravenhill

Finney preached like a lion. His sermons were life and fire; you listened whether you liked it or not. There was a holy violence about him which firmly took your attention by storm.

—*Pratney*

Sin's Explosion

Look, I am a little tired of reading about Sam Jones in the past. I want to see something in the present. I am a little tired of reading of what Charles G. Finney did. I want to know what Charles G. Finneys do today. I learned years ago that one of the great secrets of serving God is prayer and fasting.

—Martyn Lloyd-Jones

I ask once more what have been the consequences of the doctrine I have preached for the past nine years? By the fruits shall you know those of whom I speak. There is a cloud of witnesses who at this hour experience the gospel which I preach to be the power of God unto salvation. The habitual drunkard that was, is now temperate in all things. The whoremonger now flees fornication. He that stole, steals no more, but works with his hands. He that cursed or swore, perhaps in every sentence, has now learned to serve the Lord with fear and rejoice unto Him with reverence. Those formerly enslaved to various habits of sin are now brought to uniform habits of holiness.

You have without doubt had some success in opposing this doctrine. Very many have, by your unwearied endeavors, been deterred from hearing it at all, and have thereby probably escaped being "seduced into holiness," having lived and died in their sins. The time is short. I am past the noon of life, and my remaining years flee away as a shadow. You are old and full of days, having passed the usual age of man. It cannot, therefore, be long before we shall both drop this house of earth and stand naked before God. On His left hand shall be those who are shortly to dwell in everlasting fire, prepared for the devil and his angels. In that number will be all who died in their sins, including those whom you kept from repentance. Will you then rejoice in your success? The Lord grant it may not be said in that hour: "These have perished in their iniquity, but their blood I require at thy hands."

—John Wesley
speaking to religious leaders

But they mocked the messengers of God, and despised his words, and misused his prophets, until the wrath of the Lord arose against his people, till there was no remedy.

—2 Chronicles 36:16

This television message was delivered to the entire U.S. and Canada.

The epitaph of the twentieth century may be, "They gained their rights except the right to live." Ladies and gentlemen, if AIDS continues to double every 10 years, America will crumble between 1993 and 1997. Since Dr. Koop, the Surgeon General of the United States, affirms that there is no probable hope for a cure this century, we are on a collision course that may make the Statue of Liberty become the most expensive tombstone in history.

But is it strictly an American problem? No! International news releases from 100 nations including Australia, Brazil, England, Germany, Kenya, the 12 European Common Market nations, and Russia have reported that AIDS is SPREADING LIKE WILDFIRE.

Sin's Explosion

The situation is severe. Presently, two million already carry the virus in Australia, four million in America, and Switzerland has broken all records for Europe. The 12-nation Common Market alliance sees the doubling of the disease within 12 months. Because of the severity of the situation, *U.S. News & World Report* predicts that tens of millions will die if a cure is not found in the next 13 years.

There have been other plagues throughout history. Millions died through Spanish influenza, bubonic plague, yellow fever, smallpox, polio, multiple sclerosis, and cancer. However, there is nothing in the annals of history that may equal the devastating death that the AIDS virus will soon create.

David Block in a *Rolling Stone* article said, "If AIDS continues increasing at its present rate, all Americans will be killed in 12 years."

Nancy Spandous believes that 35 years from now, in 2020, the last human could be expiring on this earth from AIDS.

With the AIDS virus being exuded practically from every bodily orifice, pore, and secretion, intimate contact of any kind makes such deadly statements a possibility.

Today, the "if-it-feels-good-do-it" philosophy is definitely on the way out. Young and old who spend a night in promiscuous sex now say with Isaiah the prophet in Chapter 21, verse 4, *The night of my pleasure hath he turned into fear*.

A Fulfillment of Prophecy?

Do such alarmist statements shock you? Well, there is something even more startling. Did you know that the present sexual rage with its accompanying venereal sores and pains is prophesied in the Bible? Jesus, in describing world conditions at the time of His return to earth, said, *There shall be...pestilences* [or rare, malignant diseases] (Matthew 24:7). The Spirit of God also, through the Apostle John in Revelation 16, gives the human race a portrait of what transpires upon earth just preceding closing time. Hear Him! *Go your ways, and pour out the vials of the wrath of God upon the earth. And the first* [angel] *went, and poured out his vial upon the earth; and there fell a noisome and grievous sore upon the men which had the mark of the beast* [666], *and upon them which worshipped his image...And the fifth angel poured out his vial upon the seat of the beast; and his kingdom was full of darkness; and they gnawed their tongues for pain, and blasphemed the God of heaven because of their pains and their sores* (vss. 1,2,10,11).

The hour has finally arrived for the literal fulfillment of these predictions. Four million already carry the virus in the USA. This will multiply fourfold to 15 million by 1991. The World Health Service predicts that the dreaded AIDS disease will escalate to 150 million internationally within 48 months. GOD HAVE MERCY ON US.

Beware! Homosexuality, live-in partnerships, one-night stands and free sex can no longer be touted as a lifestyle, but rather a deathstyle. AIDS is for life. Pains, sores, and a humiliating death may become your permanent gift from a friendly sexual donor. Also, that one-night fling may sting until death do you part. One morning you may awaken with AIDS and cry, *The thing which I greatly feared is come upon me*

(Job 3:25). Soon you may say, *My skin is broken, and become loathesome* (Job 7:5). Also, *My strength faileth because of mine iniquity, and my bones are consumed* (Psalm 31:10).

Playwright Larry Kramer describing the death of his friends, said, "I am angry and frustrated beyond the bounds of what my skin, bones, body, and brain can encompass. My sleep is tormented by nightmares and visions of lost friends, and my days are flooded by the tears of funerals, memorial services, and sick friends. While I made love the other night I thought, 'Is this the one that will kill me?'"

Neighbor, you can't have it all. The beer commercial is wrong.

May I speak forcefully and plainly to all who play Russian roulette with their lives through careless sexual escapades and particularly to sexual saboteurs—yes, sexual terrorists who carry the virus and knowingly infect others. This is premeditated murder if you are a carrier. Isaiah 59:4 pictures you when it states, [You] *conceive mischief, and bring forth iniquity.*

Recently, a high-class prostitute in Texas left a note behind for her victim. It read, "Welcome to the world of AIDS." How merciless. Don't you become a victim. Presently, 50 percent of the hookers in Miami, Ft. Lauderdale, Washington D.C., New York City, and Uganda test positive for AIDS. It's worldwide. So quit listening to the Playboy philosophy that declares, "If it feels good, do it." Instead, obey God who said in Proverbs 4:14,15, *Enter not into the path of the wicked, and go not in the way of evil men. Avoid it, pass not by it, turn from it, and pass away.* Why? Because *this is the will of God, even your sanctifica-*

tion, that ye should abstain from fornication [all sexual encounters and perversions] (1 Thessalonians 4:3).

The Consequences of Sin

Friends, you can't ignore God's warnings and escape the consequences of sin. The Bible says, *Let no man deceive you with vain words: for because of these* [sins] *cometh the wrath of God upon the children of disobedience* (Ephesians 5:6). Jeremiah 16:4,11 adds, *They shall die of grievous deaths...Because* [they] *have forsaken me...and have not kept my law.* Also, *and they were haughty, and committed abomination before me: therefore I took them away* (Ezekiel 16:50).

Moses told his people what would happen if they sinned. *The Lord shall smite thee with a consumption, and with a fever, and with an inflammation, and with an extreme burning* (Deuteronomy 28:22). Because of it you shall *die in youth* (Job 36:14). Doesn't 2 Chronicles 36:16 picture the day in which we live? *The wrath of the Lord arose against his people, till there was no remedy.* TERRIFYING WORDS! You have AIDS and there is no remedy—no help and no hope.

Is free, uncontrolled, uninhibited sex really fun? Harvard therapist Dr. Armand Nicoli said, "This new sexual freedom is not what people are led to believe...It certainly does not lead to prolonged ecstatic pleasure. Quite the opposite. It leads to unwanted pregnancies, ill-advised marriages, abor-

95

tions followed by severe depressions, disillusionment, frustration, despondency, and then suicide."

Sexual liberation has produced one-and-a-half million abortions annually, 400 thousand illegitimate babies annually, three million cases of gonorrhea annually, one million cases of pelvic inflammatory disease annually, one hundred thousand cases of teenage girls becoming permanently sterilized annually, ten thousand cases of cervical cancer annually, plus 30 million cases of incurable genital herpes and venereal warts—PLUS DEATH THROUGH AIDS TO MILLIONS OF YOUNG HOMOSEXUAL MEN.

Is there a solution? The answer is found in Proverbs 3:7,8, *Fear the Lord, and depart from evil. It shall be health to thy navel, and marrow to thy bones.* How true! So stop, look, and listen—turn from wrong to right. Obey the Judeo-Christian commandments—listen to God who for your own good declares, *Thou shalt not commit adultery* [sexual promiscuity of any kind] (Exodus 20:14).

Until recently, men mocked ministers who proclaimed the judgment of God against sin as "puritanical simpletons." But it's God that says, *They that plow iniquity, and sow wickedness, reap the same* (Job 4:8). It's God that says, *Be not deceived;* [I am] *not mocked: for whatsoever a man soweth, that shall he also reap* (Galatians 6:7). Neighbor, sin is destructive! Quit fooling yourself. Cursing destroys speech; lying destroys credibility; greed destroys happiness; tobacco destroys lungs; booze destroys decency; pornography destroys the mind; and sexual promiscuity destroys THE BODY AND THE SOUL. God's Word is true. *When lust hath conceived, it bringeth forth sin: and sin, when it is finished, bringeth forth death* (James 1:15).

To this point we have considered the severity of this epidemic called AIDS. Now a greater shock confronts all of us as its source is uncovered. Did you know that leading medical specialists have traced the AIDS lentivirus to a species of monkeys in Africa called the green monkeys? Similarly, lentiviruses have been discovered in horses worldwide and sheep in the Middle East. Now hear this—it is utterly mind-boggling. Never throughout world history has anyone fully understood the most stunning Bible prophecy ever recorded. Now we do.

Chapter six of the Book of Revelation pictures the four horsemen of the Apocalypse. This quartet of killers produce an array of plagues upon planet earth that destroys 50 percent of the inhabitants. Who are the unholy four? Well, the rider of the white horse is the infamous Antichrist who leads the pack. The rider of the red horse is a barbarian who causes wars and rumors of war to flourish. The rider of the black horse is a sadist who creates the greatest era of starvation ever known to mankind. However, the fourth and final rider of the pale horse is the one who has power to destroy one-sixth of humanity through disease. If this be so—and it is, soon one out of six human beings will die through illness when this rider mounts the pale horse of suffering, disease, and death. But how does he perform his task? What does he employ as the origin of the disease? Hear it—don't miss it—this is astounding. The answer is the BEASTS OF THE FIELD (see Revelation 6:8).

Sin's Explosion

Think of it! This prophecy has become a reality in our generation because the beasts of the field, monkeys and sheep, are the source for the present plague. Wow! But how was the virus transmitted? Well, medical experts believe that the green monkeys of Africa passed their lentivirus to humans through biting and bestiality. Shocking you say. Well, one percent of Americans have committed such acts with animals. God forgive us.

Next, infected men engaged other men in sexual acts, and soon the virus spread like wildfire among homosexuals internationally. As a matter of fact, when the disease was first discovered, its original label was GRIDS, which stood for Gay Related Immune Deficiency syndrome. Soon gay lobbyists, to avoid suspicion, worked diligently to see that the twentieth century plague was renamed AIDS. Then, bisexuals, or men who enjoyed either men or women, spread the disease to the heterosexual community, and scores of such men even entered the sanctity of their homes and filled their wives with the virus. WHEW!

Paul Harvey, the famous commentator, often ends his thought-provoking discussions by saying, "And now you know the rest of the story." Could I at this juncture tell YOU the rest of the story? Don't turn me off yet. Listen and live.

The Scope of AIDS

Here are the facts concerning the scope of the disease.

The virus is found in saliva, tears, perspiration, urine, feces, breast milk, semen, vaginal secretions, vomit, blood, and brain tissue. It also infiltrates eyes, lungs, liver, spleen, kidneys, and other organs.

One single virion entering one's system will eventually destroy a person within 12 years—the length of one's incubation. What a period of imprisonment for one foolish sexual encounter.

Furthermore, the Acquired Immune Deficiency Syndrome is only a portion of the AIDS problem. A brain destroyed by the virus, causing dementia, is equally frightening.

But there is more. This hearty virus lives outside of one's body for 10 days, even in a dried out condition. The clues or tell-tale signs of AIDS may include an unexplained weight loss, drenching night sweats, persistent diarrhea, swelling of the lymph nodes, chronic fatigue, persistent flu symptoms, pneumonia, tuberculosis, small purplish spots on one's body, itching blisters or scabs, blurred vision, and ultimately skin cancer.

Is it really as bad as I just described? Should you really be concerned? Harvard pathologist William Haseltine says, "All it takes is the transmission of one microbial parasite. After it enters and researchers find it five to 10 years later—BINGO—that's it! You're gone!"

On such a solemn note, let's focus our attention on the scenario for survival. Obey the rules and live now! What rules? The "don'ts" for survival.

Don't play sex games. Sex is to be reserved for marriage. The Bible says, *Marriage is honorable in all, and the bed undefiled* [in marriage]: *but whoremongers and adulterers God will judge* (Hebrews 13:4). Don't visit prostitutes. Fifty percent of them are riddled with VD and the AIDS virus.

Don't play homosexual games. God also condemns this sin as He does adultery. And in describing homosexuality, God says, *Their women did change the natural use into that which is against nature: And likewise also the men, leaving the natural use of the woman, burned in their lust one toward another; men with men working that which is unseemly...*[THE RESULT] *Who knowing the judgment of God, that they which commit such things are worthy of death* (Romans 1:26-32).

When one goes to bed with promiscuous people, he or she goes to bed with the entire sexual history of such persons—plus all their partners along with the partners of the partners—an intertwining of sexual escapades that possibly involves a total of 4,000 contacts through one act—homosexually or heterosexually. Is it worth it?

Wait, there is more.

Don't allow blood to be transfused into your body unless it is your own or a trusted and tested friend's blood.

Don't touch blood spills or blood soiled articles of clothing unless wearing protective gloves. Don't use anyone's razor blade. Don't even allow your friendly barber to reuse a razor on you until it has been sterilized. Remember, the virion of an AIDS victim lives on that blade for 10 days if he has been nicked.

Don't allow your ears to be pierced at department stores unless a new needle is unpackaged and used.

The smallest contaminated pin prick may infect you with the virus.

Don't let medics or anyone else put unsterilized needles in your body for drug or medical purposes, especially tatoo artists.

Don't go to a sperm bank for semen. You may never live to see the baby.

Don't partake of food when the chef has accidentally nicked himself while preparing the meal. Recently, Mayor Bradley of Los Angeles advised all restaurant owners as follows, "If the chef at your restaurant cuts himself, the food over which he bled should be discarded." Hip, Hip, Hooray—what consolation this produces in the midst of a plague.

Don't allow doctors to examine you, especially gynecologists, without rubber gloves.

Don't let dentists use vacuum pumps to rid the mouth of saliva unless the equipment has been sterilized between patients. Furthermore, don't let dentists or dental assistants work in your mouth without rubber gloves.

Kissing cousins, this next tidbit is especially for you. Don't allow anyone to kiss you on the mouth, especially if you have cold sores, canker sores, blisters, or lesions around the lips or inner cheeks. The AIDS infected blood from flossing teeth mixed with saliva may lead to the kiss of death. Also, don't use anyone's toothbrush, especially after they have flossed their teeth.

Friend, though the "don'ts" are many, remember that 99 percent of all present AIDS victims succumbed to the disease through illicit sexual practices or virus-contaminated needles used during drug injections. This is why Dr. Koop, our Surgeon General, constantly warns that young people are not only at high risk but their sexual activity will determine whether our society survives the devastating disease or not. This alarm is not sounded to place one on a guilt trip but to save multitudes from excruciatingly gory deaths.

We Have to Answer to God

Now as important as life is to you, there is something infinitely more valuable than existence in a body, and that's a soul's eternal abode with God. This is why Jesus said in Matthew 10:28, *And fear not them which kill the body, but are not able to kill the soul: but rather fear him* [Satan] *which is able to destroy both soul and body in hell.*

The first death, which is bodily, means only the grave. But the second death, which is spiritual, means an eternal existence of body and soul in the Lake of Fire (see Revelation 20:14). This death is reserved for those who break God's holy laws, including sexual sins.

So though you may practice "safe sex" and though you may run around with a pocket or purse full of condoms crying out, "No glove—no love," and though you may think you are protected bodily, you are not covered spiritually.

I think I can almost hear some of you muttering, arguing, rationalizing, vilifying, maligning, and even cursing me at this point. But I hold in my hand a book written by the Spirit of God, and on the Judgment Day you will answer to God according to what He has inscribed upon the pages of this sacred volume. Here is what He has to say:

Know ye not that the unrighteous shall not inherit the kingdom of God? Be not deceived: neither fornicators, nor idolators, nor adulterers, nor effeminate, nor abusers of themselves with mankind...shall inherit the kingdom of God (1Corinthians 6:9,10). The fornicators mentioned by God in this text are single folks who practice illicit sex outside of marriage during one-night stands or live-in relationships. Adulterers are married folks who do the same. The effeminate are young boys drawn into homosexual acts by the abusers of themselves with men—chicken hawks or life-long practicing homosexuals. Now the God who does not practice discrimination says—all these groups who commit sexual sin outside of marriage, condom or no condom, are eternally excluded from eternal life unless they repent.

God again states, *Now the works of the flesh are manifest, which are these; Adultery, fornication, uncleanness, lasciviousness* [the practice of sexual aberrations with greediness—never being satisfied. THE RESULT?] *...they which do such things shall not inherit the kingdom of God* (Galatians 5:19,21).

Hear God once more. *For this ye know, that no whoremonger* [womanizer], *nor unclean person* [one who practices any kind of sexual perversion outside of marriage]*...hath any inheritance in the kingdom of Christ and of God* (Ephesians 5:5). God again says that the whoremongers (womanizers) *shall have their part in the lake which burneth with fire and brimstone: which is the second death* (Revelation

21:8). On the basis of present statistics in this sex-crazed era, millions upon millions will be outside of God's Holy City forever because they flaunted, ignored, or ridiculed God's Holy Commandments. God said what He meant, and meant what He said when before the eyes of His servant Moses He indelibly and eternally inscribed on a tablet of stone—*Thou shalt not commit adultery.*

Be like Moses. He decided to obey and follow God. He refused *to enjoy the pleasures of sin for a season* (Hebrews 11:25). He made his decision centuries ago. Presently he enjoys his eternal reward.

Some of us are like Moses, others are not. If not, is there hope for the fallen? Yes, beloved friend, and what I am about to say is exceedingly precious. Nothing I have said thus far can equal this next statement. Hear me. While AIDS blood contaminates others—the blood of Jesus Christ, God's Son, cleanses from all sin (see 1 John 1:7). When our Saviour shed His precious efficacious blood upon Calvary's cross almost twenty centuries ago, that blood flowed to make the vilest offender of God's laws clean. I don't care what you have done, how often you have done it, how wicked, abominable, hideous, heinous, degraded, depraved, distorted, or defiled your sin was or is—hear me. The blood of Jesus Christ cleanseth from all sin. Praise the Lamb of God who taketh away the sin of the world (see John 1:29). Hallelujah to Christ who loved us and washed us from our sin in His own blood (see Revelation 1:5).

Can you be forgiven? Listen: *For God so loved the world, that he gave his only begotten Son, that whosoever believeth in him should not perish, but have everlasting life.* Will you come to Calvary today? Will you repent—change your mind about your lifestyle? Will you cast all your past and present sin upon Jesus? He longs to bear it. Remember, Christ died for our sins—all of them. He wants to save you today, precious friend, if your heart is ready—if you want to be cleansed from the past—if you want your sins expiated, obliterated, and liquidated—if you want a new beginning, free from the hang-ups of the past. If you want to be saved, forgiven, cleansed, born again—then pray and ask Christ to save or restore you.

Chapter 7
The Blight of Booze

This leathern-girdled prophet with a time-limit ministry so burned and shone that those who heard his hottongued, heart-burning message, went home to sleepless nights until their blistered souls were broken in repentance. Yet John the Baptist was *strange in doctrine*—no sacrifice, ceremony, or circumcision; *strange in diet*—no winebibbing nor banqueting; *strange in dress*—no phylacteries nor Pharisaic garments.

—Leonard Ravenhill

America needs in every town, city, neighborhood, village, and hamlet, what she used to have—somebody who stands behind the pulpit on Sunday who knows God. They may not like him, but they won't cross him. They may hate him, but they won't touch him because everybody in town knows he is God's man.

—*Martyn Lloyd-Jones*

Right now, God is preparing His Elijahs for the last great earthly offensive against militant godlessness (whether political or wearing a mask of religion).

—Leonard Ravenhill

Sin's Explosion

Do you remember Billy Sunday's message "Get on the Water Wagon" sermon against the liquor traffic? Everywhere Billy Sunday went some saloons were closed, some saloon keepers were converted, and often the collective moral forces of the churches were united to vote out the saloons. Billy Sunday used slang. His words were sharp. His illustrations were pointed. He pulled off his coat. He occasionally broke a chair to pieces. He dared the devil. Sure, Billy Sunday was sensational, if you mean that he hated sin and said so. He said so in the language of the street. Common people understood what he said. His preaching against sin and booze caused multiplied hundreds of thousands to repent and to be saved.

—John R. Rice

The teachings of both Mohammed and Buddha forbid alcoholic beverages. Sad that two billion religionists have higher standards than the present-day boozers within Christendom.

—Jack Van Impe

Since you can't quit drinking, why not start your own saloon? Be the only customer and don't buy a license. Give your wife $55 to buy a case of whiskey. A case holds 240 snorts. Buy all your drinks from her at 60 cents a snort and in 12 days when it is gone, she'll have $89 to bank and $55 to start business again. If you live for 10 years and still buy all your booze from your wife and then die in your boots from the snakes, your widow will have $27,085.47 on deposit; enough to bury you respectably, bring up your children, pay off the mortgage on your house, marry a decent man, and forget she ever knew you.

—Author unknown

The Blight of Booze

The drunken man is a living corpse.

—St. John Chrysostom

Alcoholism is drinking to escape problems created by drinking...

—Panelist at Yale Center of Alcohol Studies

Alcoholism is reached when certain individuals stop bragging about how much they can drink and begin to lie about the amount they are drinking...

—American Medical Association

One drink is too many. Twenty is not enough.

—Skid-row alcoholic in medical interview

O God, that men should put an enemy in their mouth to steal away their brains.

—William Shakespeare

Drunkenness is the ruin of reason. It is premature old age. It is temporary death.

—St. Basil

Alcohol is a cancer in human society, eating out the vitals and threatening destruction.

—Abraham Lincoln

Drunkenness has killed more men than all the history's wars.

—General Pershing

Sin's Explosion

Woe unto him that giveth his neighbour drink, that puttest the bottle to him, and makest him drunken also.

—Habakkuk 2:15

Christians are divided on the question of drinking.

In America, the majority of evangelical churches take at least a nominal stand against the use of alcohol. The move is on to water down this position. Social drinking is increasing, even among fundamentalists. Some avoid hard liquor but look upon the use of beer and wine as permissible. In a recent Christian convention, the bar keepers were disgruntled because business was atrocious. However, their sorrow turned to joy as scores of these religious leaders ordered liquor for their rooms behind closed doors.

In Europe, a great number of professing Christians use wine or beer regularly under the guise of necessity because of "bad water" or "culture acceptance." A surprising number of traveling American churchgoers who are abstainers at home feel free to drink while in Europe. Even some missionaries drink where that is the custom, saying their convictions allow them to "do as the Romans do."

The whole issue is discussed by Mark A. Noll in his article, "America's Battle Against the Bottle," which appeared in *Christianity Today*.

Some evangelicals have made opinions on liquor more important for fellowship and cooperation than attitudes toward the person of Christ or the nature of salvation. This is particularly

unfortunate since the Bible speaks clearly about
Christ and salvation, but not about the question
of total abstinence.[1]

But is Noll's conclusion correct? Is there no biblical absolute on the alcohol question? Has God left us
without direction as to what our position should be on
one of the most important social and moral issues?

What Does the Bible Say?

The Bible certainly is not silent about beverage
alcohol. The word "wine" appears more than 200
times in the King James Version of the Old Testament.
This word was translated from a number of different
Hebrew words.

The first biblical record of intoxication has to do
with Noah, whom the Bible calls a "preacher of
righteousness." Commenting on Noah's drunkenness, F. B. Meyer has written:

Noah's sin reminds us how weak are the best
of men; liable to fall, even after the most marvelous deliverances. The love of drink will drag
a preacher of righteousness into the dust. Let us
see to it that we fall not into this temptation
ourselves; and that we tempt not others.[2]

Some feel that Noah was unaware of the process of
fermentation and that intoxicating wine was unknown
before the Flood. Matthew Henry alludes to this,
saying:

The drunkenness of Noah is recorded in the
Bible, with that fairness which is found only in
Scripture, as a case and proof of human weak-
ness and imperfection, even though he may have

been surprised into the sin; and to show that the best of men cannot stand upright, unless they depend upon Divine grace, and are upheld thereby.[3]

Commentators' efforts to excuse Noah might be wishful thinking. This man of faith was not the first nor the last to stumble after being greatly blessed by God. Interesting as it may be to speculate about conditions before and after the Flood, we simply do not know the facts. We do know, however, that the day after his intoxication, Noah cursed members of his family. That unpleasant result of drinking is still common today.

Fermented wine was used in Sodom. Lot's drunkenness after his deliverance from that city before its destruction testifies to the use of booze there (see Genesis 19:30-38). Lot's drinking episode ended in immorality, a frequent companion of intoxication. How different the future for Lot's descendants might have been had he or his daughters not included wine among the provisions they hurriedly put together in their last-minute escape from doomed Sodom.

The Prophet Daniel, an abstainer, tells of Belshazzar's (the king of Babylon) last night on earth. He says that on that fateful night the king made a great feast for a thousand of his lords. Wine flowed freely. As the drinking continued, Belshazzar called for the golden and silver vessels that Nebuchadnezzar had taken out of the Jerusalem temple, so that he and his friends could drink wine out of them. (Alcohol often encourages irreverence.) When the party reached its peak of impiety, God called the drinking to a halt and warned the king of coming judgment. Before morning, Belshazzar had lost his position, his kingdom, and his life (see Daniel 5).

In the Old Testament, priests were instructed not to drink wine or any kind of strong drink.

And the Lord spake unto Aaron, saying, Do not drink wine nor strong drink, thou, nor thy sons with thee, when ye go into the tabernacle of the congregation, lest ye die: it shall be a statute forever throughout your generations: And that ye may put difference between holy and unholy, and between unclean and clean; And that ye may teach the children of Israel all the statutes which the Lord hath spoken unto them by the hand of Moses (Leviticus 10:8-11).

Upon skimming these verses one might conclude that this command to abstain from all alcoholic beverages had only to do with serving in the tabernacle. A more thorough reading, however, with special attention given to verse 10, makes it clear that abstaining from beverage alcohol was to be a way of life for the priests. This lifestyle was to demonstrate the difference between holy and unholy, between clean and unclean. In this context, the use of intoxicating beverages is seen as unholy and unclean, and the aim of the priest's lifestyle was to set an example before the people.

Joseph Seiss, an outstanding Lutheran theologian of the nineteenth century, gives the following commentary on this text:

The history of strong drink is the history of ruin, of tears, of blood. It is, perhaps, the greatest curse that has ever scourged the earth. It is one of depravity's worst fruits—a giant demon of destruction. Men talk of earthquakes, storms, floods, conflagrations, famine, pestilence, depotism, and war; but intemperance in the use of intoxicating drinks has sent a volume of misery and woe into the stream of this world's history, more fearful and terrific than either of them. It is the Amazon and Mississippi among the rivers of wretchedness. It is the Alexander and Napoleon among the warriors upon the peace and good of man. It is like the pale horse of the Apocalypse whose rider is Death, and at whose heels follow hell and destruction. It is an evil which is limited to no age, no continent, no nation, no party, no sex, no period of life. It has taken the poor man at his toil and the rich man at his desk, the senator in the halls of state and the drayman on the street, the young man in his festivities and the old man in his repose, the priest at the altar and the layman in the pew, and plunged them together into a common ruin. It has raged equally in times of war and in times of peace, in periods of depression and in periods of prosperity, in republics and in monarchies, among the civilized and among the savage. Since the time that Noah came out of the ark, and planted vineyards, and drank of their wines, we read in all the histories of its terrible doings, and never once lose sight of its black and bloody tracks.[4]

No wonder the priests—the Lord's representatives—were commanded to refrain from drinking intoxicating wine. It is a destroyer of people, an enemy of those they were to lead in the way of life.

Samson's mother was commanded not to drink wine or strong drink while awaiting the birth of her child, because Samson was to be dedicated to God in a special way.

And the angel of the Lord appeared unto the woman, and said unto her, Behold now, thou art barren, and bearest not: but thou shalt conceive, and bear a son. Now therefore beware, I pray thee, and drink not wine nor strong drink, and eat not any unclean thing (Judges 13:3,4).

Rulers were forbidden to use intoxicating wine.

It is not for kings, O Lemuel, it is not for kings to drink wine; nor for princes strong drink: Lest they drink, and forget the law, and pervert the judgment of any of the afflicted (Proverbs 31:4,5).

Solomon gave a blanket command, setting forth the biblical principle that all fermented wine is to be avoided.

Look not thou upon the wine when it is red, when it giveth his colour in the cup, when it moveth itself aright (Proverbs 23:31).

The word *look* as Solomon used it means "to lust for" or "to desire." He is simply saying that we are to have nothing to do with wine after it has fermented.

Biblical Warnings Against Drinking

There are many Old Testament warnings about the effects of intoxicating wine.

Wine is a mocker.

Wine is a mocker, strong drink is raging: and whosoever is deceived thereby is not wise (Proverbs 20:1).

Sin's Explosion

Heavy drinking brings poverty.

For the drunkard and the glutton shall come to poverty: and drowsiness shall clothe a man with rags (Proverbs 23:21).

The use of intoxicating wine brings trouble physically and socially.

Who hath woe? who hath sorrow? who hath contentions? who hath babbling? who hath wounds without cause? who hath redness of eyes? They that tarry long at the wine; they that go to seek mixed wine (Proverbs 23:29,30).

Intoxicating wine ultimately harms the user.

At the last it biteth like a serpent, and stingeth like an adder (Proverbs 23:32).

Beverage alcohol is the companion of immorality and untruthfulness.

Thine eyes shall behold strange women, and thine heart shall utter perverse things (Proverbs 23:33).

The urge to drink can be so strong that it overcomes good judgment, making one forget the misery of his last binge.

They have stricken me, shalt thou say, and I was not sick; they have beaten me, and I felt it not: when shall I awake? I will seek it yet again (Proverbs 23:35).

When religious leaders indulge in strong drink, they deceive their followers as to the realities of life and the importance of getting right with God while there is time.

Come ye, say they, I will fetch wine, and we will fill ourselves with strong drink; and to morrow shall be as this day, and much more abundant (Isaiah 56:12).

Drinking makes a proud and selfish person.

Yea also, because he transgresseth by wine, he is a proud man, neither keepeth at home, who enlargeth his desire as hell, and is as death, and cannot be satisfied, but gathereth unto him all nations, and heapeth unto him all people (Habakkuk 2:5).

The description, then, of beverage alcohol as set forth in the Bible is that of an enemy attacking its users and robbing them of everything that is good in life. Human experience bears this out. To quote the eloquent Seiss again on the evils of strong drink:

Egypt, the source of science—Babylon, the wonder and glory of the world—Greece, the home of learning and of liberty—Rome with her Caesars, the mistress of the earth—each in its turn had its heart lacerated by this dreadful canker-worm, and thus became an easy prey to the destroyer. It has drained tears enough to make a sea, expended treasure enough to exhaust Golconda, shed blood enough to redden the waves of every ocean, and rung out wailing enough to make a chorus to the lamentations of the underworld. Some of the mightiest intellects, some of the most generous natures, some of the happiest homes, some of the noblest specimens of man, it has blighted and crushed, and buried in squalid wretchedness.[5]

In the Old Testament, as well as in the New, wine is often a symbol of God's judgment and wrath. In writing of God's chastening of His people, the psalmist says they have been made to drink the *wine of astonishment* (Psalm 60:3).

Sin's Explosion

The wrath of God prepared for the wicked is pictured as a cup full of fermented wine.

For in the hand of the Lord there is a cup, and the wine is red; it is full of mixture; and he poureth out of the same: but the dregs thereof, all the wicked of the earth shall wring them out, and drink them (Psalm 75:8).

The Prophet Jeremiah saw God's fury symbolized in a cup of wine.

For thus saith the Lord God of Israel unto me; Take the wine cup of this fury at my hand, and cause all the nations, to whom I send thee, to drink it. And they shall drink, and be moved, and be mad, because of the sword that I will send among them. Then took I the cup at the Lord's hand, and made all the nations to drink, unto whom the Lord had sent me (Jeremiah 25:15-17).

In summary, then, the Old Testament records specific tragedies resulting from the use of beverage alcohol. It singles out special people and groups whose lives were to be examples to others, and they are commanded not to drink intoxicating beverages. Clear Old Testament commands declare that we are not to look upon fermented wine with longing nor desire.

Intoxicating wine mocks, impoverishes, affects health, injures its users, and contributes to immorality and dishonesty. It warps character, encouraging selfishness and greed. It is seen as a symbol of God's wrath and judgment.

But there is another side to the question. Some Old Testament verses speak of wine as a blessing, a symbol of prosperity, a source of cheer and gladness. Consider these examples:

Therefore God give thee of the dew of heaven, and the fatness of the earth, and plenty of corn and wine (Genesis 27:28).

And the vine said unto them, Should I leave my wine, which cheereth God and man, and go to be promoted over the trees? (Judges 9:13).

He causeth the grass to grow for the cattle, and herb for the service of man: that he may bring forth food out of the earth; And wine that maketh glad the heart of man, and oil to make his face to shine, and bread which strengtheneth man's heart (Psalm 104:14,15).

Are There Two Kinds of Wine?

How can wine be both a curse and a blessing, a symbol of judgment and a symbol of prosperity? How shall we explain these seeming contradictions?

More than 100 years ago, Dr. William Patton struggled with these same questions. Serving as a pastor in New York City in an era when alcohol use was rampant, Patton became concerned about the detrimental effect that beverage alcohol was having on people in his community. He was disturbed that many who were heavy drinkers quoted the Bible as a defense for their drinking. Let Patton tell his story:

I soon found that the concession so generally made, even by ministers, that the Bible sanctions the use of intoxicating drinks, was the most impregnable citadel into which all drinkers, all apologists for drinking, and all vendors of the article, fled. This compelled me, thus early, to study the Bible patiently and carefully, to know for myself its exact teachings. I collated every passage, and found that they would range under three heads: 1. Where wine was mentioned with nothing to denote its character; 2. Where it was spoken of as the cause of misery; and 3. Where it was mentioned as a blessing, with corn and bread and oil—as the emblem of spiritual mercies and of eternal happiness. These results deeply impressed me, and forced upon me the question, Must there not have been two kinds of wine? So novel to my mind was this thought, and finding no confirmation of it in the commentaries to which I had access, I did not feel at liberty to give much publicity to it—I held it therefore in abeyance, hoping for more light. More than thirty-five years since, when revising the study of Hebrew with Professor Seixas, an imminent [sic] Hebrew teacher, I submitted to him the collation of texts which I had made, with the request that he would give me his deliberate opinion. He took the manuscript and, a few days after, returned it with the statement, "Your discriminations are just; they denote that there are two kinds of wine, and the Hebrew Scriptures justify this view." Thus fortified, I hesitated no longer, but, by sermons and addresses, made known my convictions.[6]

Patton's book, *Bible Wines or Laws of Fermentation and Wines of the Ancients*, has become a classic on the subject.

Having given himself to serious study of the Hebrew and Greek texts and their biblical contexts, Patton discovered the following surprising facts.

(1) The Hebrew words translated "wine" in the Bible do not always mean fermented or intoxicating wine.

(2) The Hebrew word *yayin*, most often translated "wine" in the Old Testament, means grape juice in any form—fermented or unfermented. The true meaning can only be determined by the text.

(3) The Hebrew word *tirosh*, also translated "wine," in all but one possible case means "new wine," "unfermented wine." This word was used repeatedly in the original text in the places where wine has a good textual connotation.

(4) Many wines of the ancients were boiled or filtered to prevent fermentation, and these were often considered the best wines.

So, light begins to break through. The Bible speaks of two kinds of wine: good wine and bad wine, unfermented wine and fermented wine, wine that does not intoxicate and wine that does intoxicate.

While a detailed study of every word translated "wine" in the Bible is provided in my book, *Alcohol, The Beloved Enemy*, consideration here of the two most frequently used words, *yayin* and *tirosh*, will be sufficient to put the question to rest.

New Wine — Unfermented

Tirosh, translated "wine" in the Old Testament, means "new wine or grape juice." It sometimes refers to the juice still in the grapes before pressing. Consider these examples:

Therefore God give thee of the dew of heaven, and the fatness of the earth, and plenty of corn and wine [tirosh] (Genesis 27:28).

Note the association with corn, speaking of the harvest.

All the best of the oil, and all the best of the wine, and of the wheat, the firstfruits of them which they shall offer unto the Lord, them have I given thee. And whatsoever is first ripe in the land, which they shall bring unto the Lord, shall be thine; every one that is clean in thine house shall eat of it (Numbers 18:12,13).

The wine here, *tirosh*, is part of the offering of the firstfruits, that is, the earliest gatherings of the harvest. It is brought freshly pressed to the altar.

And he will love thee, and bless thee, and multiply thee: he will also bless the fruit of thy womb, and the fruit of thy land, thy corn, and thy wine, and thine oil, the increase of thy kine, and the flocks of thy sheep, in the land which he sware unto thy fathers to give thee (Deuteronomy 7:13).

The use of *tirosh* in this text is again with corn and oil—part of the harvest. The reference is unmistakably to new wine, grape juice.

That I will give you the rain of your land in his due season, the first rain and the latter rain, that thou mayest gather in thy corn, and thy wine, and thine oil (Deuteronomy 11:14).

Note the gathering of corn and wine in the harvest with an unmistakable reference to the wine, *tirosh*, being juice still in the grapes—unfermented wine.

And the vine said unto them, Should I leave my wine [tirosh], *which cheereth God and man, and go to be promoted over the trees?* (Judges 9:13).

This interesting verse is part of Jotham's parable, in which the trees call to the vine to come and reign over them. But the vine refuses because it does not want to leave its wine, which cheers God and man. There is no doubt that the wine, or grape juice, is still in the grapes. It is in this unfermented state that wine cheers God and man, because it is part of the blessed abundant harvest.

And that we should bring the firstfruits of our dough, and our offerings, and the fruit of all manner of trees, of wine and of oil, unto the priests, to the chambers of the house of our God; and the tithes of our ground unto the Levites, that the same Levites might have the tithes in all the cities of our tillage (Nehemiah 10:37).

Again, wine, *tirosh*, is spoken of as part of the offering of the firstfruits. Fermentation would have been impossible. If any doubts remain, perhaps Nehemiah 10:39 will settle them.

For the children of Israel and the children of Levi shall bring the offering of the corn, of the new wine, and the oil unto the chambers, where are the vessels of the sanctuary, and the priests that minister, and the porters, and the singers: and we will not forsake the house of our God.

Isaiah further confirms Patton's findings.

Thus saith the Lord, As the new wine is found in the cluster, and one saith, Destroy it not; for a blessing is in it: so will I do for my servants' sakes, that I may not destroy them all (Isaiah 65:8).

Sin's Explosion

There is little wonder that Patton's study brought him to the conclusion that there are two kinds of wine—fermented and unfermented. In this passage the wine is described as still being in the cluster, and "a blessing is in it."

Now read Joel's thrilling prophecy of millennial blessings.

And it shall come to pass in that day, that the mountains shall drop down new wine, and the hills shall flow with milk, and all the rivers of Judah shall flow with waters, and a fountain shall come forth of the house of the Lord, and shall water the valley of Shittim (Joel 3:18).

We shall drink wine in the kingdom—new wine that drops from the vines in the vineyards that grow on the mountains. This wine is unfermented; it is not intoxicating.

And we shall share it together when Christ reigns as King.

While the Hebrew word *tirosh* is translated "wine" 38 times, the word used for wine most often in the Old Testament is *yayin*, which appears 141 times. *Young's Analytical Concordance* defines *yayin* as "what is pressed out, grape juice." In his article, "Did Jesus Turn Water Into Intoxicating Wine?" Lloyd Button writes:

It should be made clear that the English word "wine" used in the Bible is a translation of a number of words in the Hebrew and Greek languages referring to various products of the vine. Some Bible dictionaries insist that the usual meaning of the word wine is fermented. *Yayin* in Hebrew and *oinos* in Greek are the general terms

124

for wine, and as we note later in this article can refer to both fermented and unfermented wine.[7]

Patton quotes Professor M. Stuart on the meaning of the word *yayin*:

In the Hebrew Scriptures the word *yayin*, in its broadest meaning, designates grape juice, or the liquid which the fruit of the vine yields. This may be new or old, sweet or sour, fermented or unfermented, intoxicating or unintoxicating. The simple idea of grape juice or vine-liquor is the basis and essence of the word, in whatever connection it may stand. The specific sense which we must often assign to the word arises not from the word itself, but from the connection in which it stands.[8]

Since the word *juice* appears only once in the Old Testament (in Song of Solomon 8:2, referring to the juice of a pomegranate), and since the geographical setting of the Scriptures is a land of vineyards where grape juice was plentiful, it is understandable that many of the biblical texts having to do with the fruit of the vine refer to grape juice in its unfermented state. This is often the case with the meaning of the word *yayin*, translated "wine."

Note how *yayin* speaks of unfermented wine in the following texts:

And Melchizedek king of Salem brought forth bread and wine [yayin]: and he was the priest of the most high God (Genesis 14:18).

Remembering that fermented wine was forbidden to the priests (see Leviticus 10:9,10), we conclude that the wine Melchizedek carried was unfermented grape juice—wine that does not intoxicate.

Sin's Explosion

He causeth the grass to grow for the cattle, and herb for the service of man: that he may bring forth food out of the earth; And wine that maketh glad the heart of man, and oil to make his face to shine, and bread which strengtheneth man's heart (Psalm 104:14,15).

Because of expressions that today are associated with the use of intoxicating beverages, the reader is likely to think that "making glad the heart of man" is similar to "feeling good" as a result of drinking wine. Nothing could be further from the truth. Fermented wine does not make a person glad; it simply induces sleep in some areas of his brain.

A reading of Psalm 4:7 shows that the source of gladness in one's heart may come from corn and wine, but that this gladness reaches it peak through appreciating God's goodness. In both texts, degrees of gladness are the result of appreciating God's provision. At its height, this gladness comes from understanding God's spiritual blessings. To a lesser degree, it is a result of God's care of man in giving the harvest of food, wine, and oil.

Jeremiah says, *As for me, behold, I will dwell at Mizpah to serve the Chaldeans, which will come unto us: but ye, gather ye wine, and summer fruits, and oil, and put them in your vessels, and dwell in your cities that ye have taken* (Jeremiah 40:10).

This scene of the harvest calls for wine, *yayin*, to be brought in from the fields; it is to be gathered with the summer fruits. Therefore, it would be unfermented and nonintoxicating.

In his masterful work, *The Use of "Wine" in the Old Testament*, Dr. Robert P. Teachout, associate professor of Old Testament at Detroit Baptist Divinity School, concludes his lengthy and detailed study of *yayin* in this way:

Therefore, the unified idea which is inherent in the word *yayin* is not that of a "fermented wine" per se (with divine approval dependent upon an assumed restriction of the quantity ingested, an assumption which is not explicit anywhere in the Old Testament). Instead, the comprehensive idea which the word conveys is that of a "grape beverage" (with the implied fermentation or its lack to be determined objectively only from the divine approval or disapproval of the beverage indicated by any context).[9]

In Teachout's judgment, *yayin* is intended to mean "grape juice" 71 times and "fermented wine" 70 times in the Old Testament.

Alcoholic Wine Speaks of Judgment

Symbolically, intoxicating wine speaks of judgment and wrath. In contrast, nonintoxicating wine speaks of spiritual blessings.

Ho, every one that thirsteth, come ye to the waters, and he that hath no money; come ye, buy, and eat; yea, come, buy wine and milk without money and without price (Isaiah 55:1).

William Patton says:

In all the passages where good wine is named there is no lisp of warning, no intimations of danger, no hint of disapprobation, but always a decided approval.

How bold and strongly marked is the contrast:

The one the cause or intoxication, of violence, and of woes.

The other the occasion of comfort and peace.

The one the cause of irreligion and of self-destruction.

The other the devout offering of piety on the altar of God.

The one the symbol of divine wrath.

The other the symbol of spiritual blessings.

The one the emblem of eternal damnation.

The other the emblem of eternal salvation.[10]

The supposed riddle of the use of wine in the Old Testament is no longer a mystery. And it is encouraging to know that one does not have to be a master of the original languages to determine the type of wine spoken of in each text. Charles Wesley Ewing explains:

...if a reader will just consider the context surrounding the word he can easily understand whether fermented or unfermented grape juice was intended. Wherever the use of wine is prohibited or discouraged it means the fermented wine. Where its use is encouraged and is spoken of as something for our good it means the unfermented.[11]

How sad a commentary Christian social drinkers are in light of the fact that one billion Muslims plus one billion Buddhists who think of Christ only as a good prophet refrain from the use of alcoholic beverages. An old-fashioned, Holy Spirit-empowered revival today would do away with Christian boozers as holiness became our watchword.

But what about the New Testament? Didn't Jesus make wine? Was fermented wine used in the first Communion service? Does the New Testament sanction the use of beverage alcohol?

Let me quote two portions of Scripture to answer these questions. *Know ye not that the unrighteous shall not inherit the kingdom of God? Be not deceived: neither fornicators, nor idolaters, nor adulterers, nor effeminate, nor abusers of themselves with mankind, nor thieves, nor covetous, nor drunkards, nor revilers, nor extortioners, shall inherit the kingdom of God* (1 Corinthians 6:9,10). Galatians 5:19-21 says, *Now the works of the flesh are manifest, which are these; Adultery, fornication, uncleanness, lasciviousness, idolatry, witchcraft, hatred, variance, emulations, wrath, strife, seditions, heresies, envyings, murders, drunkenness, revellings, and such like: of the which I tell you before, as I have also told you in time past, that they which do such things shall not inherit the kingdom of God.*

Also, order my book, *Alcohol, The Beloved Enemy,* to discover what every verse using the word "wine" means from Genesis to Revelation.

---

1 Mark A. Noll, "America's Battle Against the Bottle," *Christianity Today* (January 19, 1979).

2 F. B. Meyer, *The Five Books of Moses* (Grand Rapids: Zondervan, 1955), pp. 16.

3 Matthew Henry, *A Complete Bible Commentary* (Chicago: Moody Press, n.d.), pp. 17.

4 Joseph A. Seiss, *The Gospel in Leviticus* (Grand Rapids: Zondervan, n.d.), pp. 180-181.

5 Ibid., pp. 181-182.

Sin's Explosion

6 William Patton, *Bible Wines or Laws of Fermentation and Wines of the Ancients* (Oklahoma City: Sane Press, n.d.), pp. 11-12.

7 Lloyd Button, "Did Jesus Turn Water Into Wine?" *The Baptist Bulletin* (February, 1973).

8 Patton, *Bible Wines*, pp. 56.

9 Robert P. Teachout, "The Use of 'Wine' in the Old Testament," Th.D. dissertation, Dallas Theological Seminary, 1979, pp. 312.

10 Patton, *Bible Wines*, pp. 74.

11 Charles Wesley Ewing, *The Bible and Its Wines* (Denver: Prohibition National Committee, 1949), pp. 10.

Chapter 8

Hope for Potheads and Speedfreaks

NARCOTIC: 1. Having the power to produce narcosis as a drug. 2. Pertaining to or of the nature of narcosis. 3. Pertaining to narcotics or their use. 4. Used by, or in the treatment of, narcotic addicts. 5. Any of a class of substances that blunt the senses, as opium, morphine, belladonna, and alcohol, that in large quantities produce euphoria, stupor, or coma, that when used constantly can cause habituation or addiction, and that are used in medicine to relieve pain, cause sedation, and induce sleep. 6. An individual inclined toward habitual use of such substances. 7. Anything that exercises a soothing or numbing effect or influence.

—The Random House Dictionary
English Language,
The Unabridged Edition

On the average, persons who are drug addicts live 20 to 25 years less than they would if they were not addicts. And for the poor addict, you can hardly call "life" more than a living death.

—*Dr. H. J. Anslinger*

Sin's Explosion

To be a confirmed drug addict is to be one of the walking dead. There are many symptoms to indicate a confirmed addict—any of them may be present:

The teeth have rotted out; the appetite is lost and the stomach and intestines don't function properly. The gall bladder becomes inflamed, eyes and skin turn a bilious yellow. In some cases the membranes of the nose turn a flaming red; the partition separating the nostrils is eaten away—breathing is difficult. Oxygen in the blood decreases; bronchitis and tuberculosis develop. Good traits of character disappear and bad ones emerge. Sex organs become affected. Veins collapse and livid purplish scars remain. Boils and abscesses plague the skin; gnawing pain racks the body. Nerves snap; vicious twitching develops. Imaginary and fantastic fears blight the mind and sometimes complete insanity results. Often times, too, death comes—much too early in life. Compared with normal persons, according to one authority quoted in a U.S. Treasury Department pamphlet, drug addicts die of tuberculosis at a rate of 4 to 1; pneumonia, 2 to 1; premature old age, 5 to 1; bronchitis, 4 to 1; brain hemorrhage, 3 to 1; cancer and other malignant tumors, 3 to 1; and more than 2 to 1 of a wide variety of other diseases. Such is the torment of being a drug addict; such is the plague of being one of the walking dead.

—New York City Police
Department Report

Pot is rot.

—*Jack Van Impe*

Every day in New York several babies are born who seem as normal as the hundreds of other infants who come into the world here daily. But, within hours, these few infants may jerk, jitter, and twitch, and it becomes evident that they, though only hours old, are hooked on drugs. Their agitation, which may cause them to rub their skin raw, shows they are undergoing withdrawal symptoms probably every bit as racking as those that torture other addicts when they are deprived of heroin, morphine, or barbiturates, the chief addicting drugs.

—Richard D. Lyons
Cleveland Plain Dealer

Drug-related rock festivals, are "exercises in outdoor depravity" attended by "hopped-up sex maniacs." He wrote: "OK, so I'm a senile old hater." I still say these deafening, dope-ridden, degenerate mob scenes have no more place in America than would a publicly promoted gang rape or legally sanctioned performance of the Black Mass.

—Dr. Max Rafferty

The National Institute on Drug Abuse conducted a survey of sixteen thousand seniors at 130 high schools. The results showed 5.5 percent as daily drug users; 63 percent had experimented with illegal drugs; 16 percent had some experience with cocaine; and 12 percent had tried heroin. The strong indication is that students are introduced to drugs by friends.

—Jay Strack

Dope to cope? Nope!

—Jack Van Impe

133

Sin's Explosion

For by thy sorceries [drug abuses] *were all nations deceived.*

—*Revelation 18:23*

Diane Linkletter—the beautiful, talented daughter of famous radio and television personality, Art Linkletter—in a depressed, panic-filled suicidal frame of mind, resulting from an LSD experiment, committed suicide by leaping to her death from her sixth floor apartment in Los Angeles. Her father, because of it, immediately became a champion in the anti-drug crusade.

Why was he so concerned? The following quote by Dr. Robert Sumner states it explicitly:

"Using the language of narcotic users, try to get the picture: Visualize dopers cowering in a corner, waiting to inject, sniff, or swallow. In the group are methheads, junkies, potheads, speedfreaks, acidheads, hypes, pillheads, cokies, cubeheads, and hopheads. They pop, snort, or drop yellow jackets, acid, snow, purple hearts, barbs, weed, bounding powder, smack, mary jane, red devils, speedball, happy dust, mesc, goof balls, rainbows, dexies, reefers, blue velvet, and bennies. They speak of bags, roaches, bindles, sleighrides, fixes, tracks, blanks, decks, blasts, flashes, and being strung out. They have an awesome fear of narcs, stoolies, an O.D., the fuzz, bummers, coming down, not having bread for a dealer, a crash, getting a dummy, cold turkey, freakouts, not being able to score, the cop out, flipping, lemonade, and being busted by the man when dirty. As you can easily see, it's truly a 'bad scene.'"

What has caused this alarming escalation of narcotics use—including alcohol? A booklet published by the Federal Government lists the following six factors as contributing to the great "turn on" of our day:

1. The widespread belief that "medicines" can magically solve problems.
2. The numbers of young people who are dissatisfied or disillusioned, or who have lost faith in the prevailing social system.
3. The tendency of persons with psychological problems to see easy solutions with chemicals.
4. The easy access to drugs of various sorts.
5. The development of an affluent society that can afford drugs.
6. The statements of proselytizers who proclaim the "goodness" of drugs.

Now, what does God's Word have to say about this subject?

There are a number of words used in the Bible to describe the same general subject: SORCERY. Altogether there are at least 27 references to sorcery, sorcerers, witches, witchcraft, and the art of bewitching. Of these, the last five in the New Testament are especially pertinent, for they have a direct bearing on the days in which we live.

In the books of the Old Testament, and in the historical book of the New Testament (the Book of Acts) the term *sorcery* always means "witchcraft or magic." And it is to be carefully noted that it is continually and constantly condemned in the Bible.

But the last five occurrences of the word in the New Testament mean drug addiction! Each of these five references should be considered carefully in the light of their context. Further, the study of these five references clearly reveal: (1) the present world conditions as foretold in the prophetic Scriptures; (2) the inevitable result of drug addiction in just a very few years hence; (3) the certain and definite judgment to come upon the drug pusher as well as (4) the drug victim; and finally, (5) the appraisal of this terrible sin in the sight of God Almighty. But do not stop there. God, in His mercy, has a redemption that will save the drug victim—and YOU should know about it. Consider this revelation of what the Bible says about drugs and drug addiction, and God's remedy.

World Conditions in These Days

The Book of Revelation clearly depicts the time which is immediately ahead of us. After the Rapture of the true Church, when all who have received Jesus Christ as their personal Saviour are translated to be with Him, there will break out on this earth a period of turmoil of such proportions that it is aptly called the "Tribulation." In the middle of this 7-year period, there is this description of the people who will then be living on the earth: *Neither repented they of their murders, nor of their sorceries, nor of their fornication, nor of their thefts* (Revelation 9:21). Everywhere else in the Bible (with the exception of the five verses studied here) the word *sorcery* means "magic, the magical arts, or witchcraft." But not here. Here the original Greek root word is *pharmakeia*. When it is transliterated into English, we have "pharmacy" or "drug store." But the literal and actual meaning of the Greek is "enchantment with drugs." The description, therefore, of the conditions here upon the earth during the terrible Great Tribulation is that men repented not of their enchantment with drugs!

Already we can see the prelude to this—the spread of dope used among even school children is by a hard and unrepenting society of evil mankind!

The Inevitable Results of Drug Use

Such widespread use of drugs cannot help but bring its own destruction. With all their trips and mind expansion propaganda, not one user ever is able to actually do more, or be more efficient, than he was before experimenting with drugs. The steady downward retrogression will be climaxed at the close of this Great Tribulation—when the full cup of its own judgment is measured! The last chapters of the Book of Revelation very graphically picture these resulting conditions. Chapter 18 provides intimate detail. Beginning at verse 21 there is a most comprehensive picture of the terrible results of this worldwide dope addiction:

Thus with violence shall that great city...be thrown down...— the continuation of riots and burnings, which are becoming increasingly a dreadful part of these very days! *And the voice of harpers, and musicians, and of pipers, and trumpeters, shall be heard no more at all...*—no more musicians and singers, including rock-and-roll, which is an accepted part and pattern of this age. *...and no craftsman, of whatsoever craft he be, shall be found any more...*—the unions and the laboring man will be unable to work!

Sin's Explosion

...the sound of a millstone shall be heard no more...—the factories will be shut down!

And the light of a candle shall shine no more at all...—power plants will not even be able to furnish sufficient electricity for lights! *...the voice of the bridegroom and of the bride shall be heard no more at all...*—there will be no rejoicing, no happiness, none of the carefree spirit that drugs are supposed to impart! *...thy merchants were the great men of the earth...*—commerce will come to a grinding halt! What is the reason for all this calamity? *...for by thy sorceries were all nations deceived* (vss. 21-23).

The Greek word for sorceries here is again *pharmakeia*, and can be read, "by their enchantment with drugs were all the nations deceived!" This is the result—the first time in world history that there is mass international usage of drugs! It's happening in our generation. Christ is coming soon!

Judgment of Drug Pushers Is Sure

There is a change in the next occurrence of the word translated "sorceries," and this change reveals a class of people who are doomed. It is found in Revelation 21:8, *But the fearful, and unbelieving, and the abominable, and murderers, and whoremongers, and sorcerers, and idolaters, and all liars, shall have their part in the lake which burneth with fire and brimstone: which is the second death.* The Greek root word *pharmakeus*, means "the enchanter with drugs." This would be the pusher, the seller of drugs. The text plainly declares that eight distinct groups of people will never get into heaven—these eight groups will go into the Lake of Fire (this is a description of eternal hell) and one of these groups is those who are "enchanters with drugs"! What a solemn warning against having any part in this horrible traffic!

Not the Pusher Alone Is Judged

There is one more reference to "sorcerers" in this last book of the Bible. It is almost the same as that given in Revelation 21:8, but it has a still deeper meaning. Revelation 22:15: *For without are dogs, and sorcerers, and whoremongers, and murderers, and idolaters, and whosoever loveth and maketh a lie.* Here the word is again *pharmakeus*, and definitely includes both the drugs and their use, and by extension, includes both the pushers and the users.

Now take notice: These are kept out of heaven! (It wouldn't be heaven very long if they were admitted!) There is only one place to which they can go—and that is the place of eternal punishment, separated from the presence of God! This place was prepared for Satan and his angels (see Matthew 25:41) and the Bible is explicit in its statements that there is no other place for those who refuse to repent of their sin! There they will keep on sinning forever, for it will be too late to be saved. That is why hell is eternal! Of the six classes named here, "sorcerers"—drug pushers and drug users—are named in second place (immediately following the term which describes outlaws as wild dogs)!

Drug Addiction Among 17 Vile Sins

Another word with the same meaning is given in Galatians 5:19-21, *Now the works of the flesh are*

139

manifest, which are these; Adultery, fornication, uncleanness, lasciviousness, idolatry, witchcraft, hatred, variance, emulations, wrath, strife, seditions, heresies, envyings, murders, drunkenness, revellings, and such like: of the which I tell you before, as I have also told you in time past, that they which do such things shall not inherit the kingdom of God.

The word here is translated in our English Bible as "witchcraft." It is the same word again, *pharmakeia*, and it is number six in a list of 17 kinds of sinners who shall not inherit the kingdom of God! The drug user and the drug pusher are both excluded from heaven!

The Important Question

What can be done for the one who finds himself enmeshed in this terrible traffic? Is there no hope for escape from the clutches of this binding habit? The Lord Jesus Christ came into the world for one express reason. First John 3:8 says, *For this purpose the Son of God was manifested, that he might destroy the works of the devil.* For men who are bound in the sins of the flesh, Jesus Christ, God's only begotten Son, came into the world! By His death upon the cross, He has broken the grip of Satan! So now when any guilty sinner calls upon Him for salvation, Jesus Christ immediately frees that person from the shackles of sin which bound Him. There is no limit to the saving power of the Lord Jesus Christ!

Just how does one apply this saving power of Jesus Christ to his own needs? The answer to this question is so simple, many fail to understand it. Salvation is receiving Christ. *But as many as received him, to them gave he power to become the sons of God, even to them that believe on his name* (John 1:12). The power which is given when one receives Jesus Christ as personal Lord and Saviour, is the "power to become something and someone, a child of the King"! Becoming a son of God by faith in Jesus Christ includes victory (see 1 Corinthians 15:57) over the shackles of sin, even dope! Whether you are a victim of drugs or drunkenness—or whatever hold Satan may have on you—the Bible is very plain. It clearly and definitely tells you how to find liberation from sin! Take special notice of these two verses: *Jesus answered them, Verily, verily, I say unto you, Whosoever committeth sin is the servant of sin* (John 8:34), and *If the Son therefore shall make you free, ye shall be free indeed* (John 8:36). The very fact that you commit sin—whether you admit it or not—that committing of sin soon makes you its slave! Some people have sufficient will power to break one habit, but are still bound by other habits which reveal their rebellion against God. But when an individual receives Jesus Christ as his own personal Saviour, He imparts His life into that person, and he is free indeed!

And that—to be free indeed—is what every person bound by sin needs. If you are a "servant of sin" you are a "slave of sin"!

In the Bible you will find the answer to your need. Here are just a few references to help you get started on the way to victory over the sin which binds you. Look them up, and mark them in your Bible:

Sin's Explosion

John 1:12,13; 1:29; 3:1-21; 3:36; 10:28,29; 14:6; Acts 4:12; 16:31; Romans 1:16; 3:23,24; 5:8,9; 2 Corinthians 5:17; 5:21; 8:9; 13:4; Galatians 2:20; Ephesians 2:8; Colossians 1:14; 1:27; 2 Thessalonians 3:3; 1 Timothy 1:15; 2 Timothy 1:12; Titus 1:2; 3:5; Hebrews 2:14-18; 7:25; 12:2; 1 Peter 1:18,19; 1:23; 2:24; 3:18; 1 John 1:7; 2:2; 5:12; Revelation 1:4; 5:9; 12:11, 22:17.

Then, when you have completed the references, read the New Testament beginning with the Gospel of John and mark every verse that applies to you. It will not be long before you will find that God can meet your every need through His Son, Jesus Christ.

Chapter 9

Abortion Is Murder

Abortion: On January 22, 1973, the Supreme Court decreed that unborn children had no "right to life." This decision was made in spite of the fact that the 14th Amendment of the Constitution provides that "no state...shall deprive any person of life, liberty, or property without the due process of law; nor deny to any person within its jurisdiction the equal protection of the laws." Since then, over one million babies have been killed each year. (Today it is 1,500,000 annually.)

—Pratney

In Los Angeles, February 1982, a 20x8x8 metal trash container was discovered, filled with the horrifying spectacle of numerous dead and decaying little bodies, each four pounds or more, pickled in formaldehyde and stacked in leaking tubs like ice cream containers. A week later, authorities removed hundreds more, many with perfectly formed faces and limbs from the home of the man who once owned the now defunct medical lab that had dumped its grisly stock. As well as can be determined, a total of 17,000 fetuses, in various stages of development, were discovered. County officials would not permit news and T.V. photographers near the scene;

143

Sin's Explosion

it shocked many as badly as the news of the Nazi Holocaust.

—*L.A. Reporter*

We must remember that Hitler didn't start killing Jews; he began with the mentally retarded.

Next, he killed those in retarded children's hospitals and homes; criminals in Nazi prisons; and finally, he emptied old peoples homes. Over 40,000 people were killed by Hitler before he began his anti-Semitic campaign. If the state can arbitrarily kill any of us who do not deserve to die, it can kill all of us.

—Pratney

Our people ought to know where we stand on the moral issues of the day. They ought to know where the pastor stands on divorce, on abortion, on capital punishment. God give us churches that are intolerant of evil.

—*Martyn Lloyd-Jones*

An unprecedented tidal wave of commandment-breaking, God-defying, soul-destroying iniquity sweeps the ocean of human affairs.

—Leonard Ravenhill

The revivalist always shocked some, frightened others and alienated not a few, but he knew who had called him and what he was sent to do.

—*A. W. Tozer*

The tragedy of this late hour is that we have too many dead men in the pulpits giving out too many dead sermons to too many dead people.

—Leonard Ravenhill

O that we were more deeply moved by the languishing state of Christ's cause upon the earth today, by the inroads of the enemy and the awful desolation he has wrought in Zion. Alas a spirit of indifference, or at least of fatalistic stoicism, is freezing so many of us.

—*A. W. Pink*

Lo, children are an heritage of the Lord: and the fruit of the womb is his reward.

—*Psalm 127:3*

In Exodus 20:13, God says, *Thou shalt not kill.* Jesus said in Matthew 5:21, *Ye have heard that it was said by them of old time, Thou shalt not kill.* Jesus again said in Matthew 19:18, *Thou shalt do no murder.* We are living in strange and peculiar times. Multitudes today are crying out against capital punishment on the basis of the verse I just quoted from God's Holy Word. And in many instances the same crowd is working feverishly to pass laws favoring abortion to murder little babies.

Why does this sin-sick society show leniency towards murderers, rapists, robbers, and other vicious criminals and then does an about-face by wanting to destroy these little bundles of innocence through abortive murder? Let's face the truth. The majority of those who want to get rid of what God has created in their wombs are those who want to live for self and selfish pursuits, or the unmarried who had a fling in the back seat of a parked automobile or some dingy motel room or a one-night stand based on lust instead of love. Now when the price for a night of adventure is beginning to manifest itself, they want to add to their wickedness by slaying this innocent little baby. Many have done it and will do it without any pangs of conscience. Why? Because Titus 1:15 states that *their mind and conscience is defiled*, depraved and dirty. They think that they are going to get away with their iniquity, but they will have to meet God some day after death. Hebrews 9:27 states, *It is appointed unto men once to die, but after this the judgment.* Now why will abortionists have to meet God at judgment? Because God loves children. In Psalm 127:3, the psalmist cries out, *Lo, children are an heritage of the Lord: and the fruit of the womb is his reward.*

Did you get that? *The fruit of the womb is God's reward.* Don't you destroy or murder that which God has given you. In Mark 9:42, our Saviour is speaking about little children, and wants us *never* to put a stumbling block in their path. Hear Him, *And whosoever shall offend one of these little ones that believe in me, it is better for him that a millstone were hanged about his neck, and he were cast into the sea.* Then He goes into a description of judgment for offending these little ones. Verses 43-46: *And if thy hand offend thee, cut it off: it is better for thee to enter into life maimed, than having two hands to go into hell, into the fire that never shall be quenched: Where their worm dieth not, and the fire is not quenched.*

And if thy foot offend thee, cut it off: it is better for thee to enter halt into life, than having two feet to be cast into hell, into the fire that never shall be quenched: Where their worm dieth not, and the fire is not quenched. And if thine eye offend thee, pluck it out: it is better for thee to enter into the kingdom of God with one eye, than having two eyes to be cast into hell fire: Where their worm dieth not, and the fire is not quenched.

How God must love little ones. Now why is God so against the sin of abortion? Let's consider a few facts about abortion. First of all, what is it?

Four Kinds of Abortion

There are four types of abortion. The first is a suction-type of abortion where a tube is inserted into the womb and there creates a powerful vacuum which tears the fetus from the womb in a mass of blood and tissue which is removed from the mother. This method is used in the earlier stages of pregnancy and occurs in about 75 percent of the cases in the United States and Canada.

The second type is when a spoon-shaped instrument with sharp edges is inserted and is used to cut up the baby, and separate it from the womb. Often because of inadequate dilation the surgeon who is performing the abortion has to use his hands to crush the baby's head, because it is too large to be removed successfully. This was the more common technique of the past but it is still widely used. It runs into the danger of not only possibly cutting the interior of the womb and causing hemorrhaging, but also the danger of infection and possible permanent damage, so that the mother can never again have a successful pregnancy.

The third type of abortion is the salt-brine technique sometimes called salting-down. A large needle is inserted into the womb and through this needle most of the fluids are removed and then a strong salt solution is injected into the mother. The baby thrashes around violently, and unless anesthesia is used the mother will experience extreme pain during this period. The baby is literally pickled in this salt and after a few days is delivered as a stillbirth, dead.

The fourth type is an abortion very similar to a Caesarean operation in which through abdominal surgery the baby is removed. This baby will be alive at the time. It is removed from the mother's body, it will be moving its arms and legs, often it will be crying, struggling for air. After a few hours of crying and moving and thrashing about it finally dies. Does this not sound like murder to you, my friend?

Now the next question—is the fetus a lump or a life? A blob or a baby? I quote from the handbook on abortion.

At 18 days the heart begins to beat and human brain activity can be recorded. The little human inside the mother's womb will at eight weeks grab an instrument placed in its palm and hold on. An electrocardiogram can also be done because the heart is beating regularly and it swims freely in the amniotic fluid with a natural swimmer's stroke. At 10 weeks the body is completely formed and by 12 weeks all organ systems are functional. It breathes, swallows, digests, and urinates. He is very sensitive to pain, recoiling from pin-prick and noise, and seeks a position of comfort when disturbed. Soon he will sleep and wake with his mother. If his amniotic fluid is sweetened, he will swallow more often. If it is made sour, he will quit swallowing. After 12 weeks nothing new will develop or function, only grow and mature.

I want you to get that. In other words, after 12 weeks, the baby is all he'll ever be. Nothing new will develop or function after 12 weeks, only grow and mature. Marcus Richardson was born January 1, 1972, in Cincinnati, Ohio. At exactly 20 weeks he was born, and is today a perfectly normal child.

Is the fetus then, just a lump or a life, a blob or a baby? God makes it emphatically and dogmatically clear that it is a life that's being destroyed. Therefore, it's murder. Ministers who are for abortion, only prove once again that they have turned their backs on the Holy Bible.

In Michigan I saw the names of multitudes of ministers in the Detroit area who favored abortion. Clergymen—get back to your Bibles and believe! Hear the Word of the Lord. God tells Jeremiah that He knew him even before his conception in chapter 1:5: *Before I formed thee in the belly I knew thee; and before thou camest forth out of the womb I sanctified thee, and I ordained thee a prophet unto the nations.* To paraphrase this text, God says, "I knew you when you were just seed and that seed was not even as yet injected into the womb."

The psalmist states in chapter 139:13-16, *Thou hast covered me in my mother's womb. I will praise thee;*

for I am fearfully and wonderfully made: marvellous are thy works; and that my soul knoweth right well. My substance was not hid from thee, when I was made in secret, and curiously wrought in the lowest parts of the earth. Thine eyes did see my substance, yet being unperfect; and in thy book all my members were written, which in continuance were fashioned, when as yet there was none of them. Let me repeat that. And in thy book all my members were written (or planned) when as yet there was none of them. Oh, my friend, don't tell me that God doesn't know about and love that little fetus. IT'S A LIFE, A BABY.

Isaiah cries out in chapter 49:1, *The Lord hath called me from the womb; from the bowels of my mother hath he made mention of my name.* And again says in verse 5, *The Lord...formed me from the womb to be his servant.*

A Fetus Is a Human Person

While these texts are wonderful, the greatest two proofs that the fetus is truly a human being worthy of earthly existence have to do with John the Baptist and the Lord Jesus Christ. The story is recorded in Luke 1:8-15. Zacharias is a priest and is doing his work as a priest, when an angel visits him.

And it came to pass, that while he executed the priest's office before God in the order of his course, according to the custom of the priest's office, his lot was to burn incense when he went into the temple of the Lord. And the whole multitude of the people were praying without at the time of incense. And there appeared unto him an angel of the Lord standing on the right side of the altar of incense. And when Zacharias saw him, he was troubled, and fear fell upon him. But the angel said unto him, Fear not, Zacharias: for thy prayer is heard: and thy wife Elisabeth shall bear thee a son, and thou shalt call his name John. And thou shalt have joy and gladness; and many shall rejoice at his birth. For he [John] shall be great in the sight of the Lord, and shall drink neither wine nor strong drink; and he shall be filled with the Holy Ghost, even from his mother's womb. Let me repeat that. He shall be filled with the Holy Ghost, even from his mother's womb.

From this we see that the fetus within Elisabeth was not just a piece of meat, a fleshly morsel to be extricated like a tumor, but a baby already filled with God's Spirit while in his mother's womb. Mother, don't have that abortion. God may already be doing a mighty spiritual experience in that fetus you plan to eliminate. If to this point you are blindly unconvinced, what will you do with Jesus? Here is One the Bible calls God while He is naught but a four-week-old fetus. The story is recorded in Luke 1:26-36:

And in the sixth month the angel Gabriel was sent from God unto a city of Galilee, named Nazareth, to a virgin espoused to a man whose name was Joseph, of the house of David; and the virgin's name was Mary. And the angel came in unto her and said, Hail, thou that art highly favoured, the Lord is with thee: blessed art thou among women. And when she saw him, she was troubled at his saying, and cast in her mind what manner of salutation this should be. And the angel said unto her, Fear not, Mary: for thou hast found favour with God. And, behold, thou shalt conceive in thy womb, and bring forth a son, and shalt call his name JESUS. He shall be great, and shall be called the Son of the Highest: and the Lord God shall give unto him the throne of his father David: And he shall reign over the house of Jacob for ever; and of his kingdom there shall be no end.

Then said Mary unto the angel, How shall this be, seeing I know not a man? And the angel answered and said unto her, The Holy Ghost shall come upon thee, and the power of the Highest shall overshadow thee: therefore also that holy thing which shall be born of thee shall be called the Son of God. And, behold, thy cousin Elisabeth, she hath also conceived a son in her old age: and this is the sixth month with her, who was called barren.

Mary, after receiving this startling message from God is overwhelmed with excitement and expectation. Finally after four weeks, she feels it necessary to visit Elisabeth, her cousin, to share her blessed experience that she encountered with the Almighty. When she arrives, Elisabeth exultingly exclaims in verse 43, *And whence is this to me, that the mother of my Lord should come to me?* Now, I want you to get that statement because the Lord Jesus in the womb of Mary is only four weeks old. Still, Elisabeth says, "My Lord has come." That little four-week growth is the Lord. That's right. Friend, since the Word of God teaches that, that which is formed in the womb is life, then any act by anyone to eliminate God's creative act within the womb becomes murder.

God Will Judge Abortion

In conclusion, I remind one and all that abortion will certainly be judged at the day of reckoning.

Ecclesiastes 12:14 states, *For God shall bring every work into judgment, with every secret thing, whether it be good, or whether it be evil.* Romans 2:16: *In that day God shall judge the secrets of men by Jesus Christ.* In Revelation 20:12,13, the Lord gives us a picture of the great judgment morning and says, *And the books were opened...and the sea gave up the dead which were in it; and death and hell delivered up the dead which were in them: and they were judged every man according to their works.* God has His books and your records and knows what you did. If you don't repent of your sin, you will meet God face-to-face for destroying that life He created within you at the great Judgment Day.

But let me quickly add that the Bible also states in 1 John 1:7 that *the blood of Jesus Christ his Son cleanseth us from all sin.* So, if you will come to Christ with a repentant, broken heart, you will be forgiven. Why not open your heart and absolve your tormented conscience by praying the following words:

"Heavenly Father, I am sorry for my sin. Forgive me, Lord. Come into my heart now, cleanse me and save me from all my iniquity and sin through Your shed blood, in Jesus' name."

The thief on the cross by the side of Jesus uttered a prayer for forgiveness that contained only nine words, "Lord, remember me when Thou comest into Thy kingdom." Jesus replied, "Today, shalt thou be with Me in paradise." If your prayer was from the heart, your sins were forgiven. Now, go out and live for Christ. Tell others what Jesus has done for you. If you are already the Lord's, pray that an old-fashioned, spirit-empowered revival may soon permeate the land so that this slaughter of the innocents may be stopped forever.

Chapter 10

Latter Day Sins and Signs

The Church began with men in the "upper room" agonizing—and today is ending with men in the supper room organizing. The Church began in revival; we are ending in ritual. We started virile; we are ending sterile.

—Leonard Ravenhill

My dear friends there is only one explanation for the state of the Christian church today. It is the work of the Philistines. The water is there, so why do we not see it? Why are we not able to drink of it? The Philistines have been here, and they have filled the wells with the earth and the rubbish and the refuse.

—*Martyn Lloyd-Jones*

The moon of revival has not yet risen on this hell-bound, Christ-rejecting, speeding-to-judgment generation. We don't "sit at ease" in Zion any more. We have gone past that; we just sleep. In the church, pillars have given place to pillows.

—Leonard Ravenhill

Sin's Explosion

We believers are lean, lazy, luxury-loving, loveless, and lacking.

—Leonard Ravenhill

I love musicians and I have some great musicians in my revival team, but musicians cause us to lie when we sing. Do you ever sing,

"Like a mighty army
   Moves the church of God"?

If you do, get down on your knees and ask God to forgive you for lying. If the average army moved like the average church, it couldn't win a battle against a bunch of pygmies.

—Martyn Lloyd-Jones

No wonder a modernist has declared that men will weep for souls—if the price is right—aye, like Judas, they will be weeping when it is too late.

—Leonard Ravenhill

There is nothing that is so characteristic of every period of revival than a great and a profound seriousness.

Do not take my word for these things, read them for yourselves. Read again how when the saintly Robert Murray McCheyne walked into his pulpit at Dundee, before he had opened his mouth, people would begin to weep and were broken down. Why? Well, there was a solemnity about the man. He had come from the presence of God. He did not trip into the pulpit lightly and crack a joke or two to put everybody at ease and to prepare the atmosphere. No, there was a radiance of God about him. There was a terrible seriousness.

—Martyn Lloyd-Jones

The man whose sermon is "repent" sets himself against his age and will for the time being be battered mercilessly by the age whose moral tone he challenges. There is but one end for such a man—"off with his head!" You had better not try to preach repentance until you have pledged your head to heaven.

—*Joseph Parker*

Tradition says, Paul was only four feet six inches in height, then he was the greatest dwarf that ever lived. He out-paced, out-prayed, and out-passioned all his contemporaries. On his escutcheon was blazed: "One thing I do." He was blind to all that other men gloried in.

—Leonard Ravenhill

But evil men and seducers shall wax worse and worse, deceiving, and being deceived.

—*2 Timothy 3:13*

In the second epistle of Paul to Timothy, chapter 3, verses 1 to 5, Paul deals with the hour when the church of Jesus Christ is resurrected and meets the Lord in the twinkling of an eye. The Lord Jesus Christ is coming again! Our Saviour said in John 14:2,3, *In my Father's house are many mansions: if it were not so, I would have told you. I go to prepare a place for you. And if I go and prepare a place for you, I will come again, and receive you unto myself; that where I am, there ye may be also.* First Thessalonians 4:16-18: *For the Lord himself shall descend from heaven with a shout, with the voice of the archangel, and with the trump of God: and the dead in Christ shall rise first: Then we which are alive and remain shall be caught up together with them in the clouds, to meet the Lord in the air: and so shall we ever be with the Lord. Wherefore comfort one another with these words.* First Corinthians 15:51,52: *Behold, I shew you a mystery; We shall not all sleep, but we shall all be changed, in a moment, in the twinkling of an eye, at the last trump: for the trumpet shall sound, and the dead shall be raised incorruptible, and we shall be changed.*

Signs of His Coming

Now, how do we know that the coming of the Lord draweth nigh? There are many tremendous signs given in the New Testament. Let's consider 2 Timothy 3:1-5, *This know also, that in the last days perilous times shall come. For men shall be lovers of their own selves, covetous, boasters, proud, blasphemers, disobedient to parents, unthankful, unholy, without natural affection, trucebreakers, false accusers, incontinent, fierce, despisers of those that are good, traitors, heady, highminded, lovers of pleasure more than lovers of God; Having a form of godliness, but denying the power thereof: from such turn away.*

Some say, "Haven't these signs always existed? How can these be signs pointing to His return when we have always experienced some of them?" The answer is found by comparing Romans 1:28-32 with 2 Timothy 3:1-5. Paul, in Romans 1, is speaking about the pagan world of the ungodly. However, in 2 Timothy 3, he is speaking about the conditions that shall prevail at the end of the age of Christendom among those who profess the Christian religion. Did you get that? In Romans 1, he is talking about things that are happening among the pagans. In 2 Timothy 3, he speaks about the deterioration of the professing church.

Never before have we seen signs so drastically predominant in the Christian church than at this present hour. The only comfort we find in these conditions is that they do tell us that the coming of the Lord is at hand. We must be ready every moment. Let's consider these signs one by one.

Selfishness

Men shall be lovers of their own selves...

What a picture of this present hour, when church members are so busy satisfying their flesh with the world's goodies and pleasures, that they have no time to pray or witness to lost souls. God help us! A certain scribe came to Jesus in Matthew 22:36-40, and said, *Master, which is the great commandment...? Jesus said unto him, Thou shalt love the Lord thy God with all thy heart, and with all thy soul, and with all thy mind. This is the first and great commandment. And the second is like unto it, Thou shalt love thy neighbour as thyself. On these two commandments hang all the law and the prophets.*

Sin's Explosion

But, we are so busy satisfying our bodily appetites in the professing church of Jesus Christ at the present hour, that we do not have time to pray or win souls to Him. We are lovers of our own selves. One could expect this in the ungodly world of pagans, but how sad when one sees it among those who are supposedly of the family of God.

The Love of Money

Covetousness...
They will love money in the last days. In the first century, Peter could say in Acts 3:6, *Silver and gold have I none; but such as I have give I thee: In the name of Jesus Christ of Nazareth rise up and walk.* The Church has wealth untold, but it doesn't not have the power to perform miracles. We are living in the Laodicean age mentioned in Revelation 3:15,16, *I know thy works, that thou art neither cold nor hot: I would thou wert cold or hot. So then because thou art lukewarm and neither cold nor hot, I will spue thee out of my mouth.* God says, "You make me sick!" Why? *Because thou sayest, I am rich, and increased with goods, and have need of nothing; and knowest not that thou art wretched, and miserable, and poor, and blind, and naked* (Revelation 3:17).

So many in our churches today are in the upper crust. They have money so they think they are really something. They are so important that they have no time to help people, no time to do things for Christ, no time for the church, no time for devotions, no time for anything, except getting a few more dollars. In 1 Timothy 6:10 our God says, *For the love of money is the root of all evil: which while some coveted after, they have erred from the faith, and pierced themselves through with many sorrows*. How sad it is in our day and age to pick up Christian periodicals and read, "Do you want to make $20,000 or $25,000 a year?" as though this was a believer's goal. Thank God when He blesses believers and they use it for His glory. I hope you are not one of the signs of the end. Do not try to get everything you can to build an empire here and neglect the work of Jesus Christ.

Pride

Boasters, proud...

God said, *Humble yourselves in the sight of the Lord, and he shall lift you up* (James 4:10). Satan fell because of pride. In Isaiah 14:13,14 he said, *I will ascend into heaven, I will exalt my throne above the stars of God: I will sit also upon the mount of the congregation, in the sides of the north: I will ascend above the heights of the clouds; I will be like the most High.*

Professing believers are so proud! A man recently came to me with tears in his eyes and said, "I was trying to win this young lady to Christ. Her parents are alcoholics and she had nothing to wear but an old tattered dress. I took her to our church—a fundamental, Bible-believing church. When she walked down the aisle, I heard a few snooty people behind me say, 'Why do they bring that kind of trash to our church?'" If you are so high and mighty, I pray that God will speak to your heart and show you that you are one of the signs that Jesus Christ is coming soon. Our Saviour said in Matthew 11:28,29, *Come unto me, all ye that labour and are heavy laden, and I will give you rest. Take my yoke upon you, and learn of me; for I am meek and lowly in heart: and ye shall find rest unto your souls.*

Blasphemy

Blasphemers...

Blasphemy is a sin against the Lord Jesus Christ. Paul said in 1 Timothy 1:12,13, *And I thank Christ Jesus our Lord, who hath enabled me, for that he counted me faithful, putting me into the ministry; Who was before a blasphemer....* What did he do? He murdered Christians and hated the name of Jesus Christ. There are so many like that today. Our seminaries are filled with apostates who mock the doctrine of the Lord Jesus Christ—His virgin birth, His deity, His blood atonement, and His bodily resurrection. They talk about higher criticism and blaspheme Christ in the Scriptures. Seventy percent of the ministers are either affected or infected by this malady. God help us! Jesus Christ is coming soon!

Disobedience

Disobedient to parents...

Some young people say that they love Jesus Christ, but when their parents ask them to do something, they always answer back with a smart remark. Do they really believe the Bible? Listen, young man and young lady, to Ephesians 6:1-3, *Children, obey your parents in the Lord: for this is right. Honour thy father and mother; (which is the first commandment with promise;) that thou mayest live long on the earth.* I was mightily moved not long ago as I studied John 19:26,27. Jesus Christ was hanging on the cross, dying for the sins of all sinners. Yet, in His last moments, He looked down and saw His wonderful mother, Mary, standing beneath the cross. Do you know what He said? *Woman, behold thy son! Then saith he to the disciple, Behold thy mother!* Even in the last moments of life as Christ was dying for the entire world, He still loved His mother. He came to fulfill the Law and He said in Matthew 19:19, *Honour thy father and thy mother.* You young people who are so disobedient and disrespectful are a sign that Jesus is coming soon.

Unthankfulness

Unthankful...
Look at some of the church members. They are ashamed to pray in a restaurant. When they do bow their heads, they sit there and scratch their eyebrows for a few seconds so that no one will think they are talking to the Almighty God.

Unholiness

Unholy...
What a picture of the twentieth century. Godly separation from the world, according to the Bible, is sneered at as bigotry and puritanism. When one preaches against the dirty, lewd movies, the filthiness of much of this modern music called rock, the

uncleanness of tobacco, the soul-damning habits of drug abuse and alcoholism, many church members say, "Let's not talk about secondary issues." My friend, the holiness of God and holy living are not secondary issues. First Thessalonians 4:7: *For God hath not called us unto uncleanness, but unto holiness.* First Peter 1:16: *Be ye holy; for I am holy.* Again, this sign indicates that Jesus is coming soon. I repeat—all of the signs given in 2 Timothy 3 have to do with Christendom and the professing church in the last days.

Lack of Love

Without natural affection...

This refers to the dissolution of families because of the lack of love. Look at the divorce rate, the murder of babies through abortion, the stories appearing in the papers concerning parents beating their little ones to death or strangling them, and you will know that this sign is being fulfilled.

Broken Promises

Trucebreakers...

Has someone told you a secret in order that you might pray for them? Did you keep it, or did you spread gossip about that person? Promise breaking is another sign now being fulfilled.

Lying

False accusers...

164

Churches from one end of America to the other are splitting because of the exaggerated stories (outright lies) church members tell about other people. When one does falsely accuse a brother, he breaks one of God's commandments. Exodus 20:16 says, *Thou shalt not bear false witness.* Do you know what is going to happen to false accusers? Revelation 21:8 says, *But the fearful, and unbelieving, and the abominable, and murderers, and whoremongers, and sorcerers, and idolaters, and all **liars**, shall have their part in the lake which burneth with fire and brimstone* (emphasis mine).

No Self-control

Incontinent...

This is the lack of control over sexual appetites. How often one hears today, "Live it up. Premarital and extra-marital sex is good and healthy." *Let God be true, but every man a liar* (Romans 3:4). *Marriage is honourable in all, and the bed undefiled* (Hebrews 13:4). Sex is pure and holy in marriage. God goes on to say, *But whoremongers and adulterers God will judge.* As I travel across this land of ours, I see so much of this debauchery going on among church members. Sins of all kinds are being condoned in this hour. Why? Because Jesus Christ is coming soon!

Temper

Fierce...

Some of you men would be minus your teeth if you talked to the waiter in the restaurant like you talk to your wife at home. Oh, but you love Jesus Christ. You are a great Christian at church, but what a fierce, vicious temper you have at home and at work. *Let all bitterness, and wrath, and anger, and clamour, and evil speaking, be put away from you, with all malice* (Ephesians 4:31).

The signs *despisers of those that are good, traitors, heady, highminded* are all self-explanatory.

Pleasure

Lovers of pleasure more than lovers of God...

In the last days, among professing Christians, men will be lovers of pleasure more than lovers of God. This is certainly true! Not only is this true of the world, but churches go into the entertainment business in order to draw crowds. People must be amused, and the Church must meet the craving of pleasure-mad members. How else are godless hypocrites going to be held together? How can half-hearted members be attracted to the services? The latest Christian movie and the Christian minstrel show take the place of the Word of God. Beloved, God has not called us to run a showboat, but a lifeboat. We need to get souls into the kingdom of God.

Many of our religious telecasts and crusades have to feature pagan movie stars whose lives are a mockery to God, but it is done because entertainers draw crowds. The modern evangelistic crusades feature people who are still working full-time in nightclubs, where drinking, gambling, filthy jokes, and solicitation for sex are prevalent. They say, "It does not matter, though, because the end justifies the means. If these religious fakes draw crowds, then it is the right thing to do." God forgive us!

Through it all, Christless souls are lulled to sleep and made to feel religious while every carnal desire of the flesh is gratified under the sanction of the Church. Here is God's way to reach souls in the last days, *They that sow in tears shall reap in joy. He that goeth forth and weepeth, bearing precious seed, shall doubtless come again with rejoicing, bringing his sheaves with him* (Psalm 126:5,6).

Lack of Power

Having a form of godliness, but denying the power thereof...

There is so little power today in the church of God. Again, Romans 1 is a picture of the pagan world while 2 Timothy 3 pictures the professing church just before Jesus comes. Study the 19 signs and you will come to one conclusion: Soon the trumpet of God shall sound and we shall hear three words, *Come up hither* (Revelation 4:1). We will sweep through the heavenlies and see Jesus in the twinkling of an eye. Are you saved? Are you ready? Jesus is coming soon! Let Him into your heart right now. Put Jesus Christ in first place. Soon we will see Him face-to-face. Are you ready for that day?

Chapter 11

Counterfeit Clergymen, Commies, and Cultists

Karl Marx had a sister-in-law active in the evangelical Lower Rhineland Revival, who accomplished some tremendous social improvements while Marx was growing up in Germany. Because of her, he was certainly not ignorant of Christian things.

—Pratney

When D. L. Moody came to London to preach, Karl Marx was bitter, covered in boils, and full of hate and sat in a British Museum writing Das Kapital. He hated Christians—not because he failed to see any real power to transform society, but because of his own counterfeit conversion and subsequent failures.

—Pratney

Marx's disciples were to confront another awesomely holy radical in the person of Catherine Booth, whose own fiery spiritual and practical attacks on corrupt society disturbed them so much that to this day the Salvation Army is the only religion officially banned in the Soviet Union.

—Pratney

169

Sin's Explosion

Years before that revival (I am thinking particularly of the twenties and the thirties) the Presbyterian Church in Northern Ireland had gone astray in its doctrines. It had espoused a doctrine which is called "Arianism" and Arianism denies the eternity and the Godhead of the Lord Jesus Christ. Arius taught that the Lord Jesus Christ was a created being, that He was not co-equal and co-eternal with the Father. It denied Him His Godhead. Now that was the cause of the state of the Church, its utter deadness and uselessness.

—Martyn Lloyd-Jones

No revival has ever been known in the history of churches which denies or ignores certain essential truths. I regard that as an astoundingly important point. You have never heard of a revival in churches, so-called, which denies the cardinal, and fundamental, articles of our Christian faith.

You will find very clearly in the history of the Church that such churches have always opposed, and have always persecuted, those who have been in the midst of revival.

—Martyn Lloyd-Jones

At Yale College a revival "shook the institution to its center." God's instrument here was Timothy Dwight, grandson of Jonathan Edwards. Yale, originally a Christian school, was such a hot-bed of infidelity that the students called each other by the names of Voltaire, Rousseau, and other French intellectuals.

—America's Great Revivals

By 1960, Branham, a Pentecostal healer, began to stray doctrinally, embracing a "oneness position." By 1963, he had received a "Spirit of Elijah" revelation, demanding abandonment of denomination and loyalty to his "coming messenger." On December 18, 1965, driving to Arizona, he was hit head-on by a drunken driver and died Christmas Eve.

—America's Great Revivals

Thousands of people are turning to Buddhism, in India, and in other lands. Even in this land, the cults, too, are thriving.

—*Martyn Lloyd-Jones*

Elijah made it as difficult as he could for the Lord. He wanted fire, but yet he soaked the sacrifice with water! God loves such holy boldness in our prayers, "Ask of Me, and I shall give thee the heathen for thine inheritance."

—Leonard Ravenhill

We have forgotten the martial music in the Church of the living God. We have forgotten that the Church is to be an "army terrible with banners," not an army that is just plain terrible. We have given much attention to the building and almost none to the battle. The note of war has been absent for a long time. But these things will change. God has ways of getting our attention.

—*Pratney*

Some preachers are sound enough in doctrine as far as they go, but they over-emphasize the doctrine of grace. It is well enough to preach on the love of God, but one

171

can pervert even that blessed teaching and make God seem like a doting old granddaddy with no righteousness, no holiness, no wrath against sin.

—Martyn Lloyd-Jones

Now the Spirit speaketh expressly, that in the latter times some shall depart from the faith, giving heed to seducing spirits, and doctrines of devils.

—*1 Timothy 4:1*

Since the beginning of this century, the communists have methodically encircled the free nations of the world by entrenching themselves in those nations they could capture and dominate. Presently, nearly half the world is within their grasp—Afghanistan, Albania, Angola, most of Southeast Asia, Bulgaria, China, Cuba, Czechoslovakia, Ethiopia, East Germany, Hungary, North Korea, Mozambique, West Pakistan, Poland, Romania, Somalia, South Yemen, and Yugoslavia. Communism's authority over these nations constitutes the control of nearly one-third of the world's population. In addition, socialist-aligned nations add another one billion to the count.

William H. Peterson, in an article entitled "The Red Tide Is Rolling Worldwide," states, "May Day has become the banner holiday for communists and socialists the world over, replete with huge parades, displays of military might, giant pictures of Marx and speeches denouncing capitalism. It is a propaganda extravaganza trumpeting the triumph of Marxism. And triumph it is for the communists."

Clergymen, Commies, Cultists

The current unrest in Central America and the Caribbean echoes Mr. Peterson's refrain, serving as an awesome reminder that Russia's bid for world denomination has not abated and knows no bounds.

Communism vs. Christianity

It is truly a sad day in history when leading news reports inform us of the fact that religious groups and communist guerrillas have united in their efforts to subvert and subdue nations. Christians should fight communism, for the two systems are diametrically opposed. One is ordained of God; the other, of Satan. The term, "Christian Marxism" is a blasphemous one. Likewise, "liberation theology" is an abomination. Communism is the system of the Antichrist and must be combatted by the forces of righteousness. Communism is deadly. It has no good points. It is the composite of all crime. It is indeed the politics of God-less souls.

Communism is also a system of murder. Available evidence indicates that perhaps 100 million persons have been destroyed by the communists—untold millions of them believers in Christ Jesus! Many of these dear children of God had to go through unbearable torture before their spirits were released to meet the Saviour. Without becoming grotesque, let me describe some of the immense and intense suffering hundreds of thousands have experienced at the hands of barbarous communistic executioners.

Evangelist Lee Chang Whan was killed for attempting to publish Bibles. The Red Police stripped him naked, bound him, and put him in an empty water pool. The temperature was 17 degrees below zero that day. They then filled the pool and froze Chang Whan to death!

Evangelist Kim Sun was tied between two horses which were then sent running in opposite directions. Kim Sun's crime? Refusing the placement of a communist leader's portrait in the church.

The Reverend Florescu said, "I was tortured with a red-hot poker and with knives. I was beaten badly. Then, starving rats were driven into my cell through a large pipe. I could not sleep, but had to defend myself all the time. If I rested for a moment, the rats would attack me. I was forced to stand for two weeks, day and night. Finally, they brought in my 14-year-old son and began to whip him in front of me, saying that they would beat him until I betrayed my friends. Finally, I cried out, 'Alexander, I must say what they want me to say! I can't bear your beatings any more.' My son answered, 'Father, don't do me the injustice of having a traitor as a dad. If they kill me, I will die with the words, "Jesus" and "my country" on my lips.'" The communists, in a state of enragement, fell upon the child and beat him to death.

Obviously, communism is a system of politics controlled by human beings with animalistic tendencies. Oh, how can clergymen boisterously and vehemently promote a blending of Christianity and communism through "liberation theology"? Such is impossible if one is a genuine Christian. Marxist-motivated clergy and laity may do so, but real children of God cannot.

Communism and Prophecy

The Bible teaches that religious leaders and laymen will promote this satanically inspired political philosophy in the last days. There is no doubt about it, for 1 Timothy 4:1 states, *Now the Spirit speaketh expressly, that in the latter times some shall depart from the faith, giving heed to seducing spirits, and doctrines of devils.* Clergymen who unite Marx and Christ do so because their leader is not the blessed Jesus but the god of this present world system—Lucifer! Their god has smitten them with paralysis of the spiritual optic nerve and they cannot see because of the darkness he creates.

Consider 2 Corinthians 4:4, *The god of this world hath blinded the minds of them which believe not, lest the light of the glorious gospel of Christ, who is the image of God, should shine unto them.* Ministers who proclaim "liberation theology" and participate in marches that help the communists do so because of what and who they really are—as described in 2 Corinthians 11:13-15. *For such are false apostles, deceitful workers, transforming themselves into the apostles of Christ. And no marvel; for Satan himself is transformed into an angel of light. Therefore it is no great thing if his ministers also be transformed as the ministers of righteousness; whose end shall be according to their works.*

Yes, there is a name for such clergymen and laymen who deviate from the truth of Christianity—that name is "apostate"!

What does the Bible have to say about apostates?

First of all, the Bible teaches that apostates will arise within the Christian church. Acts 20:29: *For I know this, that after my departing shall grievous wolves enter in among you, not sparing the flock.*

Secondly, the Bible describes the great damage apostates do. The passage just quoted states that they spare not the flock (God's people). Romans 16:17 informs us that they "cause divisions and offences." They also "deceive the hearts of the simple" (vs. 18). That is exactly what some of these men have done as they have come out of liberal, apostate seminaries and tried to rob people of their faith in the Bible. First Timothy 4:2 declares that they speak "lies in hypocrisy." [They] *consent not to wholesome words, even the words of our Lord Jesus Christ* (1 Timothy 6:3). *Their word will eat as doth a canker* (2 Timothy 2:17), *and* [they] *overthrow the faith of some* (vs. 18). How true and how sad!

Second Peter 2:1 states that these apostates *shall bring in damnable heresies, even denying the Lord.* Verse 12 tells us that [they] *speak evil of the things that they understand not.* In verse 15, we learn that [they] *have forsaken the right way.* Verse 18: *They speak great swelling words of vanity.*

Second John, verse 7, states that they *confess not that Jesus Christ is come in the flesh.* They also [turn] *the grace of our God into lasciviousness, and* [deny] *the only Lord God, and our Lord Jesus Christ* (Jude 4).

Karl Marx and Engels became such apostates. Both men at one time talked about their love for Christ and then turned to atheism and communism. Through hours of research and study, I found historical records that document their Christian background and show the depths of degradation those who merely profess Christianity enter. Indeed, one of my sources was a book by Richard Wurmbrand entitled, *Was Karl Marx a Satanist?*

I discovered that in his early youth, Karl Marx was a professing Christian. His first written work is called *The Union of the Faithful With Christ*. There we read these beautiful words, "Through love of Christ we turn our hearts at the same time toward our brethren who are inwardly bound to us and for whom Christ gave himself in sacrifice." He continues, "Union with Christ could give comfort in sorrow, calm trust, and a heart susceptible to human love, to everything noble and great, not for the sake of ambition and glory, but only for the sake of Christ."

When Karl Marx finished high school, the following was written on his graduation certificate under the heading, *Religious Knowledge*: "His knowledge of the Christian faith and morals is clear and well grounded."

As he began his descent into apostasy he soon wrote, "I wish to avenge myself against the One who rules above."

This change took place because Marx ran with the wrong crowd and involved himself with satanism. He became part of the "falling away" prophesied in 2 Thessalonians 3, as well as a fulfillment of one of the latter-day signs mentioned in 1 Timothy 4:1, *Some shall depart from the faith, giving heed to seducing spirits, and doctrines of devils.*

His father wrote him on March 2, 1837, deeply concerned about his son's involvement with the occult. He said, "Only if your heart remains pure and beats humanly and if no DEMON will be able to gain your heart, only then will I be happy."

His father felt this sadness because of a poem Karl had sent him on his 55th birthday entitled, "The Pale Maiden." Marx's poem said:

Thus heaven I've forfeited,
I know it full well.
My soul, once true to God,
Is chosen for hell.

By 1839 Marx wrote, "I harbor hatred against all gods." He declared that his final aim in life was to draw all mankind into the abyss and to follow laughing. He has had great success. One hundred million have been mercilessly slaughtered.

Engels, too, fulfilled these prophecies and became apostate to the core. As a teenager he wrote glowing poetry about his faith. Read the following and weep. It was penned by the man who would later become Marx's greatest accomplice in the destruction of religion:

Lord Jesus Christ, God's only Son,
O step down from Thy heavenly
    throne and save my soul for me.
Come down in all Thy blessedness,
Light of Thy Father's holiness,
Grant that I may choose Thee.
And when I draw my dying breath
    and must endure the pangs of death,
Firm to Thee may I hold;
That when my eyes with dark are filled
And when my beating heart is stilled,
In Thee shall I grow cold.
Up in Heaven shall my spirit praise

thy name eternally,
Since it lieth safe in Thee
Ever, ever, ever living,
Thee abiding to behold,
Shall my life anew unfold.

Imagine! These two men rebelled against God, apostatized, and fulfilled 1 John 2:19, *They went out from us, but they were not of us; for if they had been of us, they would no doubt have continued with us: but they went out, that they might be made manifest that they were not all of us.*

The Rotted Fruit of Apostasy—Individually

The fruit of an apostate is always rotten to the core. This was true of Marx.

Marx's marriage produced six children. Three of them died of starvation in infancy because he never accepted a job to support his little ones. He was too busy formulating his anti-God doctrines.

Two more of his children committed suicide. (Who wouldn't with a father like Marx?) Once when he received a large sum from a rich uncle, he used it for a two-month drinking spree, leaving his wife and kiddies penniless in London.

The Rotted Fruit of Apostasy—Internationally

The theories of Karl Marx are the foundation for international communism's scientific laws. They include:

Sin's Explosion

(1) "There is no God." This means that communists deny every virtue and value system originating with God. Hence,

(2) "There are no moral absolutes." All is right which advances the cause of socialism and all is wrong which impedes its progress. For the communist, to lie, cheat, steal, or even murder is perfectly moral if it advances the system. That's why Lenin said, "We do not believe in eternal morality. Our morality is entirely subordinated to the interest of the class struggle." This is the reason so many have suffered horrendously at the hands of these atheists.

Millions more may suffer in the near future. Why?

Soon the "red horse" of the Apocalypse will make her grand move. Yes, the Bible teaches that the communists will continue their campaign of international aggression until they meet their Waterloo—ISRAEL! Revelation 6:4 informs us that it is a "red" horse that brings bloodshed and destruction to the world. I do not believe it is mere coincidence that the Communist Bloc nations are all described as "red." My book, *11:59...and Counting!* provides complete details and scriptural proof regarding the catastrophic events which will soon take place in the Middle East.

The Bible also teaches that China moves against Israel (see Revelation 16:12). Presently, the Chinese are completing construction of a highway through Manchuria, Mongolia, Nepal, Tibet, West Pakistan, and Afghanistan. The road leads to the Euphrates River and Israel, and soon both communist superpowers, Russia and China, will head for the Holy Land! Some believe they will act independently while others say they will be united. The point is that both armies are there for the bloodiest battle of the ages.

America and the End

God's Word also speaks of an hour when all nations shall be involved in a horrendous international conflict—undoubtedly World War III. Isaiah gives witness to this fact in chapter 14 and Zechariah 14:2 plainly states that all nations turn against Israel at Jerusalem just prior to the Battle of Armageddon. How far are we from that point? Shockingly, in a recent poll, 70 percent of all Americans stated that they expect World War III within the next 10 years! They believe Armageddon is at the door!

I thank God for America's leaders who see the danger of communism and who have determined that America shall stand as the final bastion of freedom. They believe that Lenin meant what he said when he declared, "As long as capitalism and socialism exist, we cannot live in peace. In the end, one or the other will triumph. A funeral dirge will be sung over world capitalism." They also accept the fact that LaFerte meant what he said when he stated, "There is no use in hoping for a communist victory unless we destroy Christianity."

In the light of communism's accomplishments to date and current events in the Middle East, we may have only months, weeks, or days left to tell the world about Jesus. Therefore, we must pray for our leaders as they take a stand for liberty. We must also pray for misguided ministers who proclaim a union of communism and Christianity, known as "liberation theology." They need help spiritually. Some of you may even need to pray about your own soul's need. Perhaps you started well on the trail of Christianity, writing poems about and quoting verses from God's Holy Word. Today, like Marx and Engels, you have followed Satan's detour signs and are far from God.

Come back lest you say with Marx, "My soul once true to God is chosen for hell."

Chapter 12
The Errors of Irreverent Reverends

Tetzel painted the benefits of indulgences in the crassest terms, best seen in the proverb, "As soon as the coin in the coffer springs, the soul from purgatory's fire springs."

If Tetzel had only stayed away from Luther's turf, history would have no doubt been radically different.

—Pratney

The papal court was "served at supper by six naked girls."

—*Durant, The Reformation, pp. 344*

On Monday, January 29, I expounded twice. Then I sat up till nearly one in the morning with my honored brother and fellow-laborer, John Wesley. We debated with two clergymen from the Church of England and some other strong opposers of the doctrine of the new birth. God enabled me to declare with great simplicity what He had done for my soul. This made them look upon me as a madman. We speak about what we know and testify of that which we have seen but they won't receive our witness.

—George Whitefield

Sin's Explosion

The bishops say our going out into the highways and bridges and compelling poor sinners to come in is not proper. We ought not to plead so for them to be reconciled to God. They want to know by what authority we preach. They ask, "What sign shewest thou unto us, seeing that thou doest these things?" (John 2:18).

What further sign would they require? We did not go into the fields until we were excluded from the churches. Has not God set His seal to our ministry in an extraordinary manner? Have not many who were spiritually blind received their sight? Have not many who have been lame strengthened to run the way of God's commandments? Have not the deaf heard? the lepers been cleansed? the dead raised? and the poor had the gospel preached to them? That these notable miracles have been wrought, not in our own names or by our own power, but in the name and by the power of Jesus of Nazareth cannot be defiled. And yet they require a sign.

—George Whitefield

At Bristol I received a letter from a dear Christian brother saying that an opposing minister had said, "I believe the devil in hell is in you all. Whitefield has set the town on fire, and now he is gone to kindle a flame in the country."

Shocking language for one who calls himself a minister of the gospel!

—George Whitefield

There has only been one major revival since 1859. Oh, we have passed through a barren period, with that devas-

tating higher criticism and the evil that it has done, in pulpits.

—*Martyn Lloyd-Jones*

Beware of false prophets, which come to you in sheep's clothing, but inwardly they are ravening wolves.

—*Matthew 7:15*

Christ is God. But instead of recognizing and reverencing Christ as the God-man modern theologians and religious leaders of the liberal school tear Jesus Christ down from His throne of deity and substitute men thereon.

These ordained wolves in sheep's clothing substitute a psychedelic "trip," by way of a marijuana cigarette, a methedrine injection in the arm, or the swallowing of LSD for a "religious experience." They favor the abolition of "unjust laws" so that young people may practice perversion (called "love"), premarital relations, and every kind of abomination under the approval of the church. In uplifting men as gods and God as a mere man, they make Jesus Christ—the founder and cornerstone of the Christian church—a hippie or a clam-digger in their youth literature, they also condone the sin of teenagers by blessing their barnyard morals, by encouraging the lowering of the drinking age, and by condoning the imbibing of booze at the family table. God help us! White is black and black is white; light is darkness and darkness is light; bitter is sweet and sweet is bitter! Yes, even the movie marquee shouted, "It's a mad, mad, mad, mad world!"

Sin's Explosion

What's the problem with multiplied clergymen and their parishioners? St. John sums it up accurately and precisely in chapter 3, verse 19, when he says, *This is the condemnation, that light is come into the world, and men loved darkness rather than light, because their deeds were evil.* The Apostle Paul agrees. He says in Romans 1:21-25, *Because that, when they knew God, they glorified him not as God, neither were thankful; but became vain in their imaginations, and their foolish heart was darkened. Professing themselves to be wise, they became fools, and changed the glory of the uncorruptible God into an image made like to corruptible man, and to birds, and fourfooted beasts, and creeping things. Wherefore God also gave them up to uncleanness through the lusts of their own hearts, to dishonour their own bodies between themselves: Who changed the truth of God into a lie, and worshipped and served the creature more than the Creator, who is blessed forever. Amen.*

Wow! What a powerful portion of Scripture. Forget the ramblings of Freud, the Viennese psychologist, and believe what God has to say about the weird behaviorism of ancient, as well as modern-day, homo-sapiens. Now, most of us dislike what God says about us with a "purple passion." Why? Because created creatures think that they know as much or more than God does about them. Well, the Bible lays bare the condition of the populated world. It strips man of his hypocritical explanations of "why" he does what he does, and reveals that every human born into the world is a sinner by nature and in need of a Saviour! Hence, man can shout and argue from now until doomsday about his basic goodness and his ability to change the world—but the Bible doesn't waste time answering such silliness for a creature who can't create the breath he uses to denounce the truth!

"Liberation Theology" Is Disastrous

Karl Marx is an example of just one of the myriads of human beings who tried to supersede God's indictment of the human race and the remedy for sin through our Lord Jesus Christ. Today, his offspring are Legion, and many of them parade in ecclesiastical robes and are labeled "right reverend doctors of divinity." Well, they preach "liberation theology," a blend of Christ and Marx, and doom the souls of their hearers. In negating the truths of the gospel for the heretical teachings of bums like Lenin and Marx, they have produced disastrous results among their followers.

Paul describes the calamitous results in Romans 1:26-32, *For this cause God gave them up unto vile affections: for even their women did change the natural use into that which is against nature: And likewise also the men, leaving the natural use of the woman, burned in their lust one toward another; men with men* [homosexuality] *working that which is unseemly, and receiving in themselves that recompence of their error which was meet. And even as they did not like to retain God in their knowledge, God gave them over to a reprobate mind,* [or a mind devoid of sound judgment]*, to do those things which are not convenient; Being filled with all unrighteous-*

ness, fornication [pre-marital sex], *wickedness, covetousness, maliciousness; full of envy, murder, debate, deceit, malignity; whisperers, backbiters, haters of God, despiteful, proud, boasters, inventors of evil things, disobedient to parents, without understanding, covenantbreakers, without natural affection, implacable, unmerciful: Who knowing the judgment of God, that they which commit such things are worthy of death, not only do the same, but have pleasure in them that do them.*

There it is—God's graphic indictment against the human race, wherein the details of man's sinfulness and fulfillment of His lusts are laid out in no uncertain terms. It is a modern day picture of the moral and spiritual condition of so-called "Christian America," but God's payday is coming, for *the unrighteous shall not inherit the kingdom of God. Be not deceived: neither fornicators,* [premarital sex], *nor idolaters, nor adulterers* [extra-marital flings], *nor effeminate, nor abusers of themselves with mankind, nor thieves, nor covetous, nor drunkards* [including holiday boozers], *nor revilers, nor extortioners, shall inherit the kingdom of God* (1 Corinthians 6:9,10).

There Is Hope for Sinful Man

Now don't misunderstand. There is hope for *all*. I, once, was steeped in sin. There was a time in my life when I became intoxicated. I, too, cursed God and lived the life of a pagan. Then Jesus came. He's the Answer. He changed me—and what He did for Jack Van Impe, He can do for you, for *if any man* [or woman] *be in Christ, he* [or she] *is a new creature:*

old things are passed away; behold, all things are become new (2 Corinthians 5:17).

First, however, one must see himself as God does—a sinner. The old hymn, "Amazing Grace," tells the true story of each of us: "Amazing Grace, How sweet the sound, That saved a wretch like me. I once was lost, But now am found, Was blind, But now I see." Do-gooders within various religious environments hate this castigation of their inflated opinions of self—but that doesn't change anything. God says, *All we like sheep have gone astray; we have turned every one to his own way* (Isaiah 53:6).

David, the psalmist, inspired by the blessed Holy Spirit, said, *The Lord looked down from heaven upon the children of men, to see if there were any that did understand, and seek God.* [There were none, for:] *They are all gone aside, they are all together become filthy: there is none that doeth good, no, not one* (Psalm 14:2,3).

There is no doubt about it. The Bible concludes that sin is a universal disease. Every man is spiritually sick. No human is exempt, *For all have sinned, and come short of the glory of God* (Romans 3:23), and *so death passed upon all men, for that all have sinned* (Romans 5:12). The modern psychologists, psychiatrists, liberal theologians, sociologists, anthropologists, "doing-what-comes-naturalists," and "explainers-away-of-human-behavior" may try to obliterate the sin question and its universality in the human race, but it won't go away! For God again reminds all of us in Isaiah 64:6 that *we are all as an unclean thing, and all our righteousnesses* [plural] *are as filthy rags; and we all do fade as a leaf; and our iniquities, like the wind, have taken us away* [from God].

But wait! God does not leave us without a way of escape. A bright hope, a complete and final solution which is pleasing to Him and available to every man who accepts it is the solution found in His Son, the Lord Jesus Christ. The cure is the costliest that has ever been provided in the annals of history, but it is *free* to whosoever will come and partake of it!

The cure arrived almost 2,000 years ago, just outside the little town of Bethlehem. While shepherds watched their flocks by night, the sky was suddenly rent with a glorious light which shone round about them. Then a heavenly voice announced the greatest news the world ever heard, *For unto you is born this day in the city of David a Saviour, which is Christ the Lord* (Luke 2:11).

So it happened, God came down, the second Person of the Trinity, in the form of man to do for man what man could not do for himself—save him from sin! This He did 33 years later on Calvary's cruel cross as He shed His blood for all—including you!

Yes, *He was wounded for our transgressions, he was bruised for our iniquities: the chastisement of our peace was upon him; and with his stripes we are healed* (Isaiah 53:5). Thank You, Jesus. May I close with the greatest love story ever told? It's penned in John 3:16, *For God so loved the world, that He gave His only begotten Son, that whosoever believeth in Him should not perish, but have everlasting life*. This is God's promise to you if you will receive His gift— the death of His Son for your sin—TODAY.

Chapter 13

Gospel Dynamite

The gospel is a fact; therefore tell it simply.

The gospel is a joyful fact; therefore tell it cheerfully.

The gospel is an entrusted fact; therefore tell it faithfully.

The gospel is a fact of infinite moment; therefore tell it earnestly.

The gospel is a fact of infinite love; therefore tell it feelingly.

The gospel is a fact of difficult comprehension to many; therefore tell it with illustration.

The gospel is a fact about a Person; therefore preach Christ.

—Archibald Brown

The Reformation was due not so much to the fact that Luther was earnest, Calvin learned, Zwingli brave, and Knox indefatigable, as it was to old truth being brought to the front and to the poor the gospel was preached. Had it not been for the doctrines which they taught, their zeal for holiness, and their self-sacrifice, their ecclesiastical improvements would have been of no avail. The power lay not in Luther's hammer and nails, but in the truth of those theses which he fastened up in the sight of all men.

—C. H. Spurgeon,
The Sword and the Trowel, pp. 216.

I am solemnly impressed that the schools are to a great extent spoiling the ministers. Mrs. Finney ventured to say to a seminary man who was supplying for me on Broadway: "You are preaching over the heads of the people." The student said: "I cannot descend to the people. I must cultivate an elevated style."

Mrs. Finney later said, "I have never seen this man's name connected with revivals."

—Charles G. Finney

Jonathan Edwards was tall, spare, deliberate, White-field, only of average height, jumped about like a jack-in-the-box. Edwards spoke with quiet intensity, his thin tones reaching the dim corners of the galleries. White-field hurled gospel truths like thunderbolts, his eyes flashing (one eye squinted, a memento of measles).

Edwards' sermons were masterpieces of theological thought. He built truth upon truth until the weight of them bore down on his listeners like a pile driver. White-field's orations, unremarkable from a theological stand-point.

—*America's Great Revivals*

The gospel is not an old, old story, freshly told. It is a fire in the Spirit, fed by the flame of Immortal Love; and woe unto us, if through our negligence to stir up the gift of God which is within us, that fire burn low.

—Dr. R. Moffat Gautrey

The Church of our day should be pregnant with passionate propagation, whereas she is often pleading with pale propaganda.

—Leonard Ravenhill

"It is appointed unto man once to die," a wild, terrifying shriek came from the audience; Grimshaw, one of his workers, pressed through the crowd and cried, "Brother Whitefield, you stand amongst the dead and the dying; an immortal soul has been called into eternity, the destroying angel is passing over the congregation. Cry aloud and spare not!"

After a momentary silence, Whitefield began again, only to hear a second shriek and a second man fall dead near where Lady Huntingdon and Lady Margaret Inghan were standing. After that the entire mass of the people seemed, predictably enough, "overwhelmed" by his appeal. God had found another man He could trust; Whitefield was a light-sabre in His hand for the nations. In one single week after preaching at Moorfields, he received one thousand letters from people under spiritual concern and admitted 350 people to communion.

—The Power of the Gospel Under
the Anointing of the Spirit, Whitefield Journals

Moreover, brethren, I declare unto you the gospel which I preached unto you, which also ye have received, and wherein ye stand; By which also ye are saved, if ye keep in memory what I preached unto you, unless ye have believed in vain. For I delivered unto you first of all that which I also received, how that Christ died for our sins according to the scriptures...

—1 Corinthians 15:1-3

But though we, or an angel from heaven, preach any other gospel unto you than that which we have preached unto you, let him be accursed.

As we said before, so say I now again, If any man preach any other gospel unto you than that ye have received, let him be accursed.

—Galatians 1:8,9

I never tire of quoting the cases of certain ministers used of God in the past who would not dare to go into the pulpit to preach until they had an absolute assurance that the Holy Spirit was going to accompany them there, and was going to empower them.

—*Martyn Lloyd-Jones*

For I am not ashamed of the gospel of Christ: for it is the power [dynamite in the Greek New Testament] *of God unto salvation to every one that believeth; to the Jew first, and also to the Greek.*

—*Romans 1:16*

Ministers of the gospel of Jesus Christ, Christian educators, and Sunday school teachers have but one message to preach, and that message is the gospel. This is the Great Commission given to us by the Lord before He went into glory. He said in Mark 16:15, *Go ye into all the world, and preach the gospel to every creature.*

What is this gospel? Paul, in 1 Corinthians 15:1-4 says, *I declare unto you the gospel…how that Christ died for our sins according to the scriptures; And that he was buried, and that he rose again the third day according to the scriptures.* The gospel or "good news," then, is the death, burial, and resurrection of Jesus Christ.

There are many in our churches today—clergymen and others—who do not preach the *true* gospel. This is a dangerous position. The Holy Spirit, through Paul, said in Galatians 1:8,9, *Though we, or an angel from heaven, preach any other gospel unto you than that which we have preached unto you* [the death, burial, and resurrection of Christ], *let him be accursed. As we said before, so say I now again, If any man preach any other gospel unto you than that ye have received, let him be accursed* [or anathema]. Ladies and gentlemen, one does not preach the *true* gospel until he is proclaiming the death, the burial, and the resurrection of Jesus Christ. However, there is more to it than meets the eye.

This gospel we preach must be centered around Jesus Christ or Christological truth—in other words, *doctrine*. I heard an evangelist on nationwide television say, "I don't preach doctrine, I just preach Christ." This is impossible! Why? If one says, "God became man," he is preaching Christology. If he adds, "Christ died for sinners," his sermon includes soteriology. If he further states, "Christ is coming back as King of kings and Lord of lords," he has introduced eschatology—doctrine!

Now I know a lot of men who preach for half an hour and never quote one verse or use doctrine. They are "skyscraper" preachers. They build story upon story upon story—nine stories and a tear-jerker. No wonder their converts don't last! One cannot get people saved and find them around a year later if they come forward simply on emotion. The *Word* is what

195

is needed. *For the word of God is quick and powerful, and sharper than any twoedged sword, piercing even to the dividing asunder of soul and spirit, and of the joints and marrow, and is a discerner of the thoughts and intents of the heart* (Hebrews 4:12). When the Word is used, whether it be in a church service or a Sunday school class, it will do its work!

Yes, we need doctrine based upon God's Word—and that's why He gave us the Bible. *All scripture is given by inspiration of God, and is profitable for* **doctrine***, for reproof, for correction, for instruction in righteousness* (2 Timothy 3:16, emphasis mine). Paul said to Timothy in 2 Timothy 4:2-4, *Preach the word; be instant in season, out of season; reprove, rebuke, exhort with all longsuffering and* **doctrine***. For the time will come when they will not endure sound doctrine; but after their own lusts shall they heap to themselves teachers, having itching ears; And they shall turn away their ears from the truth* (emphasis mine). Yes, they'll want their ears scratched with pleasing platitudes rather than the Word of God. Oh, we must preach *doctrine!*

Now, what is this gospel message concerning Christ? First of all, that God came. Jesus was not just a good man, a teacher, a philosopher, or a moralizer. Christ was God from all eternity! He was *from of old, from everlasting* (Micah 5:2). His name is *Wonderful, Counsellor, The mighty God, The everlasting Father* (Isaiah 9:6).

Jesus, the Creator

Do you know that Jesus Christ created the world with the Father? Genesis 1:1 states, *In the beginning*

God created the heaven and the earth. The Hebrew text states, *In the beginning **Elohim** created the heaven and the earth.* In Hebrew—and the Old Testament was written in Hebrew—whenever a word ends with "IM" it means more than one: sereph*IM*, cherub*IM*, eloh*IM*. Yes, *In the beginning* Eloh*IM* [a PLURALITY, the TRINITY] *created the heaven and the earth.*

Some may say, "Oh, but Dr. Van Impe, I'm not a Hebrew scholar. How do I know that you're telling me the truth?" Very simple. In Genesis 1:26, God said, *Let US make man in OUR image* (emphasis mine). One doesn't have to be an Albert Einstein to know that "us" and "our" refer to more than one—and in Genesis 1:1, the reference is to Jesus. That's right, *He was in the world, and the world was made by him, and the world knew him not* (John 1:10). *For by* [Christ] *were all things created, that are in heaven, and that are in earth, visible and invisible* (Colossians 1:16).

Yes, Jesus was God from all eternity, the second member of the Trinity who came to earth to take upon himself a body containing blood so that He could shed that blood for the remission of sins. Any other message is not the true gospel! Matthew 1:23 states, *Behold, a virgin shall be with child, and shall bring forth a son, and they shall call his name Emmanuel, which being interpreted is, **God with us*** (emphasis mine). Simple, isn't it?

I like Acts 16:31. The Philippian jailer had just asked, *What must I do to be saved?* (vs. 30), and Paul and Silas replied, *Believe on the Lord Jesus Christ, and thou shalt be saved, and thy house.* What happened? The jailer [believed] *in God with all his house* (vs. 34). The "God" of verse 34 is the "Lord Jesus Christ" of verse 31! Is this your Jesus? *Christ came, who is over all, God blessed for ever* (Romans 9:5). *Great is the mystery of godliness: God was manifest in the flesh* (1 Timothy 3:16). In Hebrews 1:8, we find Jehovah the Father speaking to His own Son. Jehovah's Witnesses ought to listen to Jehovah! Listen to what He says, *Thy throne, O God, is for ever and ever*.

The Virgin Birth

Furthermore, this God came into the world through the womb of the virgin Mary. Some skeptics say, "Are you foolish enough to believe that Jesus Christ was born without a father? That's an impossibility." Listen, if God could put Adam and Eve on this earth without a father OR a mother, I'm convinced He could put Jesus here when He had one more with which to work than in the beginning.

I get a charge out of some of these new translations of the Bible. They should be titled, "The Reversed Versions." When they come to Isaiah 7:14, the translators try to say that the Hebrew word "alma" means "young woman," not "virgin," in order to destroy the doctrine of the virgin birth. Let me quote the verse, *Therefore the Lord himself shall give you a sign; Behold, a virgin shall conceive*. Now, let's use their interpretation, "Therefore the Lord himself shall give you a sign; Behold, a young woman shall conceive." That's some sign! It happens a million times a day! However, a virgin—untouched by a man—IS a sign, and that's *exactly* what happened.

God's angel said to Mary, *The Holy Ghost shall come upon thee, and the power of the Highest shall over-shadow thee: therefore also that holy thing which shall be born of thee shall be called the Son of God* (Luke 1:35).

Yes, God placed His Son into the womb of the virgin Mary through the power of the Holy Spirit. Jesus said, *A body* [my Father] *prepared me* (Hebrews 10:5). Why did Jesus enter the world in this fashion? To bypass the old nature. Had He come through the sperm or seed of a man, He would have had tainted blood. He would have had the old Adamic nature within Him—and this couldn't be if He was to be our Redeemer. Thus, God came through the womb of a virgin. Jesus was without sin.

I believe in the doctrine of the impeccability of Christ. He never sinned, nor could He ever sin because He was God! [He] *did no sin* (1 Peter 2:22). [He] *knew no sin* (2 Corinthians 5:21). [He] *is holy, harmless, undefiled, separate from sinners* (Hebrews 7:26). That's my Jesus. He was virgin born so that He might be the God-man.

There are many who say, "Oh, we can get to heaven by following the Sermon on the Mount, the 'Golden Rule,' and the Ten Commandments." *No we can't!* There is only one way, and it's Jesus Christ. Seven hundred times the Book says so! Seven hundred times the New Testament declares the fact that there is only one way for a sinner to get into the pearly gates—and that's through the blood of Jesus! *For it is the blood that maketh an atonement for the soul* (Leviticus 17:11). *Without shedding of blood is no remission* (Hebrews 9:22). [Christ] *hath purchased*

199

[the church] *with his own blood* (Acts 20:28). *In whom we have redemption through his blood* (Ephesians 1:7). [We are] *redeemed with the precious blood of Christ* (1 Peter 1:19). If one hasn't gotten in that way, he didn't get in!

He Died...and Rose Again

This is not the end of the story, for they laid Him in a tomb (see Matthew 27:60). Had He remained in that tomb—like Buddha, Mohammed, Zoroaster and the rest of the leaders who headed up religions—we would have been helplessly and hopelessly lost for all eternity. But, praise God, on the third day, Jesus Christ fulfilled all of His promises and AROSE! Yes, *the God of our fathers raised up Jesus* (Acts 5:30). [He] *was delivered for our offences* [Calvary], *and was raised again for our justification* (Romans 4:25). *Remember that Jesus Christ of the seed of David was RAISED from the dead* (2 Timothy 2:8, emphasis mine). *Now the God of peace, that brought again from the dead our Lord Jesus, that great shepherd of the sheep...make you perfect in every good work to do his will* (Hebrews 13:20,21).

Does one really have to believe that Christ was God from all eternity, that He came through the womb of a virgin, that He took a body with blood to shed for sin, and that after they buried Him He rose bodily? Does one have to accept all this to be saved? YES! That's the gospel! Can one believe the gospel if it omits the Resurrection? No! Can one get to heaven if he does not accept this teaching? No! *If thou shalt confess with thy mouth the Lord Jesus, and shalt believe in*

*thy heart that God hath raised him from the dead,
thou shalt be saved* (Romans 10:9).

Hear me, my friend. Perhaps you've been following the Sermon on the Mount, the "Golden Rule,"
and the Ten Commandments, or have been trying to
do the best you humanly can. Well, this isn't enough.
Through this discourse you have now learned that
God came, that He took a body with blood, that He
shed His blood for you, and that He rose again from
the dead. Have you ever received this Jesus? That's all
He wants you to do. That's the gospel.

Wait! There is more!

Secondly, the gospel, when it is presented, must
center around conduct. I'm one of these old-fashioned evangelists who still believes in preaching the
message of holy living or holiness! We've got too
many people who raise a hand, walk an aisle, and
send their photograph for baptism, saying, "We're
in!" There's more to it than that.

Salvation Brings Newness of Life

When a man gets saved, he begins to act differently, live differently, talk differently, walk
differently, and even smell differently! My father was
an entertainer in the Belgian nightclubs of Detroit for
10 years. He always smelled like a hangover! Then
Jesus Christ came and there was a glorious transformation. Today, however, one can call himself a Christian without ever having experienced a change of life.
Beloved, this cannot be! When one is converted, he is
raised to *newness of life* (Romans 6:4). If it didn't
happen, he was not genuinely converted.

Sin's Explosion

Second Corinthians 5:17 says, *Therefore if any man be in Christ* [not a denominational structure, but Christ], *he is a new creature* [or creation]*: old things are passed away; behold, all things are become new.* Why? Romans 10:10: *For with the heart* [not with the head] *man believeth unto righteousness.* A lot of folks have it intellectually. They know all the theological truths, all of the creeds, and can quote them verbatim—but they've never been changed. God says it is a matter of the *heart.* First John 5:4 adds, *For whatsoever* [whosoever] *is born of God* [born again] *overcometh the world.*

Because of these facts, Romans 6:12 says, *Let not sin therefore reign in your mortal body.* Christ gave himself *for our sins, that he might deliver us from our sins* (Galatians 1:4). *According as he hath chosen us in him before the foundation of the world* (Ephesians 1:4). Why? *That we should be* **holy**. This is what's missing in our churches today. There is no call for holiness. One just goes through the motions. He walks an aisle as multitudes have done. However, they had a religious exercise rather than an experience with Jesus Christ. This is not sufficient. The Saviour wants holy living.

For God hath not called us unto uncleanness, but unto holiness (1 Thessalonians 4:7). He *saved us, and called us with an holy calling* (2 Timothy 1:9). Yes, *let every one that nameth the name of Christ depart from iniquity* (2 Timothy 2:19). Thus, we are to *follow peace with all men, and holiness, without which no man shall see the Lord* (Hebrews 12:14). Again, *Be ye holy; for I am holy* (1 Peter 1:16). Jesus is coming soon, and millions—MILLIONS—who name the name of Jesus are going to be missing! They knew the dogmas and creeds, but never knew Jesus.

The Communion of Love

Thirdly, and finally, the gospel presentation must center around communion. To most people, the word *communion* means "a sacrament" or "an ordinance," but there is another beautiful meaning. *Webster's Dictionary* defines communion as "intimate fellowship." Have you ever heard the expression, "the communion of the saints"? It means "intimate fellowship with ALL believers"—all of God's people: red, golden, black, white, Baptists, Methodists, Presbyterians, Evangelical Free, Nazarenes—you name them.

I'm going to tell you something. I'm a Baptist, but I needed a new touch so that I could love a Nazarene, love a brother in the Evangelical Free Church, a brother from the Christian Reformed movement, and all brothers who are born again. I don't care what label one bears, he's my brother if he believes the truths of the gospel and has received my Jesus.

I'll tell you something else. If one does not possess the spirit of love, millions are going to miss the Rapture because they had it in the head rather than the heart. When it's in one's heart, there's love. Yes, *he that saith he is in the light, and hateth his brother, is in darkness, even until now. He that loveth his brother abideth in the light, and there is none occasion of stumbling in him. But he that hateth his brother is in darkness* (1 John 2:9-11).

Sin's Explosion

Many excuse the sin of hatred by identifying it as a part of the conflict between the old Adamic nature of man and the new nature of Christ. They say it's the old nature that hates and the new nature that loves, so don't worry about it, because it can't be controlled anyway. WRONG! John is talking about *two groups* of people—the children of God and the children of the devil—not merely two natures. Hear God: *In this the children of god are manifest, and the children of the devil* (1 John 3:10). Did you get it? He said, "children of God and children of the devil"—*children of God and children of the devil!* Let's not quibble about it. God means what He says. There are *two* groups, *two* families, and LOVE portrays the family of God while hatred pictures the other.

Who's who? *Whosoever doeth not righteousness is not of God, neither he that loveth not his brother* (1 John 3:10). Again, *Beloved, let us love one another: for love is of God; and every one that loveth is born of God, and knoweth God* (1 John 4:7). What did you say, precious Holy Spirit? *Every one that loveth is born of God, and knoweth God.* Further, *He that loveth not knoweth not God; for God is love* (vs. 8). Hear it again: *He that loveth not, knoweth not God.* PLEASE, in Jesus' name, for the sake of your soul that will live eternally—either with Christ or separated from Him for the ages of ages—*make sure it's real!* Remember: *He that loveth not knoweth not God; for God is love.*

When one puts a label in these verses, i.e., "He that loveth Baptists is of God," it's not enough. It's EVERY brother who belongs to Jesus that we are to love. *If we love one another, God dwelleth in us* (1

John 4:12). *If a man say, I love God, and hateth his brother* [ANY brother], *he is a liar* (1 John 4:20).

We like to preach about certain sins, but there is a sin that is greater than adultery, greater than fornication (premarital sex), and greater than drunkenness or drug addiction. Do you know what that sin is? *Hatred*. When did you last hear a sermon on this subject? This vicious sin has become acceptable. God forgive us!

Presently, we're so enmeshed in fighting with one another and excommunicating other brothers that we don't have time left to do what we're supposed to be doing—proclaiming the unsearchable riches of Christ—His death, burial, and resurrection—the gospel! This gospel is the cornerstone of revival. Without this good news, there can be no great move of God. Seek a genuine Christian experience. Don't look at others and criticize Christianity. Instead get the real thing and set an example.

Chapter 14

Professors or Possessors?

There is a great deal of so-called Christianity which is quite Christless.

—Martyn Lloyd-Jones

In the evening I went very unwillingly to a society in Aldersgate Street, where someone was reading Luther's preface to the Epistle to the Romans. About a quarter before nine, while he was describing the change which God works in the heart through faith in Christ, I felt my heart strangely warmed. I felt I did trust in Christ, Christ alone, for salvation, and an assurance was given me that He had taken away my sins, even mine, and saved me from the law of sin and death.

—*John Wesley*

Seven thousand, six hundred people in the West give up professing faith in Christ every day.

—Pratney

Fifty percent of all members of Satanic worshippers in California left evangelical gospel preaching churches.

—*Billy Zeoli*

Sin's Explosion

Some estimate that over 80 percent of his converts during the revivals stayed true to Christ without ever backsliding, an awesome testimony to the power of a pure life and an urgent message of holiness.

—Pratney, speaking of Charles G. Finney

The multitudes of all sects and denominations that attended Finney's sermons were enormous...it was wonderful to see the change so soon made in the manners of the inhabitants. From being thoughtless and indifferent about religion, it seemed as if all the world was growing religious; one could not walk through a town in an evening without hearing psalms sung by different families in every street.

—Ben Franklin

They profess that they know God; but in works they deny him, being abominable, and disobedient, and unto every good work reprobate.

—Titus 1:16

Christianity is in dire need of revival. Sin is rampant throughout the entire church of Jesus Christ, and instead of bowing our heads in shame and sorrow and clothing ourselves in sackcloth and ashes as Old Testament saints did, we ignore or excuse the immoralities and improprieties as normal behavior because we are saved by grace. Thus, we excuse the vilest of sins as mere weaknesses of the flesh, and unconcernedly believe that because we are under grace rather than under Law, we have a special dispensation to practice sin. If one disagrees with such reasoning, he's labeled a legalist.

We Must Be Careful That Our Grace Message Does Not Produce Disgrace

Much lopsided, unscriptural teaching abounds in our world because the devil is the instigator of confusion. He will influence a sincere Christian to become unbalanced along one doctrinal line. The believer's constant harping about his pet theory, finding every verse to support it and ignoring the complete revelation on the particular subject, causes chaos. One will become enamored over the teaching of "predestination" to the point of becoming bitter over all "whosoever will" texts. Another will constantly talk "repentance" to the exclusion of the "grace of God." Even so, multitudes will talk "grace" until the subject of "works" is considered a dirty word among enlightened "grace advocates."

Martin Luther was so dogmatic about "grace" as presented in the Book of Romans that he bitterly lambasted the "works" emphasis found in the Book of James. Had it been possible, he would have removed the writings of James from the canon of Scripture.

Let's be consistent and believe all of God's Word. It fits together beautifully when one studies it with an unprejudiced mind. Don't ever build a doctrine on one verse or one book of the Bible. It leads to false doctrine. Combine all of God's revelation together before determining the truth on any subject. *No prophecy of the scripture is of any private* [single or solo] *interpretation* (2 Peter 1:20). One can prove anything by building on the foundation of one verse. Study the text, then the context and then trace the subject throughout the entire Bible to arrive at the truth. A text out of context becomes a pretext.

When one takes all of God's Word into account concerning "grace" and "good works," he concludes that salvation is "faith plus nothing." It is all God, and nothing man does saves, or keeps him saved. Salvation is by "grace," offered freely through Christ's sacrifice, and is received by faith, apart from works. However, the completed teaching is that this salvation which is "Christ in you," manifests the "good works" that the holy nature of Christ within produces.

James discusses this in chapter 2:14-20, *What doth it profit, my brethren, though a man say he have faith, and have not works? can faith,* [this kind of faith] *save him? If a brother or sister be naked, and destitute of daily food, and one of you say unto them, Depart in peace, be ye warmed and filled; notwithstanding ye give them not those things which are needful to the body; what doth it profit? Even so faith, if it hath not works* [or does not produce works], *is dead, being alone. Yea, a man may say, Thou hast faith, and I have works: shew me thy faith without thy works, and I will shew thee my faith by my works.*

The outflow of works is a sign that an inward faith is operative. You say, "I believe, I believe, and that settles it." It does if this genuine belief produces love, holiness, and good works. However, a faith that is void of works is phony. James continues in verse 19, *The demons also believe, and tremble.* The demons who eventually fill hell believe, but never produce righteous acts or good works. Why? They make an intellectual assent to facts rather than have an experience that partakes of God's nature. Friends, if this is all you have, you will join the myriads of demons in the eternal Lake of Fire. If one lives like the devil, acts like the devil, talks like the devil, and runs with the devil, he will end up with the devil. When one truly believes, he will be "a new creature" in Christ Jesus, and the results will be holiness and good works.

Professors and Possessors

With the thought in mind that genuine Christianity produces good fruit, let's consider two texts. The one depicts a professor of religion, the other a possessor of Christ. One has to do with an intellectual acceptance of facts that does not save the soul, even though one can quote every verse on grace in the Bible. The other depicts a heart experience that manifests the fruit of salvation. Jesus describes both.

Please notice that in the first reference, Matthew 7:1, Christ says, *Judge not, that ye be not judged.* I have heard this text misconstrued, misinterpreted, and misappropriated often. Hear me. This verse refers to the judging of one's motives in Christian service. For instance, it is wrong to say, "Oh, she sings to be seen of men." This type of judgment is wrong because no one knows the motives of another. Thus, we are not to judge others regarding motives.

If people sin, they are to be judged, for Christ says in verse 16, *Ye shall know them by their fruits.* The

Sin's Explosion

Saviour then dogmatically tells us exactly what their rotted fruits produce in verses 22,23. Hear Him: *Many will say to me in that day, Lord, Lord, have we not prophesied in thy name? and in thy name have cast out devils? and in thy name done many wonderful works? And then will I profess unto them, I never knew you: depart from me, ye that work iniquity.*

This is shocking. Christ is talking about ministers who preached His Word. Wait! He is talking about a specialized group who manifest the sign gifts of Romans 7 and 1 Corinthians 12-14. In spite of their masterful expositions of Scripture and their miraculous exorcisms and healings, they are for ever lost because Christ says, "I NEVER—get it—NEVER—NEVER—NEVER—knew you."

Why? They were workers of iniquity. They lived in sin and wallowed in the mire of depravity while ministering the Word of God.

On the other hand, Christ depicts those who have been incontrovertibly saved by grace, saying in John 10:27, *My sheep hear my voice, and I KNOW THEM AND THEY FOLLOW ME* (emphasis mine).

To the one crowd of reverends and Christian workers, possessing even sign gifts, Christ says, "I NEVER KNEW YOU, YOU WORKERS OF INIQUITY."

To the other group He declares, "I KNOW MY SHEEP BECAUSE THEY FOLLOW ME."

To the wolves in sheep's clothing (see Matthew 7:15), Christ says, *Depart from me, ye that work iniquity* (Matthew 7:23).

Professors or Possessors?

To the sheep He says, *And I give unto them eternal life; and they shall never perish, neither shall any man pluck them out of my hand* (John 10:28).

WHERE DO YOU STAND?

Examine yourselves, whether ye be in the faith (2 Corinthians 13:5).

May I plead with you for honesty as you study the following truths. Eternity is a long time to either be saved or lost.

Lost Preachers and Miracle-Workers

Matthew 10:1-8 records Christ's calling of twelve men to preach. *And when he had called unto him his twelve disciples, he gave them power against unclean spirits, to cast them out, and to heal all manner of sickness and all manner of disease. Now the names of the twelve apostles are these; The first, Simon, who is called Peter, and Andrew his brother; James the son of Zebedee, and John his brother; Philip, and Bartholomew; Thomas, and Matthew the publican; James the son of Alphaeus, and Lebbaeus, whose name was Thaddaeus; Simon the Canaanite, and Judas Iscariot, who also betrayed him.*

Verse 5: *These twelve Jesus sent forth.* To do what? Verse 7: *And as ye go, preach, saying, The kingdom of heaven is at hand. Heal the sick, cleanse the lepers, raise the dead, cast out devils: freely ye have received, freely give.*

In this text Judas Iscariot was called to preach. Question...Did he preach? Did he heal? Did he perform miracles? The answer is yes! Luke 9 gives the names of the twelve, and verse 6 states, *And they departed, and went through the towns, preaching the gospel, and healing every where.* Judas usually went on preaching and healing missions with Matthew who wrote the first Gospel. However, even Matthew, a real saint, was deceived by Judas. You see, this hypocrite had mastered the theological jargon of the hour so beautifully that everyone who heard him said, "If any man has the old-time religion, he does!"

The question arises, Was Judas a saved man who lost what he had, or was and is it possible to teach, preach, witness, and heal the sick without knowing the Lord? Let's see.

In John 6:64, Jesus said, *But there are some of you that believe not. For Jesus knew from the beginning who they were that believed not, and who should betray him.* Christ knew that Judas was a fake from day one. That's why Christ added, *Have not I chosen you twelve, and one of you is a devil?* [or diabolos, "devil in the flesh"] (John 6:70).

Again, consider John 12:5,6. A woman anointed the feet of Jesus with perfume and dried them with her hair. Judas, seeing the act, said, *Why was not this ointment sold for three hundred pence, and given to the poor? This he said, not that he cared for the poor; but because he was a thief, and had the bag, and bare* [stole] *what was put therein.* Thus, Judas was a thief, a crook, and a scoundrel throughout his entire ministry. Since no practicing thief can enter heaven (see 1 Corinthians 6:10), it's obvious that Judas was a lost preacher, healer, and miracle-worker.

If that sounds far-fetched, study 1 John 2:19 about antichrists in the ministry. *They went out from us, but they were not of us; for if they had been of us, they would no doubt have continued with us: but they went out, that they might be made manifest that they were not all of us*. Let's dissect the verse. "They went out from us," were ordained and approved by us, "but they were not of us...if they had been of us, they would no doubt have continued with us: but they went out [or turned their backs on us] that it might be made manifest that they were not all of us."

Don't let mighty signs and wonders deceive you. Satan can counterfeit everything but *the fruit of the Spirit* (Galatians 5:22). Here is proof. Second Corinthians 11:13-15: *For such are false apostles, deceitful workers, transforming themselves into the apostles of Christ. And no marvel; for Satan himself is transformed into an angel of light. Therefore it is no great thing if HIS MINISTERS also be transformed as the ministers of righteousness* (emphasis mine). This is happening in abundance today!

Proof of the New Birth

How, in a day of confusion, can one know who and what is genuine? There are **two C's** that prove a man is born again, and one of the two must always be operational.

The first is the **changed life**. The new birth is not just a new label, it is a new life! When God comes into one's body, there must be a change—and that is what happens at salvation. Second Peter 1:4 says that we become *partakers of the divine nature*. No one can receive God's nature and not be different. Romans 6:4 adds that we are raised to *newness of life*. Romans 10:10: *For with the heart man believeth unto right-eousness*.

Second Corinthians 5:17: *Therefore if any man be in Christ, he is a new creature: old things are passed away; behold, all things are become new*. First John 5:4: *For whatsoever is born of God overcometh the world, even our faith*. This change means we no longer are what we were.

Watch the two tenses in the English language. Romans 6:17: *But God be thanked, that **ye were** the servants of sin, but **ye have** obeyed from the heart that form of doctrine which was delivered you*.

First Corinthians 6:9-11: *Know ye not that the unrighteous shall not inherit the kingdom of God? Be not deceived: neither fornicators* [the sex sin between the unmarried], *nor idolaters, nor adulterers, nor effeminate, nor abusers of themselves with mankind* [homosexuals], *nor thieves, nor covetous, nor drunk-ards, nor revilers, nor extortioners, shall inherit the kingdom of God. And such **were** some of you: but ye **are** washed*.

Many of the Corinthians had been such sinners, but they were changed. They no longer were the vilest of the vile. They did not remain in adultery, did not continue the practice of homosexuality, and did not continue to be alcoholics. That is what they were.

That's why 1 Peter 4:3 says, *For the **time past** of our life may suffice us to have wrought the will of the Gentiles, when we walked in lasciviousness, lusts,* *excess of wine, revellings, banquetings, and abominable idolatries.*

Revellings comes from the Greek word meaning "wild jumpings" and *banquetings* from the word meaning "wild parties." It is not the typical twentieth century banquet. Peter is simply saying that salvation delivers a man from the lustful pleasures he once enjoyed when his lifestyle centered around the satisfying of bodily appetites, including illicit sex, liquor, wild parties, and wild jumpings (modern dancing). Because of the transformation, pagans and backslidden Christians mock changed believers. Thus, Peter adds in verse 4, *They think it strange that ye run not with them to the same excess of riot, speaking evil of you.*

Friend, when one is saved, he no longer is what he was. If one still is what he was, he ain't! (That's poor grammar, but good theology!) That's why Paul sums it up masterfully and correctly in 1 Timothy 1:12 by saying, *I thank Christ Jesus our Lord, who hath enabled me, for that he counted me faithful, putting me into the ministry; Who was before a blasphemer, and a persecutor, and injurious: but I obtained mercy.*

Heaven is for those whose lives have been transformed by the power of God, because they became partakers of His holy nature through the new birth experience. This is not to say that they can never do wrong, for *if we say that we have no sin, we deceive ourselves, and the truth is not in us* (1 John 1:8). Instead, it simply means that a truly born-again Christian cannot live in sin, love sin, enjoy sin, and practice sin endlessly. *He that committeth* [or, in the Greek, practiceth] *sin is of the devil* (1 John 3:8).

One who is born of God becomes a partaker of God's nature. The result is a changed life. Thus, because God is living within the Christian, [he] *doth not commit* [practice] *sin; for his seed* [God's nature] *remaineth in him: and he cannot* [practice] *sin, because he is born of God* (1 John 3:9). So when a Christian sins, he can expect to hear from heaven.

Spiritual Spanking

In this light, let's consider the second "C," the **chastised life**. Can a believer do wrong, slip, or sin? Of course, but a sinning Christian becomes the most miserable person upon earth, because God chastises him until he returns to the pathway of holy living which he originally experienced.

God's chastening, or spiritual spanking, is discussed in Hebrews 12:5-11. *My son, despise not thou the chastening of the Lord, nor faint when thou art rebuked of him: For whom the Lord loveth he hasteneth, and scourgeth every son whom he receiveth. If ye endure chastening, God dealeth with you as with sons; for what son is he whom the father chasteneth not? But if ye be without chastisement, whereof all are partakers, then are ye bastards, and not sons. Furthermore we have had fathers of our flesh which corrected us, and we gave them reverence: shall we not much rather be in subjection unto the Father of spirits, and live?*

For they verily for a few days chastened us after their own pleasure; but he for our profit, that we might be partakers of his holiness. Now no chastening for the present seemeth to be joyous, but grievous: nevertheless afterward it yielded the peaceable fruit of righteousness unto them which are exercised thereby.

Verse 10 points out that our Heavenly Father administers chastisement "that we might be partakers of his holiness." If holy living is not part of one's Christian experience, or if repeated chastisement is not encountered in order to drive the backslider to return to his original experience, such a person did not have a genuine salvation experience. Hear God again: *But if ye be without chastisement, whereof all are partakers, then are ye bastards* [illegitimate children; false professors], *and not sons* (Hebrews 12:8). Not sons? NOT SONS! God wants all of His children to remain the "new creations" that they were when He saved them (see 2 Corinthians 5:17). When they fail, He will lovingly discipline His own to bring them back.

So desirous is God of holiness within His family that He has programmed a holy walk for every one of His children:

(A) In eternity past, He chose us to be holy. *According as he hath chosen us in him before the foundation of the world, that we should be holy and without blame before him in love* (Ephesians 1:4).

(B) Presently, He calls us to the goal of holiness that was planned for us before the foundation of the world. [God] *saved us, and called us with an holy calling* (2 Timothy 1:9). Again, in 1 Thessalonians 4:7 we find that *God hath not called us unto uncleanness, but unto holiness.*

Sin's Explosion

(C) Should we step out of line spiritually, leaving the plan and calling of God, He chastises or spanks us in order that we may return to His plan (see Hebrews 12:10).

Do you see the three steps? We are chosen, called, and chastised unto holiness. Without these proofs, one is lost.

Are YOU walking as Christ walked? Is chastisement a reality when you walk out of the Lord's will? Herein lies the verification of salvation and true Christianity. The evidence is not in knowing theological truth or in quoting the creeds and clichés of the Christian faith. Instead, the evidence is holiness unto the Lord. Those who argue in favor of liquor, drugs, tobacco, pornographic magazines, R- and X-rated movies, suggestive music, premarital sex, extramarital flings, and every ungodly pleasure in existence prove that they have experienced little, if any, of the holiness that true salvation produces. Get the real evidence—before it is eternally too late!

Does God really expect holiness within His family? Search the Scriptures:

Ye shall be holy; for I am holy (Leviticus 11:44). *For thou art an holy people, The redeemed of the Lord* (Isaiah 62:12). *Even so now yield your members servants to righteousness unto holiness (Romans 6:19).*

In Colossians 1:22, we find that Christ wants to present us holy and unblameable and unreprovable in his sight [at His coming]. Indeed, Christians are to *follow peace with all men, and holiness, without which no man shall see the Lord* (Hebrews 12:14). There is no hedging with respect to God's command: *Be ye holy; for I am holy* (1 Peter 1:16).

The evidence has been presented. Christianity is "Christ in you." When one partakes of His divine, holy nature, a change occurs. The reciting of every religious creed in the world is meaningless if one's life is polluted with the world's defilements. Those who think that anti-worldly preaching constitutes unnecessary sermonizing on secondary issues had better examine their own lives to see if they are truly in the faith. Holy living is a fruit of Holy Spirit-produced salvation. It is mandatory for entrance into God's presence.

Christ makes the difference. He died at Calvary, shedding His blood, was buried, and rose again to save you. The purpose was *that he might deliver us from this present evil world* (Galatians 1:4). Although we must live in this world, we do not have to perpetually and constantly partake of its filthiness. Christ's death, burial, and resurrection guarantees that. Receive Him now, and be genuinely saved.

For those on the path of departure from holy living, severe chastisement is coming. Consider in conclusion some of God's additional C's in administering chastisement:

1. A contrite heart
2. A catastrophe
3. A casket

Judgment is never immediate for the child of God. Before the beloved Heavenly Father makes any attempt to discipline His son, He first makes the heart of the sinning child heavy. Because the Holy Spirit dwells within believers' bodies, and because He can be grieved (see Ephesians 4:30), those in whom He lives feel the effects of His grieved heart. That's why

Sin's Explosion

David, after committing adultery, cried, *Restore unto me the joy of thy salvation* (Psalm 51:12).

However, if one sins and sin's effect does not break his heart and spirit, the indicator that he is God's is inoperative and undoubtedly proves he is lost. But if he feels broken, it proves that the grieved Spirit within is at work and that he is truly the Lord's.

Next, after step one of God's plan is administered, and one continues to sin, some (or multiplied) catastrophes will come to turn one from his wayward condition. Then if he continues to rebel and backslide, *There is a sin unto death* [a casket—a premature homegoing] (1 John 5:16).

But God loves His children, and there is a better way. It's called revival and it produces self-judgment and confession of sin. God says, *If we would judge ourselves, we should not be judged* [chastised] (1 Corinthians 11:31). So confess your waywardness and come back to the Lord Jesus Christ and His holiness. *For if we confess our sins, he is faithful and just to forgive us our sins, and to cleanse us from all unrighteousness* (John 1:9).

Chapter 15

Is Hell a Four-Letter Cuss Word?

Jonathan Edwards thundered against sin! His famous sermon, SINNERS IN THE HANDS OF AN ANGRY GOD, was all on sin and hell and judgment.

His most famous (and much maligned) sermon, *Sinners in the Hands of an Angry God* was not at all typical of his preaching. Edwards' astonishing results on the day he preached that sermon are probably much more due to the manifested power of God in answer to prayer than some convicting content in his message.

Nevertheless, the effect was awesome; people screamed aloud, clutched the backs of pews and the stone pillars of the church, lest the ground open and swallow them alive into hell.

Many of the hearers were seen unconsciously holding themselves up against the pillars and the sides of the pews as though they already felt themselves sliding into the pit.

The congregations of his day were full of lost people who attended for the social or political influence membership conferred; the pulpits likewise. "It seemed," he wrote, "to be a time of extraordinary dullness in religion, licentiousness prevailed among the youth of the town."

—Edwards, Thoughts on the Revival in New England

Sin's Explosion

I read of the revivals of the past, great sweeping revivals where thousands of men were swept into the Kingdom of God. I read about Charles G. Finney winning his thousands and his hundreds of thousands of souls to Christ. Then I picked up a book and read the messages of Charles G. Finney and the message of Jonathan Edwards on "Sinners in the Hands of an Angry God;" and I said, "No wonder men trembled; no wonder they fell in the altars and cried out in repentance and sobbed their way to the throne of grace!"

—*Leonard Ravenhill*

A great cardinal article of belief which has been ignored, is man in sin and under the wrath of God. Here is a doctrine that the natural man abominates. He feels that it is insulting to him. He has always been like that. Go back again and read the histories, and you will find in all those periods of deadness and of declension that people did not believe in sin in that way. They did not believe in the wrath of God.

—Martyn Lloyd-Jones

That night I determined that I would cry aloud against the sins of the people and bring to bear the very fires of hell as a final consequence of their rebellion. For almost two hours I literally flailed the evildoers who sat before me. I called God to witness that the judgment was not far off for them. Concluding, I gave a few moments to the mercy of God but I did that in a stern manner. I was determined that the people should for once stand face-to-face with the fact of sin and hell. That night the meeting broke and I think I never experienced such a divine demonstration.

—*Charles G. Finney*

Is Hell a Cuss Word?

We are to have a passion for souls. How we need tears today; tears and heartaches and sorrows for others! Dr. Dale of Birmingham said that D. L. Moody was the only man he knew during his day who had a right to preach on hell, because he did it with a sob in his voice and tears in his heart.

—Jesse M. Hendley

This world hits the trail for hell with a speed that makes our fastest plane look like a tortoise; yet alas, few of us can remember the last time we missed our bed for a night of waiting upon God for a world-shaking revival.

—*Leonard Ravenhill*

Knowing therefore the terror of the Lord, we persuade men.

—*2 Corinthians 5:11*

There are many who believe in a heaven but who reject God's Word concerning a place called hell. However, one cannot take the parts of the Bible that are pleasing to his limited mind and reject that which is unsuitable to him—it is all or nothing. Jesus said in Luke 16:22, *And it came to pass, that the beggar died, and was carried by the angels into Abraham's bosom.* That is heaven. Oh, is it not wonderful to be saved!

Sin's Explosion

The spiritualist used to sing, "Swing low, Sweet chariot, Coming for to carry me home; Swing low, Sweet chariot, Coming for to carry me home; I looked over Jordan, and what did I see, Coming for to carry me home; A band of angels, coming after me, Coming for to carry me home." D. L. Moody, on his deathbed, said, "Heaven is opening, earth is receding. Jesus is calling, and the angels are coming." And that is what Christ said concerning the beggar who died prepared.

But Jesus preached all the truth—He believed and preached both sides of the subject. He was not like some of these lopsided preachers today who say, "We believe everything the Bible has to say about heaven but reject what it has to say about hell." Let us be consistent!

In Luke 16:22-24, Christ proclaims the other side of the subject. *The rich man also died, and was buried; And in hell he lifted up his eyes, being in torments, and seeth Abraham afar off, and Lazarus in his bosom. And he cried and said, Father Abraham, have mercy on me, and send Lazarus that he may dip the tip of his finger in water, and cool my tongue; for I am tormented in this flame.*

There are two places. Jesus said in John 3:36, *He that believeth on the Son hath everlasting life* [heaven]; *and he that believeth not the Son shall not see life; but the wrath* [what a word!] *of God abideth on him.* Jesus said in John 6:47, *Verily, verily, I say unto you, he that believeth on me hath everlasting life* [heaven]. But He also said in John 8:24, *I said therefore unto you, that ye shall die in your sins: for if ye*

believe not that I am he, ye shall die in your sins.
Friend, that's eternal hell.

There Is a Hell

False religionists have hatched the "no-hell" plot to gain adherence to their movements. Because multitudes—even 70 percent of the preachers—no longer believe or like to even consider that such a place exists, a new group can grow quickly if they discount the claims of the Holy Bible and the Lord Jesus Christ by preaching pleasing platitudes which cater to rebellious minds. But Romans 3:4 says, *Let God be true, but every man a liar.* I don't care if every human being or preacher says, "I do not believe it." When I can find it 162 times in my New Testament, I will believe it! It is the Word—we must believe it!

A popular trend today is to take the Hebrew word *sheol* and the Greek words *hades* and *gehenna* and state that they all mean the grave, though they are translated "hell" in the Word of God in the majority of instances. Let's take the Old Testament Hebrew word *sheol*. Why would God have to use this word to picture a grave when the Hebrew word *queber* logically depicts and portrays it? Consider the following five points in the Old Testament:

1. The body never goes to *sheol* but goes to *queber* 37 times. Why? Because *queber* is the grave for bodies and *sheol* is the place for departed spirits.

2. *Sheol* is never on the face of the earth but *queber* is located there 32 times. Why? Because

graves are on the earth. *Sheol*, the place for departed spirits, is in some other realm of God's creation.

3. Man never puts another man into *sheol* but he does put a man into a *queber* 33 times. Why? Because man has the power to put other men into graves but does not have the power to put souls into *sheol*.

4. Man never digs or makes a *sheol* but he makes and digs a *queber* six times. Why? Because man has the power to make a grave but he does not have the power to make a *sheol* for departed spirits.

5. Man never speaks of a man as touching *sheol*, but he touches a *queber* five times. Why? Because, again, it is a grave on the earth and he has the power to touch it. But he has no power to do anything about *sheol*, the place for departed spirits.

To look at all the Old Testament instances involving *sheol* would take months of study. Besides, Christ has brought to light, life, and immortality—that which has to do with a never-dying soul—through the gospel or the New Testament (see 2 Timothy 1:10). Therefore, let's study *hades* and *gehenna* and see if they mean the grave or the place of eternal suffering.

You may ask, "Why did the Lord Jesus use two words—*hades* and *gehenna*? Are there two places?" Yes. Do you wish to know why?

Hades and Gehenna Explained

Let me illustrate it this way: All of us know the difference between a local jail and a penitentiary. If a

man is taken in a crime, he is not put into the penitentiary until he has had a trial. When he has had his trial
and is found guilty, he is transferred to the penitentiary. Get this next statement, for it is so important to a
direct understanding of the Bible subject of hell.
When Jesus uses the word *hades*, He is referring to
the local jail, the place where the sinner is held until
the judgment morning. Then, at Judgment Day, all
sinners come out of the local jail (*hades*), appear
before the Judge, are found guilty, and then transferred to *gehenna*, the final penitentiary for souls.

Let me also add that the term *gehenna* is synonymous with the Lake of Fire. Revelation 20:13,14:
*The sea gave up the dead which were in it: and death
and* [hades—that is the Greek word for hell] *delivered
up the dead...And death and hell* [hades] *were cast
into the lake of fire* [gehenna]. This is the second
death. I repeat that *hades* is the local jail and *gehenna*,
the final penitentiary. Any sinner who dies, even at
this hour, does not go to *gehenna*, but to *hades*, where
the rich man is located (see Luke 16:23). At Judgment
Day, he comes out of *hades*, meets Christ at the trial,
and then is transferred to the final penitentiary of lost
souls—*gehenna*.

Let's consider eleven instances Christ uses in the
New Testament to depict and describe *hades*—the
temporary local jail.

Matthew 11:23: *And thou, Capernaum, which art
exalted unto heaven, shalt be brought down to hell*.
That is the Greek word *hades*, where the rich man of
Luke 16:23 is located.

Matthew 16:18: *Thou art Peter, and upon this rock I
will build my church; and the gates of hell* [hades]
shall not prevail against it.

Luke 10:15: *And thou, Capernaum, which art exalted to heaven, shalt be thrust down to hell* [hades].

Luke 16:22,23: *The rich man also died, and was buried: And in hell* [hades] *he lifted his eyes, being in torments.*

Acts 2:27: *Thou wilt not leave my soul in hell* [hades].

Acts 2:31: *His soul was not left in hell* [hades].

1 Corinthians 15:55: *O death* [hades], *where is thy victory?*

Revelation 1:18: *I am he that liveth, and was dead; and, behold, I am alive for evermore, Amen; and have the keys of hell* [hades] *and of death.*

Revelation 6:8: *Death, and Hell* [hades] *followed with him.*

Revelation 20:13,14, *Death and hell* [hades] *delivered up the dead which were in them...And death and hell* [hades] *were cast into the lake of fire.* Plain isn't it? After sinners were judged, death and *hades* were cast into the final penitentiary—*gehenna*—synonymous with the Lake of Fire.

Gehenna differs from *hades* in that *gehenna* is a place where there are degrees of suffering. After one is judged, after he has been examined as to how much light he experienced, how often he heard the gospel, and rejected it, he is assigned to degrees of punishment in the final penitentiary. Romans 2:5 proves this statement, *After thy hardness and impenitent heart treasurest up* [stores up, saves up] *unto thyself wrath...*[administered in *gehenna*, the penitentiary].

Gehenna is used by Christ 12 times:

Matthew 5:22: *Whosoever shall say Thou fool, shall be in danger of hell* [gehenna] *fire.* Let us put the cultists substitute there—grave—for they say hell is the grave. Jesus would then be saying, "Sinners shall be in danger of grave fire." That must be strange fire in the grave—I have never heard of it, have you? So Jesus must not be talking about a grave.

Matthew 5:29,30: *And if thy right eye offend thee, pluck it out, and cast it from thee: for it is profitable for thee that one of thy members should perish, and not that thy whole body should be cast into hell* [gehenna]. *And if thy right hand offend thee, cut it off, and cast it from thee: for it is profitable for thee that one of thy members should perish, and not that thy whole body should be cast into hell* [gehenna].

Matthew 10:28: *And fear not them which kill the body, but are not able to kill the soul: but rather fear him which is able to destroy both soul and body in hell* [gehenna].

Matthew 18:9: *And if thine eye offend thee, pluck it out, and cast it from thee: it is better for thee to enter into life with one eye, rather than having two eyes to be cast into hell fire* [gehenna].

Matthew 23:15: *Woe unto you, scribes and Pharisees, hypocrites! for ye compass sea and land to make one proselyte* [convert], *and when he is made, ye make him twofold more the child of hell* [gehenna] *than yourselves.*

Matthew 23:33: *Ye serpents, ye generation of vipers, how can ye escape the damnation of hell* [gehenna]?

In Mark 9:43-47, Jesus says, *If thy hand offend thee, cut it off: it is better for thee to enter into life maimed, than having two hands to go into hell* [gehenna], *into the fire that never shall be quenched:*

Where their worm dieth not, and the fire is not quenched. And if thy foot offend thee, cut it off: it is better for thee to enter halt into life, than having two feet to be cast into hell [gehenna], *into the fire that never shall be quenched: Where their worm dieth not, and the fire is not quenched. And if thine eye offend thee, pluck it out: it is better for thee to enter into the kingdom of God with one eye, than having two eyes to be cast into hell* [gehenna] *fire.*

Every time Jesus mentions this place, *gehenna*, He always says it is the place where the worm dieth not and the fire is never quenched (see Mark 9:44,46,48). Do not let some cultist tell you this is the grave when the Word of God makes it explicitly clear that this is a place where there is agony, suffering, burning, where the memory dies not, and where the fires never cease.

Luke 12:5: *I will forewarn you whom ye shall fear: Fear him, which after he hath killed hath power to cast into hell* [gehenna]; *yea, I say unto you, Fear him.*

Then in James 3:6, He says, *The tongue is a fire, a world of iniquity: so is the tongue among our members, that it defileth the whole body, and setteth on fire the course of nature; and it is set on fire of hell* [gehenna].

Thus we discover there are eleven passages concerning *hades*, and twelve passages concerning *gehenna*. *Hades* is the local jail where the sinner awaits the judgment morning. At that time he comes out, is judged, and then is transferred to *gehenna*. Do not let any false religionist, any cultist, tell you that is merely a grave. Hear me, my friend. When Jesus stood on this earth, He pointed to the Valley of Hinnom. In the Old Testament it was a place of sacrifice to pagan gods. In the New Testament it became the garbage dump. The fire burned 24 hours a day to get rid of all the refuse, and Jesus said that hell was going to be like the fires at the Valley of Hinnom.

Hell Is Not the Grave

As we have just observed, there are many today who say that the words *hades* and *gehenna* always mean the grave—period. That is just not so. But even if it were so, we could prove there is such a place as hell by the many expressions throughout the New Testament which indicate, through the terminology used, that such a place exits—though it is not called hell.

For instance, Matthew 3:12 states, *He* [Christ] *will burn up the chaff with unquenchable fire.* This speaks about sinners at the end of time. What is this unquenchable fire if there is no hell? Matthew 13:42: *And shall cast them into the furnace of fire: there shall be wailing and gnashing of teeth.* What is this furnace of fire if there is no hell? In Matthew 25:41, Jesus says to those on the left hand, *Depart from me, ye cursed, into everlasting fire.* Matthew 25:46: *These shall go away into everlasting punishment.* There must be a place where this everlasting punishment takes place.

In Mark 3:29 Jesus said, *He...is in danger of eternal damnation.* Not eternal sleep in a grave, but eternal damnation. John 3:36: *He that believeth not the Son shall not see life; but the wrath of God abideth on him.* The abiding wrath continues beyond the grave, for it is forever.

233

Sin's Explosion

John 5:28,29: *Marvel not at this: for the hour is coming, in the which all that are in the graves shall hear his voice, and shall come forth; they that have done good, unto the resurrection of life; and they that have done evil, unto the resurrection of damnation.* If the grave is hell and is all the damnation mankind receives, why raise them out of the grave for the resurrection of damnation if they are already in the place of damnation? Simple logic proves again that it cannot be the grave.

Second Thessalonians 1:8,9: *In flaming fire taking vengeance on them that know not God, and that obey not the gospel of our Lord Jesus Christ: Who shall be punished with everlasting destruction from the presence of the Lord.* Does this sound like the grave?

Hebrews 6:6,8: *If they shall fall away...*[what then?] *Whose end* [or ending, consummation] *is to be burned.* But where, if there is no hell, if the grave ends it all?

Hebrews 9:27: *And as it is appointed unto men once to die, but* [there is more] *after this the judgment.* Second Peter 2:9: *The Lord knoweth how to...reserve the unjust unto the day of judgment to be punished.* The grave does not end it. Jude 7: *Suffering the vengeance of eternal fire...* Jude 23: *Others save with fear, pulling them out of the fire.* Revelation 14:11: *And the smoke of their torment ascendeth up for ever and ever: and they have no rest day nor night.* Revelation 21:8 says, *The fearful, and unbelieving, and the abominable, and murderers, and whoremongers, and sorcerers, and idolaters, and all liars, shall have their part in the lake which burneth with fire and brimstone.*

So, you see, here are a number of expressions (there are 132 of such in the New Testament—I deal with most of them in my recorded sermon, "Hell Without Hell," proving that even if the word *hades* or *gehenna* meant the grave, you would still have 132 verses which indicate there is something besides the grave.

Also, if you were to make an alphabetical study of all the following words, you would have to believe there is something beyond the grave: accursed, anguish, Beelzebub, blackness of darkness, bottomless pit, burn, condemn, cursed, damnation, darkness, demons, destruction, devil, end, eternal, everlasting, fearful, fiery, fire, flame, forever, furnace, harvest, indignation, judgment, Lucifer, perdition, perish, punish, recompence, soul, suffer, tares, torment, tribulation, unquenchable, vengeance, wail, weep, wicked, and wrath. My friend, do not tell me the grave ends it all. That is positively ridiculous in light of the Holy Scriptures.

Believe me, it is terrible to be lost, but let me give you the good news concerning Christ's love. John 3:17 says, *For God sent not his Son into the world to condemn the world; but that the world through him might be saved.* Jesus did not come to condemn—He came to save. He said, *I lay down my life for the sheep* (John 10:15). He came and shed His precious blood on Calvary's cross that ALL might have eternal life. You can have your name written in the Book of Life, you can have a home in heaven forever if you receive God's offer of salvation, but if you reject Christ, there will be an endless hell.

Sin's Explosion

You Are Responsible for the Lost

In conclusion let me talk to God's people about soulwinning. Revival has always produced hell-fire preaching. No man can omit the multiplied Bible texts of this subject from his preaching vocabulary and be used of God. It is impossible. A revived heart will proclaim all God's truth. Furthermore, I pray that every Christian may grasp anew the seriousness of hell and that if he does not pull sinners out of the fire, he is responsible (see Jude 23). Read the following and renew your soulwinning vows.

Barrenness, or neglect of the souls of men, is sin. James 4:17: *Therefore to him that knoweth to do good, and doeth it not, to him it is sin.* God's Word not only tells us that there are sins of commission (the wrong we do), but there are sins of omission (that which God wants us to do servicewise, which we neglect to do). So, *to him that knoweth to do good and doeth it not, to him it is sin.* Barrenness is also the deadliest sin for a believer to practice because it allows never-dying souls to go into the regions of the doomed and damned for all eternity without warning them.

Barrenness is without doubt the sin of blood-guiltiness because God holds Christians responsible in this matter of witnessing. Ezekiel 3:17-19 says, *Son of man, I have made thee a watchman unto the house of Israel: therefore hear the word at my mouth, and give them warning from me. When I say unto the wicked, Thou shalt surely die; and thou givest him not warning, nor speakest to warn the wicked from his wicked way, to save his life; the same wicked man shall die in his iniquity; but his blood will I require at thine hand.*

236

Yet if thou warn the wicked, and he turn not from his wickedness, nor from his wicked way, he shall die in his iniquity; but thou hast delivered thy soul. God says that if one does not warn those with whom he comes into contact, and they die in their sins, their blood will be upon his hands. However, if one does warn them and they won't listen, his hands will be clean at the Judgment Seat of Christ.

What does it mean when the Bible says that blood will be upon a Christian's head or hands?

Well, Paul had been preaching in Ephesus about three years. He is about to leave, and the leaders of the Church are standing around him. Paul says in Acts 20:31, *Therefore watch, and remember, that by the space of three years I ceased not to warn every one night and day with tears.* Then in verses 26 and 27 adds, *Wherefore I take you to record this day, that I am pure from the blood of all men.* [Pure? Why?] *For I have not shunned to declare unto you all the counsel of God.* He didn't win everyone, but he was faithful in his preaching, his presentation, his proclamation, his praying—he tried.

Thus his hands were clean. His conscience also was clear, therefore he could say, *I say the truth in Christ, I lie not, my conscience also bearing me witness in the Holy Ghost. That I have great heaviness and continual sorrow in my heart. For I could wish that myself were accursed from Christ for my brethren, my kinsmen according to the flesh: Who are Israelites* (Romans 9:1-4).

Imagine! Paul said that he would be willing to be like the rich man in hell crying for a trickle of water for all eternity, if his presence in hell could mean the salvation of one of his people. He was talking about Jews he had never met or would meet; he was talking about Gentiles he had never known nor would know. However, he had such a love in his soul for sinners that he would be willing to be separated from the Jesus he loved for the ages of ages if his separation from Christ would mean the salvation of souls. Paul didn't say he would give up a few extra dollars or a few extra pleasures and conveniences or a few enjoyable activities to win the lost. He said he would give his soul in eternal hell fire forever and forever and forever to win the lost.

Christian, confess this deadly sin of barrenness in your life. Then determine by the grace of God that you are going to be different from this day onward.

Chapter 16

Roadblocks to Revival

And it grieved Samuel; and he cried unto the Lord all
night.

—1 Samuel 15:11

*Moses prayed; and how he prayed! Ezra prayed.
Nehemiah prayed. All the prophets prayed. Elijah
prayed. Elisha prayed. Isaiah prayed. Jeremiah prayed.
Jesus prayed. Paul prayed. Wesley prayed. Luther
prayed. If these men, who were so gigantic, prayed, how
much more do we need to pray! The preparation of
intercession! Oh, my friends, when I come to a revival
meeting and am told, "We have had seasons of prayer,"
my heart leaps with joy. When I come for a revival
meeting, and the first night, and the second night, and
the third night the prayer rooms are full, I know in my
heart that there are not enough devils in hell to stop us.*

—*Hyman J. Appelman*

Thomas Goodwin in his exposition of the sealing of the
Spirit in Ephesians 1:13 uses a wonderful term. He
says, "Sue Him for it, sue Him for it." Do not leave
Him alone. Pester Him, as it were, with His own prom-

ise. Tell Him that what He has said He is going to do. Quote the Scripture to Him. And you know, God delights to hear us doing it, as a father likes to see this element in his own child who has obviously been listening to what his father has been saying. It pleases him. The child may be slightly impertinent, it does not matter, the father likes it in spite of that. And God is our Father, and He loves us, and He likes to hear us pleading His own promises, quoting His own words to Him, and saying, "In the light of this, can You refrain?" It delights the heart of God. Sue Him!

—Martyn Lloyd-Jones

The first great revival of Christian history had its origin on the human side in a 10-day prayer meeting. We read of the handful of disciples. These all continued with one accord in prayer and supplication (Acts 1:14).

—*R. A. Torrey*

Every true revival has had its earthly origin in prayer.

It was a master stroke of Satan when he got the church to so generally lay aside this mighty weapon of prayer.

—R. A. Torrey

And everywhere, it was a revival of prayer. There was no hysteria, no unusual disturbances. Just prayer.

—*America's Great Revivals*

Jonathan Edwards' son-in-law, David Brainerd, (who prayed in the snow until it melted around him and was stained by his blood as he coughed away his life with tuberculosis), prevailed in prayer for revival among the American Indians. He describes in his journal how it finally began in 1745: "The power of God seemed to descend on the assembly like a rushing mighty wind and with an astonishing energy bore all down before it. I stood amazed at the influence that seized the audience almost universally and could compare it to nothing more aptly than the irresistible force of a mighty torrent. Almost all persons of all ages were bowed down with concern together and scarce one was able to withstand the shock of the astonishing operation.

—Edwards, The Life and Diary of
David Brainerd, pp.142-143

Mr. Moody's wonderful work in England and Scotland and Ireland, then afterwards in America, originated in prayer. Mr. Moody made little impression until men and women began to cry to God. Indeed, his going to England at all was in answer to the persistent cries to God by a bed-ridden saint.

—R. A. Torrey

I praise God that in His providence Brainerd should die in my house so that I might hear his prayers, so that I might witness his consecration.

—Anthony Edwards

Does God ever need more patience with His people than when they are "praying"? We tell Him what to do and how to do it. We pass judgments and make appreciations in our prayers.

—Leonard Ravenhill

Sin's Explosion

There can be no revival when Mr. Amen and Mr. Wet-Eyes are not found in the audience.

—Charles G. Finney

Finney's sermons were followed immediately by confession, repentance, tears, and many conversions.

—America's Great Revivals

Moody never pretended to be a great preacher. He told a newspaperman, "I am the most overestimated man in this country. For some reason the people look upon me as a great man, but I am only a lay preacher, and have little learning."

—America's Great Revivals

Revival upset the status quo. Things no longer ran smoothly. Satan opposed. And even those used of God were in danger of becoming proud, arrogant, rash. But Satan could not stop the revival of the Great Awakening.

—America's Great Revivals

Forbearing one another, and forgiving one another, if any man have a quarrel against any: even as Christ forgave you, so also do ye.

—Colossians 3:13

The greatest verse in the Bible on the subject of revival is found in 2 Chronicles 7:14. This truth, delivered to Israel centuries ago, is preeminently applicable for believers in the twentieth century. The text states, *If my people which are called by my name, shall humble themselves, and pray, and seek my face, and turn from their wicked ways; then will I hear from heaven, and will forgive their sin, and will heal their land.*

Humility

The first thing a believer can do to bring the blessing of God back upon his experience is to seek humility. Pride fills the arena of Christendom today. Christian services, including evangelistic crusades, are filled with performers seeking praise. Carnal performers seek the exaltation of self. Christ is the only One worthy of praise.

Tempermental artists, charging exorbitant sums, want glory. These prima donnas must have worshipers or they will not perform. God deliver us from egotistical, haughty performers, and give us more old-fashioned, Holy Spirit-filled soloists who want Christ to be uplifted. How embarrassed this crowd will be at the Judgment Seat of Christ when motives are investigated.

First Corinthians 4:5 states, *Therefore judge nothing before the time, until the Lord come, who both will bring to light the hidden things of darkness, and will make manifest the counsels* [or motives—Greek] *of the hearts.* When God tests motives in that day, many will have nothing but an incinerated pile of ashes to throw at Christ's feet in place of crowns (see 1 Corinthians 3:11-15).

Let's see what God has to say about pride. In Proverbs 16:18, He states, *Pride goeth before destruction, and a haughty spirit before a fall.* Sir, lady— high and mighty—a destructive fall is predicted for your life and ministry. Fall on your knees and repent of this hindering sin in your life. Oh, how we need to be like Jesus who said in Matthew 11:29, *Take my yoke upon you, and learn of me; for I am meek and lowly in heart: and ye shall find rest unto your souls*.

We need the humility of John the Baptist who cried out in John 3:30, *He must increase, but I must decrease. He must be exalted and I abased.* When one genuinely practices this truth, God will exalt the sincere soul. *Humble yourselves in the sight of the Lord, and he shall lift you up* (James 4:10). God says that the way up is down to self.

Glory seekers will never have the blessing and power of God upon them because God *resisteth the proud, but giveth grace unto the humble* (James 4:6). Let's ask God to forgive us for the sin of thinking that we are latter day gifts to the Church. Instead, *Humble yourselves therefore under the mighty hand of God, that he may exalt you in due time* (1 Peter 5:6). The glory is coming at the Judgment Seat when rewards are distributed to the faithful. Do what you can for Christ and the souls of men now, and crowns to lay at Christ's feet will be yours at that great Coronation Day.

So child of God, be faithful—even when no one seems to care—*For so an entrance shall be ministered unto you abundantly into the everlasting kingdom of our Lord and Saviour Jesus Christ* (2 Peter 1:11). Remember, *Whosoever shall exalt himself shall be abased; and he that shall humble himself shall be exalted* (Matthew 23:12).

Prayer

Prayer is a necessity if one is to experience true revival in his heart. God says, *If my people, which are called by my name, shall humble themselves, and pray and seek my face, and turn from their wicked ways; then will I hear from heaven, and will forgive their sin, and will heal their land* (2 Chronicles 7:14).

Modern Christians know little about this most effectual ministry. Jesus did. He said in Luke 18:1, *Men ought always to pray and not to faint.* Christ rose up early in the morning to pray (see Mark 1:35). He *continued all night in prayer to God* (Luke 6:12). Multitudes will rise up early to fish, ski, and golf, while others will sit up until the small hours of the morning watching vampires, witches, and blood-suckers on "Shock Theatre." How different these Christians are from Christ, after whom Christianity is named. These so-called followers need a heaven-shaking revival of body and soul.

Paul, who said in 1 Corinthians 11:1, *Be ye followers of me, even as I also am of Christ,* practiced what he preached. He continued instant in prayer (see Romans 12:12); *praying always with all prayer and supplication in the Spirit* (Ephesians 6:18); [and prayed] *without ceasing* (1 Thessalonians 5:17).

In other periods of American history, entire cities and counties were deluged with revival as thousands per week—up to one million total—were converted. The secret was prayer.

Sin's Explosion

Finney describes the times of agonizing prayer that transpired in his day to produce revival. In his book, *Revival Lectures*, he states, "Men prayed until their clothing was soaked through with perspiration. Some bled like Christ did in Luke 22:44. Two prayed themselves to death before the age of 40. To many it appeared as foolishness, but cities were turned upside down for Christ."

Would to God that we had prayer warriors like this in every major city where the Jack Van Impe Crusades are conducted. Oh, to see a revival where sin is put out of business; where movie houses, brothels, massage parlours, and pornography dens are barricaded because the power of God, through prayer, has padlocked Satan's establishments because a Holy Ghost revival has hit. Oh Christian, pray without ceasing.

Confession

Prayer, however, is meaningless without confession because God's holiness demands it. *If I regard iniquity in my heart, the Lord will not hear me* (Psalm 66:18). *Behold, the Lord's hand is not shortened, that it cannot save; neither his ear heavy, that it cannot hear: But your iniquities have separated between you and your God, and your sins have hid his face from you, that he will not hear* (Isaiah 59:1,2). This is why 1 John 1:9 states, *If we confess our sins, he is faithful and just to forgive us our sins, and to cleanse us from all unrighteousness.*

Bitterness

Bitterness is one of the greatest sins of the hour. There is nothing that is damaging the church of Jesus Christ and destroying one's spiritual life more than bitterness. This spirit of animosity surely is not of God. If one is controlled by hatred, he certainly should question his profession of faith. *Beloved, let us love one another: for love is of God; and everyone that loveth is born of God, and knoweth God. He that loveth not knoweth not God; for God is love* (1 John 4:7,8).

A Spirit-filled Christian is known by the love he has for others. *The fruit of the Spirit is love, joy, peace, longsuffering, gentleness, goodness, faith, meekness, temperance* (Galatians 5:22,23).

You may say, "I have experienced the second work of grace." Do you have love for other believers who may not claim to have your experience?

You may say, "I have spoken the heavenly language, yea the vocabulary of angels." But are you filled with love? First Corinthians 13:1 declares, *Though I speak with the tongues of men and of angels, and have not charity* [love], *I am become as sounding brass, or a tinkling cymbal*. The Holy Spirit says that heavenly languages, when boasted about without the evidence of love, become nothing but manifestations of the flesh.

The real evidence of the Spirit is found in verses 4-8: *Charity suffereth long, and is kind; charity envieth not* [is not jealous]*; charity vaunteth not itself, is not puffed up* [hey, look at my gifts], *doth not*

Sin's Explosion

behave itself unseemly, seeketh not her own, is not easily provoked [made mad], *thinketh no evil; Rejoiceth not in iniquity, but rejoiceth in the truth; Beareth all things, believeth all things, hopeth all things, endureth all things. Charity never faileth.*

This is the love the crucified Saviour manifested at Calvary. After they battered nails into His hands and feet, jammed a crown of thorns into the flesh of His head, ripped His beard from the facial area, scourged His back and chest into mutilated shreds of flesh, then—after all their brutality was heaped upon Him—He lovingly cried, *Father, forgive them; for they know not what they do* (Luke 23:34).

Some carnal mind is already excusing self for the bitterness he holds by saying, "This was Christ, and He was God. Because of His Deity, He could love in the midst of hate. Our humanity limits us in loving the unlovely." Let me immediately answer you with the example of Stephen in Acts 7:51-60.

This mere mortal man, filled with the Holy Spirit, manifested the same loving kindness that his Saviour did upon Calvary's tree. The Scriptures picture Stephen preaching a strong, sin-denouncing sermon. The enraged crowd can't take the truth and so verse 57 says, *Then they cried out with a loud voice, and stopped their ears, and ran upon him with one accord, and cast him out of the city, and stoned him; and the witnesses laid down their clothes at a young man's feet, whose name was Saul. And they stoned Stephen, calling upon God, and saying, Lord Jesus, receive my spirit.* Now please get verse 60, *And he kneeled down, and cried with a loud voice, Lord, lay not this sin to their charge. And when he had said this, he fell asleep.*

Think of it...as they stoned him to death—crushed his head with rocks—he asked his Lord not to hold them accountable for what they had done. Verse 55 tells us why his heart was so filled with love—he was filled with the Holy Spirit. There is the evidence.

A man can talk about every experience in the book and still be a trouble-making church-wrecker, but when the Spirit is truly in control, he won't have to say a word. Instead, the love that flows from his heart to the saved and lost will indicate that the blessed Spirit of God is at the helm of his life. When the world sees this love in the Christian, a genuine moving of God will take place.

Now what is the primary cause for bitterness, the hurt one bears because of another's words? The tongue.

Nothing in the history of mankind has wrought more havoc and sorrow then the uncontrolled tongue of human beings. A wise proverb states, "He that thinketh by the inch and speaketh by the yard should be kicked by the foot." Again, "Loose tongues get their owners into tight places."

God says in James 3:6, *The tongue is a fire, a world of iniquity: so is the tongue among our members, that it defileth the whole body, and setteth on fire the course of nature; and it is set on fire of hell.* Verses 9,10: *Therewith bless we God, even the Father; and therewith curse we men, which are made after the similitude of God. Out of the same mouth proceedeth blessing and cursing. My brethren, these things ought not so to be.*

A slanderous, vile, malicious tongue is indicative of one of two conditions:

(1) The slanderer may be a hell-bound sinner. *If any man among you seem to be religious, and bridleth not his tongue, but deceiveth his own heart, this man's religion is vain* (James 1:26). A wagging tongue is usually a symbol of an empty heart. God said so.

In Galatians 5:19-21, the Holy Spirit lists seventeen abominations, and eight of these include: unclean-ness (a dirty, smut-filled mouth), hatred, variance, emulations, wrath, strife, heresies, and envyings—all have to do with the REASON FOR or the RESULT OF a poison-filled, uncontrollable tongue and those practicing these eight sins are under the anthema or condemnation of God. The devil's reward, at the end of the trail, for gossipers is stated in verse 21, *They which do such things shall not inherit the kingdom of God.*

God hates these sins. How easy it is for self-righteous church members to condemn the sins of the flesh practiced by some, and overlook the wickedness of their own lives as they lacerate, mutilate, and cut to shreds other members of the human race with their razor-sharp tongues. Proverbs 6:16-18 states, *These six things doth the Lord hate: yea, seven are an abomination unto him: A proud look, a lying tongue, and hands that shed innocent blood, an heart that deviseth wicked imaginations, feet that be swift in running to mischief, a false witness that speaketh lies, and he that soweth discord among brethren.*

Friends, what about the deadly tongue you possess? Will your tongue, described in the Bible as a fire, lead you into the fires to eternal doom? Fall on your face, confess your sin, get washed in Christ's blood and be saved for eternity.

(2) Second, a loose-tongued person may be saved, but carnal. Each hearer must determine his own spiritual condition before God. Both situations are taught in God's Holy Word, and a true messenger must present both viewpoints, and then allow the individual, under the direction of the Holy Spirit, to determine his own personal state before God.

The Corinthian church was filled with fighting, carping Christians. Paul, in writing to this carnal assembly, says, *I, brethren, could not speak unto you as unto spiritual, but as unto carnal, even as unto babes in Christ. I have fed you with milk, and not with meat: for hitherto ye were not able to bear it, neither yet now are ye able. For ye are yet carnal: for whereas there is among you envying, and strife, and divisions, are ye not carnal, and walk as men?* (1 Corinthians 3:1-3).

Fighting, bickering, and sowing discord among brethren is not a sign of spirituality, but of extreme carnality. Many who claim to be dominated by the Holy Spirit are constantly running off at the mouth. You are professing a lie if this is the case. It is easy to call the working of the Holy Spirit a second work of grace, an infilling a baptism, and loudly proclaim an experience with the third member of the Trinity through signs and wonders. The real evidence, however, is in a love-filled heart and Spirit-controlled tongue. You don't believe it? Hear God in James 3:2, *If any man offend not in word, the same is a perfect man.* Again, *The fruit of the Spirit is love, joy, peace, long-suffering, gentleness, goodness, faith, meekness, temperance* (Galatians 5:22,23).

Some of you have roast preacher every week. You talk against every spiritual leader of the Church. One day your children will curse God and turn their back on religion, and your uncontrollable tongue will have been the cause. God hates gossip. The Word proves it, *Lying lips are abomination to the Lord* (Proverbs 12:22).

A true witness delivereth souls; but a deceitful witness speaketh lies (Proverbs 14:25).

Pleasant words are as an honeycomb, sweet to the soul, and health to the bones (Proverbs 16:24).

A false witness shall not be unpunished, and he that speaketh lies shall perish (Proverbs 19:9).

Speak the truth in love (Ephesians 4:15).

Let your speech be always with grace (Colossians 4:6).

An Unforgiving Spirit

Some of you reading this book have been hurt by another's vicious remarks. Because of it, you have harbored ill-will toward that person. This is human, I know, but it is not divine. We who are filled with the Spirit can live on a higher plane. "To err is human; to forgive divine." If animosity, envy, ill-will, and jealousy continue, this internal bitterness will destroy one's communion with his Lord.

In Ephesians 4:30 we find, *And grieve not the holy Spirit of God, whereby ye are sealed unto the day of redemption.* It is evident that when the Spirit of God, living within a believer, is grieved, the believer feels the mood of the grief-stricken Spirit and shares in the misery. Because of it, fellowship with God is broken.

What causes the Holy Spirit to be grieved? Verses 31,32: *Let all bitterness, and wrath, and anger, and clamour, and evil speaking, be put away from you, with all malice: And* [get it, please] *be ye kind one to another, tenderhearted, forgiving one another, even as God for Christ's sake hath forgiven you.*

It is easy to "fly off the handle," and gossip about others, and run around with a grudge while talking about the power of the Holy Spirit—but it is all a farce. His Spirit will make one turn the other cheek; will make one love the unlovable, and will never seek revenge by hurting the one who hurt him.

God says if one wants to spare himself heartache and divine judgment, he should judge this sin in his own life and put it away. Remember, *If my people, which are called by my name, shall humble themselves, and pray, and seek my face, and turn from their wicked ways; then will I hear from heaven, and will forgive their sin, and will heal their land* (2 Chronicles 7:14).

Chapter 17

Tame That Tongue

They were just words. There's no such thing. It's like saying, "After all it's just an atomic bomb."

—Joseph Stowell

How long will ye...break me in pieces with words?

—Job 19:2

A tongue is like having dynamite in our dentures.
Life is a combustile commodity—douse your tongue.

—Joseph Stowell

Slander is the open, intentional sharing of damaging information.

—Joseph Stowell

The word translated brag in James 4:16 means "a wandering quack."

—Joseph Stowell

Sin's Explosion

Flattery is a compliment shared to manipulate another for personal gain.

—Joseph Stowell

He that thinketh by the inch and speaketh by the yard should be kicked by the foot.

—Jack Van Impe

Lie not.

—Colossians 3:9

The poison of asps is under their lips.

—Romans 3:13

The Hebrew word for slander means "to betray a confidence."

—Jack Van Impe

Let no corrupt communication proceed out of your mouth.

—Ephesians 4:29

The same church members who yell like Comanche Indians at a ball game on Saturday sit like wooden Indians in church on Sunday.

—Vance Havner

For in many things we offend all. If any man offend not in word, the same is a perfect man, and able also to bridle the whole body.

—James 3:2

T*his know also, that in the last days perilous times shall come. For men shall be lovers of their own selves, covetous, boasters, proud, blasphemers, disobedient to parents, unthankful, unholy, without natural affection, trucebreakers, false accusers, incontinent, fierce, despisers of those that are good* (2 Timothy 3:1-3).

How true this description of latter day mankind is as animosity, envy, jealousy, and lovelessness abound even in the church of the Lord Jesus Christ! Certainly we are living in the final hours of the dispensation of grace because the present situation is undoubtedly as bad, if not worse, than any period in church history.

As believers, most of us feel comfortable whenever sin is blasted from the pulpit because we are definitely not guilty of adultery, alcoholism, drug addiction, fornication, extortion, or thievery. However, we forget how despicable a slanderous tongue is to the eyes and ears of Almighty God. In fact, this sin is so great that the Holy Spirit says in Proverbs 6:16-19, *These six things doth the Lord hate: yea, seven are an abomination unto him: A proud look, a lying tongue, and hands that shed innocent blood, an heart that deviseth wicked imaginations, feet that be swift in running to mischief, a false witness that speaketh lies, and he that soweth discord among brethren.*

Usually this discord is sown by a devastating weapon called the tongue. Its deadly power is described in James 3:6,8-10, *The tongue is a fire, a world of iniquity: so is the tongue among our mem-*

bers, that it defileth the whole body, and setteth on fire the course of nature; and it is set on fire of hell. But the tongue can no man tame; it is an unruly evil, full of deadly poison. Therewith bless we God, even the Father; and therewith curse we men, which are made after the similitude of God. Out of the same mouth proceedeth blessing and cursing. My brethren, these things ought not so to be.

Is it any wonder that God gives multiplied commands against gossip and slander? He says, *Thou shalt not go up and down as a talebearer among thy people* (Leviticus 19:16); *Let all bitterness, and wrath, and anger, and clamour, and evil speaking, be put away from you, with all malice* (Ephesians 4:31); *Speak not evil one of another, brethren* (James 4:11); *Wherefore laying aside all malice and all guile, and hypocrisies, and envies, and all evil speakings...*(1 Peter 2:1).

The reason God so opposes the proverbial "forked tongue" is because of the horrendous damage it produces. *The words of a talebearer are as wounds* (Proverbs 18:8). Dr. Wilkerson says, "How many great men and women of God lay prostrate each night—lost in a stream of tears as they try to understand how and why they are victims of lies and gossip. They give their very lifeblood to the work of Christ and they have learned to expect satanic attacks when they storm the gates of hell. But there is no hurt like the deep cutting of cruel gossip that is passed on by the very ones who should be encouraging and praying for them.

"You expect gossip from liars, cheats, and street people. You expect it in politics and public life. But no gossip is as vicious, as damaging, and as hurtful as comes from God's own people [or ARE they?]. Hear me! We can no longer afford the indulgence of gossip. We can no longer allow ourselves to give our lips and voices to the service of Satan to malign, to destroy, to assassinate with gossip. It matters not whether the gossip is true or not—let God take care of that! It is our part to defend our brothers and sisters in Christ. And even if the most vicious gossip were true, we should be spending all our time in restoring, healing, and lifting up the fallen."

God says, *Brethren, if a man be overtaken in a fault, ye which are spiritual, restore such an one in the spirit of meekness; considering thyself, lest thou also be tempted* (Galatians 6:1). Beloved, how long has it been since you observed this ministry of healing in the many religious papers and magazines to which you subscribe? God help us to have a revival that will fill servants of God with the love of God for the brethren. Then we will be able to "rescue the perishing" and lift up the fallen. Until such a time, we will continue gleefully massacring our brothers by tongue and the printed page. How sad. Remember, a tongue three inches long can kill a man six feet tall!

It is a well-known fact that physicians often determine the diseases of the body by an examination of the tongue. Therefore, we should listen intently as one speaks, for the same tongue also reveals the spiritual health of one's mind and soul!

Dr. Horace F. Dean states, "Scripture says that our speech is governed from within our own hearts. *A good man out of the good treasure of his heart bringeth forth that which is good; and an evil man out of the evil treasure of his heart bringeth forth that which is evil: for of the abundance of the heart his mouth speaketh* (Luke 6:45). In other words, if our lips are to speak that which is good, edifying, and acceptable in God's sight, our hearts must first be clean and filled with that which our Lord calls 'good treasure.' Thus, the speech of the Christian should be different. Yes, his heart has been cleansed, and, by the grace of God, he is now a possessor of new life—the life of Christ Jesus, the spotless, Holy Son of God. So, the believer should practice Colossians 4:6 which states, *Let your speech be always with grace, seasoned with salt, that ye may know how ye ought to answer every man.*"

God's Judgment of the Tongue

I continue our discussion by dealing with the solemnity of the judgment upon this malignant weapon, the tongue, and its users in the world to come. The psalmist asked, *Lord, who shall abide in thy tabernacle? who shall dwell in thy holy hill?* [The answer], *He that walketh uprightly, and worketh righteousness, and speaketh the truth in his heart. He that backbiteth not with his tongue, nor doeth evil to his neighbour, nor taketh up a reproach against his neighbour* (Psalm 15:1-3). Again, *Whoso privily slandereth his neighbour, him will I cut off* (Psalm 101:5).

Now get ready for a shock. In Romans 1:29-32, God lists 22 sins that shall not escape His judgment—and 11 of them deal with the carnal spirit manifesting itself through the tongue or pen. Read the following words carefully and seriously. *Being filled with all unrighteousness, fornication, wickedness, covetousness, maliciousness; full of envy, murder, debate, deceit, malignity; whisperers, backbiters, haters of God, despiteful, proud, boasters, inventors of evil things, disobedient to parents, without understanding, covenant breakers, without natural affection, implacable, unmerciful: Who know the judgment of God, that they which commit such things are worthy of death, not only do the same, but have pleasure in them and do them.*

Second Corithians 13:5 states, *Examine yourselves, whether ye be in the faith; prove your own selves. Know ye not your own selves, how that Jesus Christ is in you, except ye be reprobates* [or counterfeits]? Keep this verse in mind as we define 11 of the 22 sins mentioned in Paul's description of "unrighteousness" in Romans 1:

1. *Maliciousness*—A desire to injure another.

2. *Envy*—A bitterness arising in one's heart toward another who is above him, who is what he is not or who possesses that which he does not have.

3. *Murder*—A hatred of others. First John 3:15 says, *Whosoever hateth his brother is a murderer.*

4. *Debate* (or strife)—The beating and battering down of another in argument or contention.

5. *Malignity*—Taking everything in an evil way, and spreading it.

6. *Whispering*—Secret slander.

7. *Backbiting*—Open slander by attacking another person through speech or the printed page.

8. *Despite* (or insolence)—Taking pleasure in insulting another.

9. *Covenant breakers*—Those who do not plan to carry out pledged promises unless doing so satisfies their selfish purposes.

10. *Implacable*—Refusing to cease from hostilities or consent to a truce of peace and love.

11. *Unmerciful*—An unwillingness to show mercy.

Is it not heartbreaking that these sins inundate Christendom? I plead with leaders and laymen alike to consider the seriousness of this listing! Remember: *They which commit such things are worthy of death.*

As shocking as this is, there is something even more shocking, and that is the remainder of Paul's statement—that those who will eventually suffer judgment for such sins *not only do the same, but have pleasure* [or take delight] *in them that do them.* Dear Father, help us. We are so sick!

The listing of sins in Galatians 5:19-21 also includes numerous sins of the flesh and human spirit. *Now the works of the flesh are manifest, which are these; adultery, fornication, uncleanness, lasciviousness, idolatry, witchcraft, hatred, variance, emulations, wrath, strife, seditions, heresies, envyings, murders, drunkenness, revellings, and such like: of the which I tell you before, as I have also told you in time past, that they which do such things shall not inherit the kingdom of God.*

Wow! May I remind you that hatred, variance, emulations, wrath, strife, seditions, and envyings are the sins that produce an overworked tongue or writer's cramp! Further, we see that those who are guilty of such works are listed along with the adulterers, fornicators, heretics, murderers, and drunkards who miss God's eternal city, heaven! Under the scrutinizing searchlight of God's Holy Word, it behooves each of us to investigate our hearts and make whatever changes are necessary to be right with the Lord. Let's ask the Father to forgive us for the error of our way, and then begin to ask those we have injured to forgive us also. This is the only way to peace and spiritual prosperity (see Ephesians 4:32 and Colossians 3:13).

The Importance of Love

Love is the proof of one's salvation as well as the Spirit-controlled life. So, *Beloved, let us love one another: for love is of God; and everyone that loveth is born of God, and knoweth God. He that loveth not knoweth not God; for God is love* (1 John 4:7,8). May I repeat verse eight? The statement is so important that one's eternal existence in heaven or hell depends on it. Hear it again: *He that loveth not knoweth not God; for God is love.* First John 3:15 states, *Whosoever hateth his brother is a murderer and no murderer has eternal life abiding in him.*

Think of it! This is astonishing. Hatred becomes murder in God's eyes, and no murderer (hater of others) has eternal life abiding in him. Rather, a life of hate classifies one as a child of the devil, for God says in 1 John 3:10, *In this the children of God are manifest, and the children of the devil: whosoever doeth not righteousness is not of God, neither he that loveth not his brother.*

Imagine! Folks who fight, fuss, bicker, backbite, gossip, slander, malign, and criticize others are "children of the devil!" One cannot, cannot, CANNOT live a life of hate when God abides within, for "God is love." Thus, love is evidence of one's born-again experience. So, *If we love one another, God dwelleth in us* (1 John 4:12). That's why Jesus said in John 13:35, *By this shall all men know that* [you] *are my disciples,* [because] *you have LOVE one for another* (emphasis mine).

It is sad that hatemongers who honestly believe that bigotry, prejudice, and malice are acceptable standards for church members fill the ranks of religion. What a shock they will experience at the Judgment Day! Then they'll know God meant what He said in James 1:26, *If any man among you SEEM to be religious, and bridleth not his tongue, but deceiveth his own heart, this man's religion is vain.* Then they'll suffer judgment for the seven sins God hates mentioned in Proverbs 6:16-19. Perhaps these should be called "The Seven Deadly Sins."

Yes, when it is eternally too late, those guilty of these sins will discover that the unrighteous—including "railers"—do not inherit the kingdom of God (see 1 Corinthians 6:9). *Webster's Dictionary* defines *railers* as "individuals who revile or scold in harsh, insolent, or abusive language." God help us! Our ranks include both leaders and members who carry on in this manner. Through their obnoxious, hateful insolence, organizations and churches are split, and souls are lost for all eternity!

If YOU are guilty, repent! Change your mind and your ways before it is eternally too late.

If ye be willing and obedient, ye shall eat the good of the land: But if ye refuse and rebel, ye shall be devoured with the sword: for the mouth of the Lord hath spoken it (Isaiah 1:19,20).

Chapter 18
Religious Bigots

Zwingli and Luther did not get along with each other. Besides this disagreement, another problem with the Reform approach was their stress on doctrine rather than character, concept rather than life. Stress on being godly was overshadowed by the the stress on being right.

—Pratney

What the sham of fighting preachers caused in the heart and spirit of the greatest revivalist in history...
Physical strain, and a growing disunity Evan Roberts attempted to correct in some divisive breakaway works among the Northern churches, led to one of the strangest endings of a ministry in history. Offered a retreat at the home of the godly Jesse Penn-Lewis and her husband, Roberts, leader of the famous Welsh Revival, accepted and never returned to ministry!

—Pratney

I fear not the tyranny of man, neither yet what the devil can invent against me.

—John Knox in "A Godly Letter"

Sin's Explosion

No man is ever fully accepted until he has, first of all, been utterly rejected.

—Author unknown

All did not speak well of me. As my popularity increased opposition also increased. At first, many of the clergy were my admirers, but some soon grew angry and complained that the churches were so crowded that there was no room for the parishioners and that the pews were being soiled. Some called me a spiritual pickpocket. Others thought I used a charm to get the people's money.

—George Whitefield

All the opposition I met, joined with the consciousness of my daily infirmities, was not enough ballast to keep me from overturning.

—George Whitefield

Can we learn from our differences and concentrate on our common convictions, as this conversation between Charles Simeon and John Wesley proves? "Pray, sir," said Simeon, (an evangelical Calvinist, to Wesley, the Armenian champion of his day) "do you feel yourself a depraved creature, so depraved you would have never thought of turning to God if God had not first put it into your heart?"

"Yes," said the veteran Wesley, "I do indeed."

"And do you utterly despair of recommending yourself to God by anything that you can do and look for salvation solely through the blood and righteousness of Christ?"

"Yes, solely through Christ."

"But, sir, supposing you were first saved by Christ, are you not, somehow or other, to save yourself afterwards by your own works?"

"No, I must be saved by Christ from first to last."

"Allowing then that you were first turned by the grace of God are you not, in some way or other, to keep yourself by your own power?"

"No."

"What then, are you to be upheld every hour and every moment by God, as much as an infant in its mother's arms?"

"Yes, altogether."

"And is all your hope in the grace and mercy of God to preserve you unto His heavenly Kingdom?"

"Yes, I have no hope but in Him."

"Then, sir, with your leave, I will put up my dagger again; for this is all my Calvinism; this is my election, my justification by faith, my final perseverance; it is, in substance, all that I hold and as I hold it."

—Martyn Lloyd-Jones

But if we walk in the light as he is in the light, we have fellowship one with another.

—1 John 1:7

Religion never got anyone into heaven and never will. Instead, millions will be eternally separated from God because their religion kept them from a genuine experience with Christ.

Religion is usually connotated with evil and hypocrisy. Even in Bible times James had to add the qualifying word *pure* before the term *religion* to make it respectable (see James 1:27).

Sin's Explosion

Religion has been responsible for the death of millions over the centuries. It is still true today. That's why the Hindus and Sikhs are constantly at one another's throats in India.

That again explains why the Sunni and Shiite Mohammedans slaughter one another at the front lines in Iraq and Iran.

That again accounts for the fact that the Catholics and Protestants of Ireland as religious warriors have murdered thousands of victims.

It's obvious that religion often produces bigotry, envy, malice, hatred, and even murder.

However, before we criticize others, let's look at what is happening on our own turf. Bitterness, hatred, and infighting also inundate the American religious scene. Though we may not be slaughtering one another as religionists do in India, Iran, Iraq, and Ireland, nevertheless lovelessness abounds within our denominations and churches. In God's eyes this equals murder. First John 3:15 states, *Whosoever hateth his brother is a murderer: and ye know that no murderer hath eternal life abiding in him.*

This spirit of lovelessness presently permeating Christendom is destroying us from within. Communism, Nazism, Fascism, Humanism, and other culticisms do great harm, but religious warriors destroy all that Christ and Christianity represent—LOVE.

These warriors often propagate animosity and bitterness by misapplying labels. This brings good and godly men into disrepute. I am a historic fundamentalist and would gladly give my life for the five-point position our forefathers originated and defended at the turn of the century. However, today one can believe in inerrancy, the deity of Christ, His virgin birth, His atoning death, His bodily resurrection, and His bodily return and still be an outcast because he differs on secondary issues and rejects the additional rules and regulations he sees forced upon the people of God.

The Cult of Neo-Fundamentalism

Dr. Tarr of Toronto, Ontario, labels such leaders as neo-fundamentalists as I did in my book, *Heart Disease in Christ's Body*. He states, "Neo-fundamentalists have come up with a new cultic position and have advanced as 'fundamentals' items that are unrelated to the original 'fundamentals.' I see in neo-fundamentalism, recurring basic tenets and life outlooks that are completely unrelated to the fundamentals of the faith, but which are being pressed as determinates of orthodoxy." I use only two of Dr. Tarr's 10 points. They are:

1. *Identification of spiritual Christianity with passing fads.* Check a neo-fundamentalist paper to discover that the preacher-authors vie with each other in their intemperate blasts against long hair, beards, and other passing fads and styles. A perceptive observer must find it confusing to read a sermon by Spurgeon, Wesley, or Booth in those same periodicals— and doubly confusing if a picture of the preacher is included! Spurgeon, with his beard and shaggy head of hair, wouldn't look out of place in today's youth culture. Wesley's hair length would be considered well beyond the

most extreme of our day. And how about General Booth's beard (founder of the Salvation Army)?

2. *Condemnation of the sins of the flesh and little rebuke for the sins of the spirit.* Neo-fundamentalist literature has a tendency to define sins largely in terms of outward acts. They warn Christians against movies, dancing, drinking, smoking, and card playing. The tragic decline in morality today certainly demands that Christian standards of sexual purity and personal honesty be emphasized. But is it not possible that the emphasis on the sins of the flesh is onesided? Should we not as energetically condemn the sins of the spirit which too frequently rear their ugly heads in all of us? Neo-fundamentalists have little to say about lovelessness, censorious judging, or character assassination.

Dr. Tarr is definitely correct in his observation of the neo-fundamentalist movement. Now, should anyone disagree with such conclusions on secondary separation, the neo-fundamentalists (militants) immediately label or mislabel such critics as moderate fundamentalist, pseudo-fundamentalists, evangelicals, neo-evangelicals, or the young evangelicals. Often these names are purposely applied to rejected brothers to stir up the wrath and ire of one leader against another.

Since writing my book *Heart Disease in Christ's Body*, I have received five thousand letters from prominent Christian leaders and laymen. Scores of them tell the story of battered, broken, and bleeding hearts within the constituency of neo-fundamentalist churches. Scores more testify to the destructive force the militant movement has been in destroying multiplied churches—and this under the banner of orthodoxy.

Let me give you documented evidence as to what is happening across America as I quote from various sources.

"I was excommunicated from my church because of my love for other men of God."

"My pastor taught me to dislike black people."

"One year ago we left a militant church after being threatened many times."

"I left the church because I was sick of all the knocking of others from the pulpit. Thank you for taking a stand against all this hatred."

"We have experienced the hate tactics of this group."

"Our church is torn apart by this militant philosophy."

"My pastor would no longer allow me to serve in the church because I went to Tennessee Temple University."

"Our church was destroyed by a militant pastor. It has taken two years to undo the damage."

"We have witnessed the tearing asunder of the body of Christ, and it has become a source of real grief."

"Missionaries are suffering and losing support because they are in the wrong fundamentalist group."

"We had a militant speak at our church. He threw stones at God's servants by name for an hour and a half. The church was packed with unsaved people, and it was an unfortunate situation. The spirit continues and today there are not enough members to pay the bills."

"Our pastor is always majoring on minors. We cry out for sanity within Christendom."

"Last summer a dear friend was speaking at another church. The pastor forbid him to have a meal with us because we were allegedly not true separatists."

"There have been several occasions when I have been labeled 'liberal, compromiser, neo-evangelical,' and not for any areas of compromise, lowering of standards, preaching of heresy; but rather for simply refusing to join in the neo-fundamentalist games of backbiting, gossip, and sowing discord among the brethren. I have refused to join the Anti-Falwell, Anti-Sword of the Lord, Anti-Hyles, Anti-Robertson, and yes, Anti-Van Impe Clubs. For these reasons I must be a liberal. Truly the Body is ravaged with occlusions that will send a destructive failure through our ranks. Sadly, there appears to be no end in sight. Thank you for saying what many feel."

Is it any wonder that a minister's wife wrote and said, "I am appalled at the immaturity of pastors in the service of Christ. It's no wonder that so many of our people are going to psychiatrists and psychologists to find the answers."

Are you shocked at what you have just read? I have but skimmed the surface. Hundreds of letters make identical statements and in practically every instance, the source of the trouble originates with one militant group within fundamentalism.

Can such attitudes be from God? Are such actions prompted by the flesh or the Spirit? James 4:1 answers the question plainly. *From whence come wars and fightings among you? come they not hence, even of your lusts that war in your members?* The fruit of such fighting is depicted by the same apostle in James 3:16 when he declares, *Where envying and strife is, there is confusion and every evil work.* Paul tells us this is so because *ye are carnal...and walk as men* (1 Corinthians 3:3).

God Is Love

To this point we have observed what religion produces. Now let's look at the greatest four-letter word ever coined in the English language—LOVE. This is what Christ and genuine Christianity produces. This is what an old-fashioned conversion experience creates within the newly born-again believer's heart.

When one is saved, regenerated, or born again, he immediately becomes a partaker of God's nature (see 2 Peter 1:4)—which includes the attribute of love. Thus, the new believer now possesses a new nature capable of loving to the same degree that God loves. Why? Because it is the very nature of God implanted within him through the miraculous, divine operation of the Holy Spirit. The believer's old nature could only hate, bicker, fuss, fight, fume, criticize, and malign other human beings. Now, at salvation, God's nature begins to change the past.

The new nature of God, received through a genuine conversion experience, now makes true love the natural outflow of that experience. First John 4:7,8 states, *Beloved, let us love one another: for love is of God; and every one that loveth is born of God, and knoweth*

God. He that loveth not knoweth not God; for God is love.

Upon the authority of this text and others, I am going to dogmatically affirm that if one's heart is always full of bitterness toward others, it is undoubtedly the greatest sign that salvation is missing. Don't fail to grasp the utter simplicity of these words: *We know that we have passed from death unto life, because we love the brethren. He that loveth not his brother abideth in death.*

Notice this text does not say that one who hates is in danger of death! In the next verse, John clarifies any misunderstanding which could arise by stating, *Whosoever hateth his brother is a murderer: and ye know that no murderer hath eternal life abiding in him.* This is not a state of broken fellowship with the Lord but rather a state of damnation because no murderer—including the one who has hate which God equates with murder—has eternal life abiding in him. Oh, get right with God! Godly love is the greatest proof that your salvation experience is real!

The Mainspring of Christianity

The Lord Jesus, in His high priestly prayer, also made it emphatically clear that the authenticity of Christianity rests on this matter of love, unity, and oneness. He said, [Father] *as thou hast sent me into the world, even so have I also sent them into the world. Neither pray I for these alone* [my sent ones], *but for them also which shall believe on me* [converts of future generations] *through their word; THAT THEY ALL MAY BE ONE; as thou, Father, art in me,*

276

and I in thee, that they also may be one in us: that the world may believe that thou hast sent me (John 17:18,20,21, emphasis mine).

Imagine, God in the flesh prayed that all Christians in all eras of time might have love for one another as a sign that the Father really sent the Son and that Christianity is genuine. Is it any wonder that Jesus said in John 13:35, *By this shall all men know that ye are my disciples, if ye have love one to another.*

Since love is the mainspring of Christianity, I spent hours researching the term throughout the pages of the New Testament. In Chapter 13 of my book, *Heart Disease in Christ's Body*, I list literally hundreds of verses that command and demand love for others.

May I quote scores of God's commandments, under various headings from His Book and mine as we proceed? Those who practice these verses are obedient fundamentalists and evangelicals, or better still, Spirit-filled Christians. I still prefer the latter term for all blood-bought children of God.

1. DISSENSION AMONG BROTHERS
Second Timothy 2:24: *The servant of the Lord must not strive; but be gentle unto all men.*

Hebrews 12:14,15: *Follow peace with all men, and holiness, without which no man shall see the Lord: Looking diligently lest any man fail of the grace of God; lest any root of bitterness springing up trouble you, and thereby many be defiled.*

James 4:11,12: *Speak not evil of one another, brethren...who art thou that judgest another?*

2. FELLOWSHIP WITH BROTHERS
Luke 9:49-56: *And John answered and said, Mas-*

ter, we saw one casting out devils in thy name; and we forbade him, because he followeth not with us. And Jesus said unto him, Forbid him not: for he that is not against us is for us.

And it came to pass, when the time was come that he should be received up, he steadfastly set his face to go to Jerusalem, and sent messengers before his face: and they went, and entered into a village of the Samaritans, to make ready for him. And they did not receive him, because his face was as though he would go to Jerusalem.

And when his disciples James and John saw this, they said, Lord, wilt thou that we command fire to come down from heaven, and consume them, even as Elias did? But he turned, and rebuked them, and said, Ye know not what manner of spirit ye are of. For the Son of man is not come to destroy men's lives, but to save them.

First John 1:7: *But if we walk in the light, as he is in the light, we have fellowship one with another, and the blood of Jesus Christ his Son cleanseth us from all sin.*

3. LOVE FOR OUR BROTHERS

Romans 12:10: *Be kindly affectioned one to another with brotherly love; in honour preferring one another.*

First Corinthians 14:1: *Follow after charity* [love], *and desire spiritual gifts.*

Galatians 5:13: *Use not liberty for an occasion to the flesh, but by love serve one another.*

Ephesians 4:1-3,15: *Walk worthy of the vocation wherewith ye are called, with all lowliness and meek-*

ness, with longsuffering, forbearing one another in love; Endeavoring to keep the unity of the Spirit in the bond of peace. [Speak] the truth in love.

Colossians 3:14: Put on charity [love], which is the bond of perfectness.

First Thessalonians 4:9: Love one another.

Hebrews 13:1: Let brotherly love continue.

First Peter 2:17: Honour all men. Love the brotherhood.

First Peter 4:8: Above all things have fervent charity [love] among yourselves: for chariy [love] shall cover the multitude of sins.

Jude 21: Keep yourselves in the love of God.

4. MAKE PEACE WITH OUR BROTHERS

Psalm 34:14: Seek peace, and pursue it.

Mark 9:50: Have peace one with another.

Romans 12:18: Live peaceably with all men.

Second Corinthians 13:11: Live in peace.

Colossians 3:15: Let the peace of God rule in your hearts.

First Thessalonians 5:13: Be at peace among yourselves.

Hebrews 12:14: Follow peace with all men.

5. FORGIVENESS OF BROTHERS

Luke 17:3,4: If thy brother...trespass against thee seven times in a day, and seven times in a day turn again to thee, saying, I repent; thou shalt forgive him.

Ephesians 4:32: And be ye kind one to another, tenderhearted, forgiving one another, even as God for Christ's sake hath forgiven you.

6. SHOW MEEKNESS TOWARD BROTHERS

First Peter 3:4: [Put on] *the ornament of a meek and quiet spirit, which is in the sight of God of great price.*

Galatians 6:1,2: *Brethren, if a man be overtaken in a fault, ye which are spiritual, restore such an one in the spirit of meekness; considering thyself, lest thou also be tempted. Bear ye one another's burdens, and so fulfil the law of Christ.*

7. BE LONGSUFFERING TOWARD BROTHERS

Second Corinthians 6:3-6: [Give] *no offence in any thing, that the ministry be not blamed: But in all things* [approve yourselves] *as the ministers of God, in much patience...by pureness, by knowledge, by longsuffering, by kindness...by love unfeigned.*

Ephesians 4:1,2: *Walk worthy of the vocation wherewith ye are called, with all lowliness and meekness, with longsuffering, forbearing one another in love.*

8. DO GOOD TO ALL BROTHERS

Matthew 5:44: *Love your enemies, bless them that curse you, do good to them that hate you, and pray for them which despitefully use you, and persecute you.*

Galatians 6:10: *Let us do good unto all men.*

9. BE KIND TO BROTHERS

Romans 12:10: *Be kindly affectioned one to another with brotherly love.*

Ephesians 4:32: *Be ye kind one to another.*

10. BE GENTLE TO BROTHERS

Second Timothy 2:24: *The servant of the Lord must...be gentle unto all men.*

Titus 3:2: *Speak evil of no man to be no brawlers, but gentle.*

James 3:17: *The wisdom that is from above is...gentle.*

11. HAVE COMPASSION ON BROTHERS

First Peter 3:8: *Be ye all of one mind, having compassion one of another, love as brethren...be courteous.*

12. PRAY FOR BROTHERS

First Thessalonians 5:25: *Brethren, pray for us.*

Perhaps your heart was convicted as you studied the many instructions of God in this message. If so, why not surrender yourself anew to His leadership in your life? Make the following prayer your desire, today and forever.

"Heavenly Father, as Your child I have fallen short of the image of Christ in so many ways. Forgive me. I recommit myself to You today and seek the fullness of Your Spirit in my life. Help me put away all bitterness, criticism, envying, and selfishness, replacing them with the love, understanding, compassion, and tenderness of Your Son, my Saviour. I want to know and love others as He does—looking beyond their faults and seeing their needs. Revive me again, fill my heart with Thy love. In Jesus' name!"

Chapter 19

Your Prejudice Is Showing

Whitefield, influenced deeply by Jonathan Edwards, was a Calvinist; Wesley, the scholar, moved toward a more Armenian view of the gospel. One censorious professor of religion, knowing the sharp theological differences between them, asked if Whitefield thought he would see John Wesley in heaven. "I fear not," he said, "he will be so near the throne and we at such a distance that we shall hardly get a sight of him."

—Pratney

The American frontier was set ablaze. The Presbyterians and Methodists immediately caught fire, and then the flame broke out among the Baptists in Carroll County on the Ohio River. Great personalities emerged from this awakening. Men like Peter Cartwright, Charles Finney, and the Methodist circuit riders.

—*Pratney*

Three things stand out in Finney's astonishing life: his willingness to change, his deep and loving devotional life, and his radical message of practical and immediate holiness. Denounced by clergy and secularist alike for his innovations in evangelism, he was intolerably ahead of his time. One preacher (Lyman Beecher) threatened to oppose him with cannon if he dared venture into his parish (Beecher later relented and extended an invitation to Finney).

—Pratney

The doctrine of "free will" seems to have been universally accepted in the Early Church. Not a single church figure in the first 300 years rejected it and most of them stated it clearly in works still existent...We find it taught by the leaders of all the main theological schools. The only ones to reject it were heretics like the Gnostics, Marcions, Valentinus, Manes (and the Manichees), etc.

—*America's Great Revivals*

All our revivalists of the First and Second Awakenings, whether Calvinist or Armenian, believed and strongly practiced human responsibility. Some, like Whitefield, fearlessly preached Augustine's view of divine election as selection, trusting that those who responded were the elect, and those who did not were not. But they did not let it hinder them from stressing, "Ye must be born again!"

—Pratney

If the Church today had as many agonizers as she had advisors, we would have a revival in a year!

—*Leonard Ravenhill*

As the coming babe dislocates the body of the mother, so does the growing "body" of revival and soul-travail dislocate the Church.

—Leonard Ravenhill

But a revival also, invariably, has another effect, and that is that it creates a new and fresh division. And it does so, because those who have experienced the blessing and the power of God are naturally one and they come together. But there are others who dislike it all, and who criticize it, and condemn it all, and who are outside it all, and the division comes in.

—Martyn Lloyd-Jones

Whosoever shall do the will of my Father which is in heaven, the same is my brother.

—Jesus, in Matthew 12:50

I met Jesus and was gloriously saved 40 years ago, and I shall never forget my newfound joy in the Lord. The precious Christians who led me to Christ taught me a love for all of God's people. They were Christians first—then Baptists. I often heard messages that incorporated the following truth: When one is a Christian, he can travel anywhere globally and experience intimate fellowship with brethren of like precious faith.

How true it was in my early days of serving Christ. These were happy days of loving the people of God regardless of their denominational affiliation. Unfortunately, those days did not last.

Fundamentalism's Roots

The harmony I experienced and enjoyed was the natural outgrowth of fundamentalism's roots.

Sin's Explosion

Dr. George Dollar in his book, *A History of Fundamentalism in America*, reports that the who's who of first-generation fundamentalists consisted of leaders identified with the following denominations: Presbyterian, Reformed, Reformed Episcopal, Methodist, Anglican, Baptist, Lutheran, Wesleyan (holiness), and Congregational. In fact, Billy Sunday was a Presbyterian and the Reverend D. L. Moody, a Congregationalist as was C. I. Scofield.

What do our roots teach us? Simply that the amalgamated mixture of first-generation fundamentalists included numerous groups composed of Calvinists and Armenians, eternal security advocates and "falling from grace" proponents, pre-millennialists and a-millennialists, sprinklers and immersionists, sacramentalists and non-sacramentalists who opted for ordinances. Nevertheless, all were rooted in one heart and spirit around the five points of historical fundamentalism:

1. The inspiration and inerrancy of Scripture.
2. The deity of Jesus Christ.
3. The virgin birth of Christ.
4. The substitutionary, atoning work of Christ on the cross.
5. The physical resurrection and the personal, bodily return of Christ to earth.

These five points constituted the basis for withdrawal from liberalism and apostasy, and men from all backgrounds took their stand on these issues—nothing additional.

Today, the waters have become muddied and bloodied by militant leadership. In fact one may no longer be considered a genuine fundamentalist even though he is so devoted to these five points that he would gladly give his life for his beliefs.

How has all this confusion, bigotry, prejudice, and lovelessness become so pervasive and predominant in a good and God-honoring movement that had such a grand beginning? It happened simply because men whose hearts brimmed with love toward others—men who were basically shy and unassuming—sat idly by and never protested the creation of neo-fundamentalism—a movement that continually added rules, regulations, and resolutions to the five original points at the conferences, convocations, and congresses of fundamentalism.

Dr. Truman Dollar, a prominent leader in the Baptist Bible Fellowship movement of Springfield, Missouri, writes, "The men who contributed to the fundamentals had widely diverse backgrounds. They were united by their common commitment to the basics ('fundamentals') of the Christian faith, they *refused* to be divided over denominational distinctives or personal biases.

"Since that early coalition, the situation has dramatically changed. There are those within the fundamentalist movement who want to add their own beliefs and practices to the five fundamentals. Their list continually expands until it eventually excludes everyone who disagrees with any position they represent. The issue is no longer a commitment to the five fundamentals but rather allegiance to what they claim are the 7 fundamentals, the 10 fundamentals, the 20 fundamentals, the 50 fundamentals, and so on."

Dr. Dollar adds, "Who are the real psuedo-fundamentalists [I prefer the term, 'neo-fundamentalist'—

JVI]? From a historical perspective they are those who have added their personal preferences to the fundamentals and have demanded allegiance to every jot and tittle of THEIR LAW. Within fundamentalism are those who want to saturate the movement with their own brand of additives dangerous to the health of the movement and, unrestrained, may produce a cancer that will destroy its life and vitality. Perhaps the time has come to perform major surgery in order to deal with the cancer."

Love for All the Family of God

God bless you, Dr. Dollar. You have expressed my sentiments precisely! Since I released my article entitled, "That They All May Be One," I have discovered that there are hundreds in our ranks who are heartsick over the bitterness, prejudice, and name-calling that abounds. These fundamentalists have hearts filled with love and want change. God help us to "walk tall" at such an hour as this and protest whatever the cost. Let's oppose the manmade labels placed upon good and godly men whose only crime is that they will not bow to man as they reject the 7, 10, 20, or 50 fundamentalism's roots.

Let's also reject the harsh, crude, and intemperate language neo-fundamentalists use in describing others.

There was a period of time in my life when I, too, thought God was pleased with such abusive verbal assaults on other men and movements. Then the Holy Spirit began to do a deep work within my being, convicting me of my ungraciousness. I now know that *the servant of the Lord must not strive: but be gentle unto all men* (2 Timothy 2:24).

In the flesh, this is an impossibility. However, through the infilling of the Holy Spirit, it becomes a reality. Then *love, joy, peace, longsuffering, gentleness, goodness, faith, meekness,* [and] *temperance* (Galatians 5:22,23) will become evident. When the Spirit controls men and movements, we will be *kindly affectioned one to another* (Romans 12:10) and will *do good unto all men, especially unto them who are of the household of faith* (Galatians 6:10). Then we will *increase and abound in love one toward another* (1 Thessalonians 3:12) and overlook the faults of others, as love covers a multitude of sin (see 1 Peter 4:8). Then love will no longer be thought of as a sentimental sickness inherent in compromisers, but a healthy wholesomeness within Spirit-controlled brethren.

I have read many fundamentalist publications and heard numerous innuendoes concerning my position. None of the statements and accusations are true. I am a historic fundamentalist who would !ay down my life for the five foundational points because they center around my wonderful Lord and the Book so precious to me. As such, I will love all blood-bought members of God's family because this is a scriptural principle preached and practiced by historic fundamentalists. I stand where the late Dr. John R. Rice stood when he so often stated with great dogmatism in The Sword of the Lord, *I am a companion of all them that fear thee* (Psalm 119:63).

Eight years ago, Rexella and I vowed before the Lord that LOVE FOR ALL THE FAMILY OF GOD would be our new position until Christ calls us home.

Sin's Explosion

We agreed that if this conviction cost us the loss of numerous supporters, or even the dissolution of our national television ministry, we would gladly pay the price. In fact, we prepared the following letter for the great number we thought would cancel their prayer and financial support.

Dear Brother,

With respect to your concern about the direction I am taking, may I immediately state that the only change is that the sweet Spirit of the Lord has broadened my convictions to practice all of God's Word, including John 13:35 and 1 John 4:7,8,12,20.

In my article entitled, "That They All May Be One," I said, "I promise God and all members of His family that the remainder of my life will be spent proclaiming the message of reconciliation and love for ALL the brotherhood (see 1 Peter 2:17)." I meant this. I will live and die for this biblical principle called love.

If my position causes you to withdraw your church's prayer and financial support, that must be your decision before God. Even if all men follow your example and I become financially unable to continue my ministry, I will know that I have obeyed God and His commandment to love one another—and nothing else matters.

Sincerely in Christ,
Jack Van Impe

Fundamentalism's Marching Orders

Is love for one another regardless of denominational affiliation a scriptural principle? Were our

Founding Fathers right or were they wrong? God has given me 50 marching orders for believers to follow showing us why we must all love one another. There can be no revival until the Holy Spirit, who moved upon His servants to pen these commands, is obeyed.

ORDER #1: EVERY BORN-AGAIN BELIEVER IS A MEMBER OF THE BODY OF CHRIST.

In Christ's great priestly prayer, recorded in John 17:11,21-23, He prayed for unity four times. His prayer was answered about 10 weeks later on the Day of Pentecost when the first convert was placed into the body of Christ. From that time onward, covering a period of 2,000 years, everyone who has believed has been placed into that Body. People in tens of thousands of denominations spanning centuries have become part of Christ's body. *For by one Spirit are we all baptized into one body, whether we be Jews or Gentiles, whether we be bond or free; and have been all made to drink into one Spirit* (1 Corinthians 12:13).

In the early centuries we had Arnoldists, Henricians, Paulicians, the Humiliati, Lollards, Waldenses, and Ana-Baptists. Today we have multiplied denominations preaching the true gospel. And by one Spirit are we all—past, present, and future—baptized into one body.

Presently, it is the duty of every Christian to keep the unity the Holy Spirit has already begun and continued for 20 centuries (see Ephesians 4:1-3). This is God's commandment, and no set of manmade resolutions can alter God's marching orders.

ORDER #2: EVERY BORN-AGAIN BELIEVER IS A MEMBER OF THE FAMILY OF GOD.

Ephesians 3:15 speaks of the family as being *in heaven and* [upon] *earth*. What does this mean? Those who have died in Jesus are already present in glory, *absent from the body...present with the Lord* (2 Corinthians 5:8). Hence, all family members—spanning 2,000 years of Christendom—are now in heaven await the homecoming of family members still upon earth.

These believers in heaven and upon earth got there by being saved in thousands of denominations in which they were members during their lifetime. Since there is no way one can get rid of his spiritual relatives in heaven or upon earth, let's love them—especially the ones still breathing!

ORDER #3: EVERY BORN-AGAIN BELIEVER IS A SON OR DAUGHTER OF GOD.

As many as received him, to them gave he power to become the sons of God (John 1:12). Since none of us has the right to eliminate or ignore our brothers and sisters within the family of God, I suggest that we begin to *love the brotherhood* (1 Peter 2:17). Galatians 3:26 says, *For ye are all the children of God by faith in Christ Jesus.* Are we to reject brothers and sisters because they have a different label than us? Heaven forbid.

ORDER #4: EVERY BORN-AGAIN BELIEVER IS THE LORD'S BY ADOPTION (see Ephesians 1:5).

Scriptural adoption means that the new "babe in Christ" has been placed into the family of God with all the rights and privileges of one who has reached legal age. These rights make every child an heir of God and *joint-heirs with Christ* (Romans 8:17).

ORDER #5: EVERY BORN-AGAIN BELIEVER HAS BEEN CLEANSED BY THE BLOOD OF JESUS (see 1 John 1:7).

Acts 11:9 tells us, *What God hath cleansed, that call not thou common* [or unclean].

ORDER #6: EVERY BORN-AGAIN BELIEVER HAS BEEN FORGIVEN.

In [Christ] *we have redemption through his blood, the forgiveness of sins, according to the riches of his grace* (Ephesians 1:7). Our sins have been forgiven and forgotten by God. Hebrews 10:17 says, *Their sins...will I remember no more.* I don't care what you've done or how often you've done it, when you come to Jesus and throw your sins on Him, they're gone. He casts your sins behind His back (see Isaiah 38:17). He removes them as far as the east is from the west (see Psalm 103:12). He buries them in the depths of the sea (see Micah 7:19) and puts up a sign for Satan saying, "No fishing allowed!" And that happens to every believer.

ORDER #7: EVERY BORN-AGAIN BELIEVER HAS BEEN REDEEMED OR BOUGHT BACK FROM THE SLAVE MARKET OF SIN AND SET FREE THROUGH THE PRECIOUS BLOOD OF JESUS (see 1 Peter 1:19).

This includes every child of God saved in every gospel-preaching denomination.

ORDER #8: EVERY BORN-AGAIN BELIEVER HAS BEEN RECONCILED (see 2 Corinthians 5:19,20).

This means that every brother in Christ is eternally at peace with God. Since God has been so gracious to us, we in turn should *follow peace with all men and holiness, without which no man shall see the Lord* (Hebrews 12:14).

ORDER #9: EVERY BORN-AGAIN BELIEVER HAS BEEN REGENERATED (see Titus 3:5), MEANING THAT LIFE AND THE DIVINE NATURE HAVE BEEN IMPARTED TO HIM (see Hebrews 12:14).

When a husband and wife have a child, he has the nature of both parents. When the little girl is sweet, Mommy says, "She's sugar and spice and everything nice, just like me." When the little boy is a monster, she says, "You're just like your father." That little one has both natures.

When one comes to the cross and gets regenerated, God places in him His holy divine nature. Christians become *partakers of the divine nature*, says 2 Peter 1:4. Do you realize what this means? Here is a man who is a Presbyterian or a Mennonite who has God's own nature in him. However, just because he doesn't bear our label doesn't mean we're not allowed by our leaders to say, "I love you" to this brother. That, beloved, is unscriptural.

ORDER #10: EVERY BORN-AGAIN BELIEVER HAS BEEN "MADE NIGH" OR CLOSE TO GOD BY THE BLOOD OF JESUS (see Ephesians 2:13).

No one is any closer to God than another on the basis of denominational merit. Instead, his nearness is based on a blood relationship—that of the Lamb of God. I thank God that this is so, for there are presently 20,780 distinct Christian denominations locatable in Christian atlases internationally, and a great percentage of them uplift, exalt, and trust only in Jesus. Since they are all close to God's heart by the blood of Jesus, we should reinvestigate our position that looks upon them as untouchables.

ORDER #11: EVERY BORN-AGAIN BELIEVER HAS BEEN ACCEPTED IN THE BELOVED (Jesus) (see Ephesians 1:6).

Our acceptance is on the basis that we have become the *righteousness of God in Christ* (2 Corinthians 5:21). This includes all believers found in all gospel-preaching churches. If every child of God is *accepted in the beloved,* we should show a little more kindness to all of our relatives in Christ Jesus.

ORDER #12: EVERY BORN-AGAIN BELIEVER IS A CITIZEN OF HEAVEN.

Philippians 3:20 declares, *For our conversation* [citizenship] *is in heaven.* Because of it, we *are no more strangers and foreigners, but fellow citizens with the saints and the household of God* (Ephesians 2:19). This citizenship is bestowed upon red, golden, black, and white, completed Jews and Gentiles, Calvinists and Armenians, pre-tribulationists and post-tribulationists, pre-millennialists and a-millennialists. Anyone who has his faith and trust in Christ has a passport for heaven, and no militant group passing resolutions making good men "pseudo-fundamentalists" or "neo-evangelicals" can change that.

ORDER #13: EVERY BORN-AGAIN BELIEVER HAS BEEN "JUSTIFIED" OR DECLARED ABSOLUTELY RIGHTEOUS—JUST AS IF HE HAD NEVER SINNED.

This is because of the merits of the shed blood of Jesus (see Romans 5:9). When one gets saved, God looks at him as though he had never committed a sin. He is absolutely holy and righteous. Yet, religious leaders won't even allow us to shake hands with other absolutely righteous brothers. How wrong biblically.

ORDER #14: EVERY BORN-AGAIN BELIEVER IS A MEMBER OF THE "ROYAL PRIESTHOOD" (see 1 Peter 2:9).

Even this status symbol is ignored in our separatist "caste system."

ORDER #15: EVERY BORN-AGAIN BELIEVER HAS BEEN (Calvinists will love this point):

A) Chosen in Him before the foundation of the world (Ephesians 1:4).

B) Elected (Romans 8:33).

C) Called with an holy calling (2 Timothy 1:9; Hebrews 1:14).

D) Drawn by the Father (John 6:44).

E) Given to Christ by the Father (John 6:44).

F) Predestined to be conformed to the image of His Son (Romans 8:29).

Imagine, the omniscient, all-knowing God planned in centuries past to save His children in thousands of denominations spanning a period of approximately 2,000 years. He placed the first convert into the body of Christ at Pentecost and will continue the process until the final member completes the Body. This includes every saved person in Baptist, Presbyterian, Methodist, Episcopalian, Lutheran, Reformed, Wesleyan, Free Methodist, Pilgrim Holiness, Nazarene, and Pentecostal churches. And since it does, we must recognize that God did it and accept His eternal plan. Then we need to love and accept all those He included. He made no mistakes. We do when we reject His foreordained plan.

ORDER #16: EVERY BORN-AGAIN BELIEVER IS ALREADY SEATED IN HEAVENLY PLACES IN CHRIST JESUS (see Ephesians 2:6).

Theologically and biblically, this is acceptable. But the militant fundamentalists don't practice this truth. They won't even sit in a restaurant with anyone not in their group lest they be suspected of compromise!

ORDER #17: EVERY BORN-AGAIN BELIEVER IS THE SALT OF THE EARTH (see Matthew 5:13).

ORDER #18: EVERY BORN-AGAIN BELIEVER IS THE LIGHT OF THE WORLD (see Matthew 5:14).

ORDER #19: EVERY BORN-AGAIN BELIEVER POSSESSES EVERLASTING LIFE (see John 3:36).

ORDER #20: EVERY BORN-AGAIN BELIEVER IS ONE OF GOD'S SHEEP (see John 10:27).

ORDER #21: EVERY BORN-AGAIN BELIEVER IS A SAINT (see Romans 1:7).

ORDER #22: EVERY BORN-AGAIN BELIEVER HAS BEEN BAPTIZED INTO CHRIST (see Romans 6:3-5).

ORDER #23: EVERY BORN-AGAIN BELIEVER IS FREE FROM CONDEMNATION (see Romans 8:1).

ORDER #24: EVERY BORN-AGAIN BELIEVER IS INSEPARABLE FROM THE LOVE OF GOD (see Romans 8:38,39).

ORDER #25: EVERY BORN-AGAIN BELIEVER IS SANCTIFIED (see 1 Corinthians 1:2).

ORDER #26: EVERY BORN-AGAIN BELIEVER IS A PARTAKER OF GOD'S GRACE (see 1 Corinthians 1:4).

ORDER #27: EVERY BORN-AGAIN BELIEVER IS CONFIRMED TO THE END (see 1 Corinthians 1:8).

ORDER #28: EVERY BORN-AGAIN BELIEVER IS CALLED INTO THE FELLOWSHIP OF HIS SON (see 1 Corinthians 1:9).

ORDER #29: EVERY BORN-AGAIN BELIEVER IS PART OF GOD'S BUILDING (see 1 Corinthians 3:9).

ORDER #30: EVERY BORN-AGAIN BELIEVER IS THE TEMPLE OF GOD (see 1 Corinthians 3:16).

ORDER #31: EVERY BORN-AGAIN BELIEVER IS THE TEMPLE OF THE HOLY SPIRIT (see 1 Corinthians 6:19).

ORDER #32: EVERY BORN-AGAIN BELIEVER DRINKS THE SAME SPIRITUAL DRINK (see 1 Corinthians 10:4).

ORDER #33: EVERY BORN-AGAIN BELIEVER PARTAKES OF ONE BREAD (see 1 Corinthians 10:17).

ORDER #34: EVERY BORN-AGAIN BELIEVER IS GIFTED (see 1 Corinthians 12:7).

ORDER #35: EVERY BORN-AGAIN BELIEVER IS SEALED (see 2 Corinthians 1:22).

ORDER #36: EVERY BORN-AGAIN BELIEVER IS A SWEET SAVOUR OF CHRIST (see 2 Corinthians 2:15).

ORDER #37: EVERY BORN-AGAIN BELIEVER HAS A NEW HOUSE OR BODILY COVERING AWAITING HIM IN HEAVEN (see 2 Corinthians 5:1).

ORDER #38: EVERY BORN-AGAIN BELIEVER IS A NEW CREATION (see 2 Corinthians 5:17).

ORDER #39: EVERY BORN-AGAIN BELIEVER IS AN AMBASSADOR FOR CHRIST (see 2 Corinthians 5:20).

ORDER #40: EVERY BORN-AGAIN BELIEVER IS ONE OF GOD'S PEOPLE (see 2 Corinthians 6:16).

ORDER #41: EVERY BORN-AGAIN BELIEVER IS A CHILD OF ABRAHAM (spiritually) (see Galatians 3:7).

ORDER #42: EVERY BORN-AGAIN BELIEVER HAS BEEN REDEEMED FROM THE CURSE OF THE LAW (see Galatians 3:13).

ORDER #43: EVERY BORN-AGAIN BELIEVER IS CHRIST'S PURCHASED POSSESSION (see Ephesians 1:13,14).

ORDER #44: EVERY BORN-AGAIN BELIEVER IS SAVED BY GRACE (see Ephesians 2:8,9).

ORDER #45: EVERY BORN-AGAIN BELIEVER IS GOD'S WORKMANSHIP (see Ephesians 2:10).

ORDER #46: EVERY BORN-AGAIN BELIEVER IS A CHILD OF LIGHT (see Ephesians 5:8).

ORDER #47: EVERY BORN-AGAIN BELIEVER HAS BEEN DELIVERED FROM DARKNESS (see Colossians 1:13).

ORDER #48: EVERY BORN-AGAIN BELIEVER HAS AN ETERNAL INHERITANCE (see Hebrews 9:15).

ORDER #49: EVERY BORN-AGAIN BELIEVER IS ALREADY PERFECTED IN CHRIST (see Hebrews 10:14).

ORDER #50: EVERY BORN-AGAIN BELIEVER IS A KING (see Revelation 5:9).

After studying this tremendous list as to what every child of God is or shall be, I find it sad that we often reject brothers and sisters in whom God has performed such mighty works. I am not talking about anyone forfeiting his denominational distinctives or giving up his doctrinal position. I *am* saying that because of our unity, as members of the one Body, (Christ's body), we must love one another—for which we will be judged if we fail to show it.

When Jesus comes I don't know everything for which we will be held accountable in that hour. I do know we'll give account for soulwinning (see 1 Thessalonians 2:19) and for our finances (see 2 Corinthians 9:6). But there is something more important than these things—yes, even more important than being martyred for Christ. This great and often missing ingredient is love. First Corinthians 13:3 says, *Though I give my body to be burned, and have not charity* [or love], *it profiteth me nothing.* Let's pray, then, for hearts of love lest we end up empty-handed at coronation day.

Sin's Explosion

At this point it should be asked, Who is my brother? Jesus answered that when He said, *Whosoever shall do the will of my Father which is in heaven, the same is my brother, and sister, and mother* (Matthew 12:50). All who do the will of God then, regardless of denominational affiliation, are Christ's brothers, and if they are His brothers they had better be ours also.

It took the Holy Spirit seven years to bring me to the place where I could honestly look at myself and see my lack of love. I came to this point and asked forgiveness of both God and men. The Scriptures were plain, and I had to obey. Will you? If your heart has been hardened and prejudiced against other brothers and sisters in Christ and the Lord has used these Scriptures to show you your lack of love, I urge you right now to pray for forgiveness. Let the Holy Spirit fill you with love for all those of the household of faith.

Don't let any carnal leader misguide you so that you lose your rewards (see 1 Corinthians 13:4). Remember: *Now abideth faith, hope, charity* [or love]*; these three, but the greatest of these is love* (1 Corinthians 13:13). So, *let brotherly love continue* (Hebrews 13:1).

Chapter 20

He Loves Me,
He Loves Me Not

I remember sometime ago I held a meeting in a very aristocratic Presbyterian church. I like the Presbyterians. Did you ever stop to think how much they have done for evangelism? Billy Sunday was a Presbyterian; Chapman was a Presbyterian; Torrey was a Presbyterian, though he was a Congregationalist to start with; Biederwolf was a Presbyterian. I could go on and call the roll. A large percentage of the great evangelists in America were Presbyterians.

—Bob Jones, Sr.

It is hard for those who admire Beecher to explain how he persecuted Finney from Dan to Beer-Sheba, actually joining forces with anti-revival people, though he himself was an ardent evangelical. His private correspondence left off just a little short of making Finney a horse-thief;

"Untruthful!...Spirit of lying...Not to be believed at all...make a manful stand against Finney."

True, at the end of the picture, Beecher was all for Finney. But the years when he and poor, dehydrated Nettleton went tommy-hawking after Finney are quite a bit too much off color for explanation.

—*America's Great Revivals*

Sin's Explosion

Finney was severely criticized for certain "new measures" he put into use in his revivals. He prayed for sinners by name. He introduced the "anxious seat," a bench in the front of the church to which people who were in the struggle of rebirth were invited. He permitted women to pray in public. He spoke in everyday language. He used assistants to speak to people about their soul's welfare. All these things were highly irregular and criticized.

—America's Great Revivals

The history of revivals proves this very clearly. Even when you have had a revival, if the spirit of contention comes in, if men begin to divide on doctrines that are not absolutely essential to salvation, the Spirit is quenched. You find it in the eighteenth century, in the disputing between Wesley and Whitefield, and their various followers. The work was arrested for a while. You had it in Wales. There was a dispute between Daniel Rowland and Howell Harris which went on from 1751 to 1763 and it was an arid and a barren period. Then they came together once more, and the Spirit came down again. Contentiousness is of the devil.

—Martyn Lloyd-Jones

There has never been anything that has so promoted spiritual unity as revival.

—Martyn Lloyd-Jones

I perceive something bordering on envy toward a brother. When shall I come to rejoice in others' gifts and graces as much as in his own? I am resolved to wrestle with Jesus Christ by faith and prayer till He gives me humility.

—*George Whitefield*

Whitefield had a deep humility, and broad charity toward loving all others who loved Jesus in sincerity. If other Christians misrepresented him, he forgave them; if they refused to work with him, he still loved them.

—Pratney

Luther, whose life first split a world church over truth, oddly enough died attempting personal unity for others. He became sick from over-exposure after a cold January journey in an attempt to reconcile two friends who had quarreled. By February, it was plain he was on his death-bed. Friends, gathering around him heard him quote John 3:16 and say "Father, into Thy hands I commend my spirit; Thou hast redeemed me, Thou true God."

—*America's Great Revivals*

In the opinion of this writer, George Whitefield exemplified in church history, more than any evangelist, the sacrifice of a ministry for the ministry of another. George Whitefield could have been founder of the Whitefield denomination if followers of his day had their way. Whitefield renounced the matter with the sword of swift decision as one church after another fell to John Wesley and Methodism. He could have brought a permanent hurt to Wesley theology if he had lived to save only his own Whitefield ministry. He renounced it all. He renounced his own ministry for the ministry of others. It was not imperative to Whitefield to save his ministry. It was all for the gospel; it was all for the Lordship of Jesus Christ! And the last nine years of his ministry, he spit blood each time he preached.

How many, in our day, would be willing to sacrifice their own ministry for the success of another ministry? This is a question of character. Whether it be our own ministry or the outbreak of a revival, we should be willing for other biblical ministries to succeed if ours should fail; we should agonize before God for revival in another place if He does not deem it His will to give us a revival in our own place.

—O. Talmadge Spence

The two essential conditions of revival are unity and prayer. All together in one place..with one accord continued steadfast in prayer (Acts 1:14).

—*Pratney*

That they all may be one; as thou, Father, art in me, and I in thee, that they also may be one in us: that the world may believe that thou hast sent me.

—*John 17:21*

At a huge ministerial conference, I made the following statement, "I can no longer tolerate the dissension and division occurring among the brethren. It hinders genuine revival and makes a mocking world reject the message of Christ. I will no longer go into areas for future evangelistic campaigns unless there is a new spirit of love and unity among our leaders."

Unfortunately, the love and unity for which my soul cried out did not occur. In fact, the divisiveness became worse. My heart was crushed.

During the past eight years Rexella and I have ministered to the entire nation via weekly television. Throughout these years, I have also spent hundreds of hours in the Word and prayer seeking a scriptural answer to the separatist problem. My in-depth study allowed me to write a book entitled *Heart Disease in Christ's Body*.

The sub-title, "Fundamentalism...Is It Side-tracked?" describes the contents of this volume. It is shocking. In it I prove that I have not compromised my position by calling for Christian unity. Instead, I have shown with hundreds of texts that it is God's will that every believer, regardless of denominational tag, should [forbear] *one another in love; Endeavouring to keep the unity of the Spirit in the bond of peace. There is one body, and one Spirit, even as ye are called in one hope of your calling; One Lord, one faith, one baptism, one God and Father of all, who is above all, and through all, and in you all* (Ephesians 4:2-6).

I have paid a tremendous cost in standing for this particular truth in God's Word. I will continue to pay whatever price I must to unify the broken, bleeding body of Christ because it is God's command to all His children.

Out of my suffering has come joy.

Five thousand Christian leaders and laymen have written to tell me of their change of heart, mind, and attitude.

Sin's Explosion

Heart Disease in Christ's Body is already circulating in 50 nations.

The Christians of Kuwait have asked for permission to translate the material for all Arabic Christians in numerous nations.

GOD IS AT WORK.

Now I am entering a new era—it is a new beginning. Redemption and reconciliation will be my double-barreled message. I will attempt, under that anointing of the blessed Holy Spirit, to call lost sinners to Christ and call the fractured members of Christ's Body to love and togetherness.

I must do so because I felt the heart cry of Jesus, who prayed, *Father, keep through thine own name those whom thou hast given me, that they may be one, as we are…. Neither pray I for these alone, but for them also which shall believe on me through their word; That they all may be one; as thou, Father, art in me, and I in thee, that they also may be one in us: that the world may believe that thou hast sent me* (John 17:11,20,21).

The prayer of our Saviour was answered on the Day of Pentecost as the first blood-bought believer was placed into the body of Christ and continues to be answered as thousands, daily, are added to His Body.

The big issue all of us must face is that there are presently 20,780 Christian denominations within the world, and the majority of them uplift Christ. Thus, it is not one group but thousands of Christian denominations who belong to and add members to the one body of Christ.

During the past 2,000 years, since the first member was added to Christ's Body, some 250,000 to

500,000 different denominations (only God knows the astronomical number) have been responsible for bringing millions into His Body through their efforts. How ridiculous, then, when one hears a separatistic brother saying, "I am the only one who is standing true to God in my city."

First Corinthians 12:13 declares, *For by one Spirit are we all baptized into one body.* This is not a Baptist, Nazarene, Pentecostal, Wesleyan, Methodist, Christian and Missionary Alliance, or Evangelical Free Church body. Rather, it is the one body of Jesus Christ composed of all born-again believers from tens of thousands of denominations since Pentecost until the present moment.

Today, instead of dividing the body of Jesus, it is every believer's duty to [endeavor] *to keep the unity of the Spirit in the bond of peace* (Ephesians 4:3). Thus, *I must obey God, not men...if I pleased men, I should not be the servant of Christ* (Galatians 1:10).

My dual message, then, must center around God's love for lost mankind and the believer's love for every brother and sister who is a member of God's family and Christ's Body.

Love Proves Salvation Is Genuine

This is the truth God has burned into my heart, and is found in 1 John 4:7,8, *Beloved, let us love one another: for love is of God; and every one that loveth is born of God, and knoweth God. He that loveth not knoweth not God; for God is love.*

Upon the authority of this text and others, I must dogmatically affirm that if one's heart is always full of bitterness toward others, it is undoubtedly the greatest sign that salvation is missing. Don't miss the utter simplicity of these words—*He that loveth not, knoweth not God.*

First John 3:14 states, *We know that we have passed from death unto life, because we love the brethren. He that loveth not his brother abideth in death.* Notice it does not say that the one who hates is in danger of death, but that he abides in the state of death. John continues in the next verse, clarifying misunderstandings that could arise, by saying, *Whosoever hateth his brother is a murderer: and ye know that no murderer hath eternal life abiding in him* (vs. 15).

Friend, this is not a state of broken fellowship with the Lord. It is rather a state of damnation because no murderer, including anyone who hates his brother, has eternal life abiding in him. Many of you reading these words today religiously carry out church functions. You sing the anthems, pray the prayers, recite the creeds, give your tithes, and take your stand for orthodoxy and fundamentalism. However, you overlook a sin in your life which will doom your soul—the malicious hatred being harbored toward others. Oh, how wrong! Godly love is the greatest proof one has that his experience is real. Now, if one knows his experience to be genuine, but still lacks the fruit of the Spirit, love and forgiveness toward others, he should immediately repent (change his mind) about his attitude, confess the abominable sin and in the spirit of revival, obey God's commands and follow Christ's example.

Hear God: *And be ye kind one to another, tenderhearted, forgiving one another, even as God for*

Christ's sake hath forgiven you (Ephesians 4:32). *Forbearing one another, and forgiving one another, if any man have a quarrel against any: even as Christ forgave you, so also do ye* (Colossians 3:13).

We are to forgive others as Christ forgave us. Most of us were a mess when Jesus lovingly forgave us. We were covered with vile, loathsome sins. From the soles of our feet to the tops of our heads, there was no soundness in us—only wounds, bruises, and putrefying sores (see Isaiah 1:6). We had no goodness and all our righteousnesses were as filthy rags (see Isaiah 64:6).

God looked down from heaven to see if there were any that did understand and seek Him. We were altogether filthy. There was none—NONE—that did good (see Psalm 14:2,3). Nevertheless, His love sent Him to die for adulterers, blasphemers, drunkards, drug addicts, extortioners, fornicators, homosexuals, killers, liars, railers, rapists, Satanists, sadists, traitors, tramps, and the rest of society's villians— because He loved us and wanted to wash us from our sins in His own blood (see Revelation 1:5).

When Jesus' earthly trial occurred, they tore His body to shreds with a Roman cat-o-nine-tails. They stuck thorns in the form of a crown, around the flesh of His skull. They pulled His beard out by the roots, and they bruised, battered, and beat His body into a mass of mutilated, bleeding flesh. Still, this God of love cried out from the cross, *Father, forgive them; for they know not what they do* (Luke 23:34).

Beloved, if God so loved us, we ought also to love one another (1 John 4:11). Is it possible that we humans could possess this kind of love? Stephen did.

When the angry crowds crushed his head and body with rocks because of his strong preaching, he cried, *Lord, lay not this sin to their charge. And when he had said this, he fell asleep* [died] (Acts 7:60).

Oh, dear God, we are such needy people and we so desire this supernatural love that will make us forgive a man "seventy times seventy," or 490 times, for the same sin. Give us Thy love in a greater measure through the Holy Spirit. Then 1 Corinthians 13:4-7 will become a reality. [Love] *suffereth long, and is kind; [love] envieth not; [love] vaunteth not itself, is not puffed up, doth not behave itself unseemly, seeketh not her own, is not easily provoked, thinketh no evil; Rejoiceth not in iniquity, but rejoiceth in the truth; Beareth all things, believeth all things, hopeth all things, endureth all things.*

Do you and I have this love today? Love is the fruit of real Christianity. If you and I hate—we will be the losers. Those who hate are classified as murderers, and no murderer has eternal life abiding in him. Is your experience with Christ real? Why not test it with God's Word.

In this the children of God are manifest, and the children of the devil: whosoever doeth not righteousness is not of God, neither he that loveth not his brother (1 John 3:10).

If we love one another, God dwelleth in us.... If a man say, I love God, and hateth his brother, he is a liar (1 John 4:12,20). Remember, a brother or sister in Christ is anyone who has received Jesus as Saviour, and brothers and sisters are found in hundreds of denominations.

He Loves Me, He Loves Me Not

I have written this message to help some needy heart seek God. Animosity, bitterness, backbiting, criticism, envy, hatred, jealousy, malice, and constant railing against others indicates that there is a serious problem in one's life, even a minister's. Revival will not come until it begins in the house of God. When the world sees a revived, unified body of believers, they will truly believe the Father sent the Son.

Chapter 21

Prayer Hindering Marriages

When we get to heaven, we will not receive a reward for remaking our partner but instead for allowing God to remake us.

God holds you accountable for your actions, not your mate's reactions.

As long as we harbour ill will, we have not forgiven.

We must accept one another as we are. If you wanted a classy Cadillac and got a dented Volkswagon, accept her as she is, you chose her.

Let your mate finish his or her sentences.

—Florence Littauer

Marriage is honourable in all.

—*Hebrews 13:4*

Don't hold back on sex in marriage. It violates God's commands.

—·1 Corinthians 7:1-5

Sin's Explosion

Today's couples, when not controlled by God's Spirit, believe that the answers are found in swinging, switching, swapping, sampling, slugging, and splitting.

When you are old enough to leave home, leave and then cleave to your mate—forsaking all others.

If you treat your wife at home as well as you do the girls at work, home would be like heaven.

—Leonard Ravenhill

If some men talked to waiters in restaurants as they do their wives at home, they would be minus their teeth.

—Jack Van Impe

Submit yourselves one to another.

—Ephesians 5:21

Seek not to be understood, but to understand.

—St. Francis

To understand your child is not just important, it is crucial.

—Fritz Ridenour

There will always be a generation gap.

—Jack Van Impe

Provoke not your children to wrath.

—Ephesians 6:4

Feeling loved and cared for is at the heart of good self-esteem and self-respect.

Avoid gunslinger terms with your teenagers such as: "Hi, Tubby, been in the fridge again?" "Going out with your punk friends again?"

—*Fritz Ridenour*

In a blizzard a little toddler saw his father's foot prints and followed them. Dad, mother, where would your children end up following your steps?

—Jack Van Impe

When contentious words cause division at home, we destroy not only the joy of oneness, but also the reflection of God in our home.
When contentious words divide our spirits at home, we destroy the picture of Christ and His Church.

—*Joseph Stowell*

Pride breeds quarrels.

—Proverbs 13:10

The man of like passions at 75 records his own heartbreak at her going (Finney is speaking):
That beloved wife of mine died. It was to me a great sorrow. The night after she died, I was lying in my room alone, and some kind Christian friends were sitting in the parlor, watching out the night. I had been asleep awhile, and as I awoke, the thought of my bereavement flashed over my mind with such power! My wife was

gone! I should never speak to her again or see her face! My children were motherless! What should I do? I rose instantly from my bed exclaiming, "I shall be deranged if I cannot rest in God." The Lord calmed my mind, for that night, but still at times seasons of sorrow would come over me.

—Finney's notes on revival

Likewise, ye wives, be in subjection to your own husbands; that, if any obey not the word, they also may without the word be won by the conversation of the wives.... Likewise, ye husbands, dwell with them according to knowledge, giving honour unto the wife, as unto the weaker vessel, and as being heirs together of the grace of life; that your prayers be not hindered.

—1 Peter 3:1,7

Do you want to improve the quality of your family life? I believe there is no better place to find help than in the pages of the Bible. God has provided a model there for parents and their children.

Someone has said that a happy family is but an earlier heaven. How true. The breakdown of the family has reached pandemic proportions; that is, it is widespread, universal, encompassing the country. Hardly a family is exempt from some degree of misery related to a disruption within the home. If it isn't the parents themselves, it is one or more of the children within the home—even very little children—causing such disharmony that the climate within the home resembles a war zone. Untamed, such undisciplined youngsters grow into unruly teenagers, unmanageable, rebellious, and selfish. On the other hand, I have heard of little children who were sweet, who were capable of being disciplined, and who gave their parents little or no trouble but who overnight, it seemed, turned into what one parent called "monsters." For such families, this is not heaven on earth.

What Is Needed?

That evil forces have ripped into family relationships cannot be denied. Perhaps that is expressing it far too mildly. It should be clearly understood by all family members that we have an adversary—a very strong adversary—on the rampage in the world today. Coming to grips with that fact is the thing, I believe, that is needed first.

Know Who the Real Enemy Is

Be sober, be vigilant; because your adversary the devil, as a roaring lion, walketh about, seeking whom he may devour: Whom resist stedfast in the faith, knowing that the same afflictions are accomplished in your brethren that are in the world (1 Peter 5:8,9).

Do you know and understand the full implications of these verses? This adversary is not just some wild-eyed little gremlin dressed in a red suit with a pitch-fork in his hand, like some carricatures portray. No, the devil is a reality, a force, an evil power. He is fierce, like a lion roaring, on the prowl for that which will satisfy his voracious appetite. Still, God has given us a Book by which satanic forces can be defeated by all family members.

A Healthy, Happy Home Life

So, what are God's requirements for a healthy, well-balanced family—physically and spiritually? First, consider the husband and father, *Husbands, love your wives, even as Christ also loved the church, and gave himself for it* (Ephesians 5:25). The husband is to take charge in the home, but he is to love his wife with the same self-sacrificing love Christ manifested when He died for our salvation.

The role of being the head of the home is a privilege, but it is also a grave responsibility. The man, if he is to obey Paul's injunction, must renounce all selfishness and always seek the best for his wife, even dying for her if necessary. This kind of love involves consideration, protection, and support.

Likewise, ye husbands, dwell with them according to knowledge, giving honour unto the wife, as unto the weaker vessel, and as being heirs together of the grace of life; that your prayers be not hindered (1 Peter 3:7). The man is to be considerate and protective because his wife is the "weaker vessel." This does not mean that the woman is inferior as a person to her husband, for Peter declares that they are "heirs *together* of the grace of life."

In salvation, a man and his wife are absolute equals in standing before God and in eternal destiny. *There is neither Jew nor Greek, there is neither bond nor free, there is neither male nor female: for ye are all one in Christ Jesus* (Galatians 3:28). The man's responsibility as the leader in the home is to strengthen, support, and protect his wife. He must create a spirit of mutuality in which his wife as a woman and he as a man share the joys and sorrows, the delights and disappointments, the laughter and tears of human existence. Certainly, he should never be unreasonable or overbearing, and his consideration and sacrificial spirit will make it easy and pleasant for his wife to accept his leadership.

Concerning the man's leadership, C. M. Ward states, "In order for marriage to work, leadership must be exercised by the male. This is not to imply that man does not benefit from the counsel and talent of his "help meet." A husband needs help—all the help he can get. But there can be only one leader in a marriage, and God's Word makes it very clear which partner that is to be.

"But I would have you know, that the head of every man is Christ; and the head of the woman is the man.... For the man is not of the woman; but the woman of the man. Neither was the man created for the woman; but the woman for the man (1 Corinthians 11:3,8,9). Thus, the husband must maintain the spiritual authority in the home or lose his God-given position. *As for me and my house, we will serve the Lord* (Joshua 24:15) should be the motto of every Christian husband and father."

Now, leadership must be administered in love. When love reigns, a woman responds. C. M. Ward continues, "The writer of Proverbs says, *Let thy fountain be blessed: and rejoice with the wife of thy youth. Let her be as the loving hind and pleasant roe; let her breasts satisfy thee at all times; and be thou ravished always with her love* (Proverbs 5:18,19). Only in marriage can we experience such magnificent dimensions of pleasure and joy.

Sin's Explosion

"Although Isaac and Rebekah's romance certainly included the sexual dimension, their relationship went far beyond physical pleasure. A finer, more delicate texture can be felt in this marriage. Their intimate devotion to one another combined the joy of sharing common goals with an unswerving purpose to fulfill God's will."

There is more to marriage than sex, but Hollywood and Broadway's warped formula of "love" seldom goes beyond the bedroom. The finer ingredients of mutuality and responsibility are excluded from the screen's version of romance. Yet, without these deeper qualities, sex cannot hold a marriage together.

Many times the Bible uses the word "know" to describe the intimate, physical relationship between a man and a woman. In the case of Isaac and Rebekah, however, another word is used, Isaac "loved her" (see Genesis 24:67). A permanent and enduring partnership is built on the second word, love, not on the first, know.

The root meaning of love is "to give." In this sense, Isaac was a true lover. He knew how to take and draw comfort from Rebekah's love, but he also knew how to be at her side and give her strength when she needed it. During a difficult time in their marriage, Isaac stood by his wife in prayer: *Isaac intreated the Lord for his wife, because she was barren: and the Lord was intreated of him, and Rebekah his wife conceived* (Genesis 25:21). What an excellent example of the fact that *the effectual fervent prayer of a righteous man availeth much* (James 5:16).

Too many husbands make widows of their wives in spiritual things. While she goes to prayer meeting, he spends the evening at the bowling alley. This, however, was not the case with Isaac and Rebekah. They were true partners.

A Lesson for the Wife

Second, consider the wife and mother. God says in Ephesians 5:22-24, *Wives, submit yourselves unto your own husbands, as unto the Lord. For the husband is the head of the wife, even as Christ is the head of the church: and he is the saviour of the body. Therefore as the church is subject unto Christ, so let the wives be to their own husbands in every thing.*

First Peter 3:1 adds, *Likewise, ye wives, be in subjection to your own husbands; that, if any obey not the word, they also may without the word be won by the conversation* [or lifestyle] *of the wives; while they behold your chaste* [holy] *conversation coupled with fear.* There is no doubt about it, God demands that a Christian woman be in subjection to her husband! This is a command of God, and refusal to comply with God's demands constitutes an act of disobedience and sin. James 4:17 declares, *To him* [or her] *that knoweth to do good, and doeth it not, to him* [or her] *it is sin.*

Dear sister, God cannot bless you until you are willing to obey Him.

Perhaps your family is suffering presently because of your willful transgression of God's command. Nothing can destroy a marriage or home more rapidly than a domineering wife. When a Christian woman, filled with the Holy Spirit, begins to obey God and allows her husband to be the head of the home, it usually results in a new relationship and changes the husband's attitude so that he can begin to love his wife even as Christ loved His Church and gave himself for it. Try it—it works! God said it, and how can God be wrong? In a successful marriage, submission is not an option—it is a command.

Wives, you'll be surprised what a smile and a gentle spirit can do! A meek and quiet spirit is the most precious and valuable adornment you can put on. In the sight of God, this kind of attitude is of "great price" (see 1 Peter 3:4).

Do you want to be loved? Then show the man God gave you some loving submission. It will work wonders.

Some husbands are starved for tender, caring affection. In all their years of marriage, they have never known what it means to be loved. I know men who are bound by the fetters of family finance, insurance, property, education, and transportation, but they receive no compensation for their efforts. These husbands feel, "My wife doesn't care for me—only for what I can provide."

Women were created with a compassionate and caring nature that reaches out to others. God told Eve, *Thy desire shall be to thy husband* (Genesis 3:16). You will find your greatest satisfaction and fulfillment in loving and caring for the man God has given you.

The bridegroom in the Song of Solomon says, *How fair and how pleasant art thou, O love, for delights!* (7:6). Can your husband say that about you?

C. M. Ward describes the ideal wife, "The ideal wife is an asset to her husband. *She will do him good and not evil all the days of her life* (Proverbs 31:12).

This is the ideal wife's main objective in her marriage—to do her husband good. Her steady, unwavering devotion gives him strength to face the world with courage.

"In public, he doesn't have to worry about what she will say about him or how she will act. A wife who wants to make her husband look good doesn't jump in with the punchline when he is telling a story. She never discounts him publicly by saying, 'Oh, you never tell it right!' Instead she builds him up and always protects him from ridicule. The husband of the Proverbs woman is *known in the gates, when he sitteth among the elders of the land* (vs. 23). How do you think he reached such a high position of prestige and authority in his community? His wife encouraged him, always telling him he could do better. She listened to his ideas, supported his opinions, and helped him reach his goals."

A well-known sales and marketing consultant made this rather revealing statement, "I have never known a totally competent man who succeeded without the belief and admiration of a woman behind him." That conclusion supports the often-expressed conviction that "behind every successful man is a great woman." If you help your husband reach his full potential, you will be the main recipient of his success.

Some wives, however, are more of a hindrance than a help to their husbands' careers. Jezebel, as the Bible records, was a hindrance. *There was none like unto Ahab, which did sell himself to work wickedness in the sight of the Lord, whom Jezebel his wife stirred up* (1 Kings 21:25). Ahab's wife blunted every decent impulse this man ever had, and she made a mockery out of his title, "King of Israel."

The wife of Louis Pasteur, the great scientist, resolved from the first days of their marriage that "the laboratory must come before everything." She kept her vow.

Mrs. Pasteur's unwavering support of her husband and his goals enabled this gifted man to fight disease and make medical history. Many lives have been saved as a result of his valuable discoveries. Your husband's success or failure in life may lie in your hands. Such a wife is loved to the end. Major Bowes who hosted "The Amateur Hour" said about his darling, "I hope she may live a thousand years, and I, a thousand less one day: So that I may never know she has passed away."

Rexella has been such a wonderful wife to me throughout our married life. As a young evangelist, barely eking out an existence, she would say, "Don't worry about the finances, honey. I will stretch every dollar to cover our basic needs. Don't allow financial woes to hinder your work for the Lord. Satan would like to discourage you, but press on to victory."

When a minister's wife told Rexella that preachers can easily become proud and must be deflated by their wives, Rexella retorted, "God's men get enough public criticism. A wife who needles her man even more is one who is not submissive to the will of God."

I can honestly identify with the stories of leaders who were successful because of having a loving, loyal help meet. Oh, what men's ministries could become if they all were as blessed with the wife of my youth who best exemplifies the virtuous woman of Proverbs 31.

The Parent-Child Relationship

Third, consider the parent-child relationship. Christian parents must take seriously the scriptural admonition, *Train up a child in the way he should go: and when he is old, he will not depart from it.* What does this mean?

Dr. Charles Swindoll states, "Some contemporary religious interpretations would paraphrase the verse, 'Be sure your child is in Sunday school and church regularly. Cement into his mind a few memorized verses from the Bible plus some hymns and prayers. Send him to Christian camps during the summers of his formative years, and certainly, if at all possible, place the child in a Christian school so he can be educated by people whose teaching is based on the Bible. Because, after all, someday he will sow his wild oats. For sure, he will have his fling. But when he gets old enough to get over his fling, he will come back to God.'

"I don't know about you, but that doesn't bring much encouragement to a parent! It doesn't seem to be much of a divine promise: when he is old and decrepit, finished with his fling, he'll come back to God. Big deal! What parent is really motivated to train his child, knowing he's training a prodigal who will ultimately turn against his parents and not return to the Lord until his later years?

Sin's Explosion

"Not only is that not much of a promise—it isn't true. You and I can name people forced by sheer determination on the part of strict parents to be in church every Sunday, to read the Bible consistently, to memorize portions of Scripture, to attend camp and Christian school. They went into rebellion as soon as they were launched from their home (often before) and are still in that state, having never returned to the 'training' they first experienced.

"I can recall a couple of childhood friends who not only rebelled, but died in their rebellion. They never did return to God.

"That is no promise at all, and I am convinced it is not what the verse is saying. The Book of Proverbs, of course, was originally penned in the Hebrew language. Invariably, things are lost in the process of translation that must be recovered by a study of the original text. So allow me to dig back into the Hebrew tongue to help bring some understanding and color to what is being said.

"First of all, what is meant by 'train up'? You may be surprised to know the original root word is the term for 'the palate, the roof of the mouth, the gums.' In verb form, it is the term used for breaking and bringing into submission a wild horse by a rope in the mouth.

"Train up a child...I want to stop here for a moment, because when we read the word child we invariably think of a little one between the time of infancy and ages four or five. But it's more than that.

"The Hebrew word *child* in 1 Samuel 4:21 refers to a newborn infant. But 1 Samuel 1:27 refers to a young boy who had just been weaned. Genesis 21:16 uses the same word of Ishmael in his pre-teen years. Genesis 31:2 uses the same word for Joseph when he was seventeen. Genesis 34:19 uses the word for a young man ready for marriage.

"The term *child* is broad. It covers all the years the child is under the roof of the parent, every age from infancy to young adulthood. The entire time is called the period of being 'trained up.'

"Train up—create a thirst in—build into the child the experience of submission (as you would train a horse that had been wild) a child of all ages in the realm of the home—in the way he should go.

"Now a man doesn't start growing a beard when he is ninety. He begins to grow a beard when he is approaching maturity. The promise is that when your child reaches maturity, when he is ready to leave home, he will not depart from his training. It's not a promise concerning people ninety years old. It's a promise for those who, having been trained correctly, are leaving the nest and entering into maturity."

Now let me continue my thoughts on the training of children. God is speaking about the disciplining of children. A youngster must know that his parents are in charge. The writer of Proverbs declares, *Chasten thy son while there is hope, and let not thy soul spare for his crying* (Proverbs 19:18). Yes, the infliction of a spanking is sometimes indispensable in disciplining one's children. The parent who refrains from discipline because he "can't stand to see the child cry" is making a serious mistake.

Another inspired proverb says, *Foolishnes is bound in the heart of a child; but the rod of correction shall drive it far from him* (Proverbs 22:15). The word translated *foolishness* refers to "self-will." A tendency of a child to go his own way is part of his very nature, and physical punishment—properly used on his seat, not his head or face—will teach him to submit to those who have authority over him. Many children do not require frequent spankings, but others do. The "board of education" applied to the "seat of understanding" is often a necessity. Still, fathers and mothers must be careful how and when they administer physical punishment.

Many children are beaten severely when parents lose their tempers. Others never know why they are being punished, for the parents are inconsistent, sometimes letting them get by with a serious offense but occasionally manifesting extreme severity over a minor infraction. A child should not be punished physically every time he displeases his parents. Such treatment should be reserved for instances of rebellion when he defies mother or dad, or when he engages in impudent backtalk. Also, every act of discipline should be administered in love and tenderness. This is the Heavenly Father's method.

Hebrews 12:5-11 says, *My son, despise not thou the chastening of the Lord, nor faint when thou art rebuked of him: For whom the Lord loveth he chasteneth, and scourgeth every son whom he receiveth. If ye endure chastening, God dealeth with you as with sons; for what son is he whom the father chasteneth not? But if ye be without chastisement, whereof all are partakers, then are ye bastards, and not sons. Furthermore we have had fathers of our flesh which corrected us, and we gave them reverence: shall we not much rather be in subjection unto the Father of spirits, and live? For they verily for a few days chastened us after their own pleasure; but he for our profit that we might be partakers of his holiness. Now no chastening for the present seemeth to be joyous, but grievous: nevertheless afterward it yieldeth the peaceable fruit of righteousness unto them which are exercised thereby.*

Christian parents should also establish a time for family worship. The reading and discussion of a Bible passage followed by prayer makes a deep spiritual imprint upon a child. Moses underscored the importance of instructing children in spiritual truth when he said:

Hear, O Israel: The Lord our God is one Lord: And thou shalt love the Lord thy God with all thine heart, and with all thy soul, and with all thy might. And these words, which I command thee this day, shall be in thine heart: And thou shalt teach them diligently unto thy children, and shalt talk of them when thou sittest in thine house, and when thou walkest by the way, and when thou liest down, and when thou risest up (Deuteronomy 6:4-7). Yes, God's Word in one hand and a "paddle of inducement" in the other is the Lord's way to train up a child. If one disobeys this plan, he will one day be clobbered by his undisciplined son.

12 Rules for Raising Disobedient Children

Here are 12 rules for raising disobedient children.

1. Begin with infancy to give the child everything he wants. In this way he will grow up to believe the world owes him a living.

2. When he picks up bad words, laugh at him. This will make him think he's cute.

3. Never give him any spiritual training. Wait until he is 21 and then let him "decide for himself."

4. Avoid use of the word "wrong." It may develop a guilt complex. This will condition him to believe later, when he is arrested for stealing a car, that society is against him and he is being persecuted.

5. Pick up everything he leaves lying around. Do everything for him so that he will be experienced in throwing all responsibility on others.

6. Let him read any printed matter he can get his hands on. Be careful that the silverware and drinking glasses are sterilized, but let his mind feast on garbage.

7. Quarrel frequently in the presence of your children. In this way they won't be so shocked when the home is broken up later.

8. Give a child all the spending money he wants. Never let him earn his own.

9. Satisfy his every craving for food, drink, and comfort. See that every sensual desire is gratified.

10. Take his part against neighbors, teachers, and policemen. They are all prejudiced against your child.

11. When he gets into real trouble, apologize for yourself by saying, "I never could do anything with him."

12. Prepare for a life of grief. You will be likely to have it.

Finally, to the children themselves, God commands in Ephesians 6:1-3, *Children, obey your parents in the Lord: for this is right. Honour thy father and mother; (which is the first commandment with promise;) That it may be well with thee, and thou mayest live long on the earth.*

Jesus set a beautiful example for all children and teenagers to follow. In fact, let's go further by remembering that the love and respect Christ showered upon His sweet mother occurred when He was 33 years of age. The lesson unfolded is very moving.

Mary was the instrument God used to bring His Son into the world. This pure young lady was a virgin who had never known man in an intimate way (see Luke 1:35). She became impregnated through the miracle-working power of the Holy Spirit—a special act of creation. Joseph had nothing to do with the birth of Christ and was only called father because he adopted Christ.

Years later as Christ hung upon the cruel cross, dying for the sins of an entire world, Joseph was unable to be present because he was dead. Jesus looked at the lonely little woman who bore Him and His tender heart was grieved. He wanted assurance that someone would take care of His mother after His departure. He looked at Mary, and at His beloved disciple John, and said, *Woman, behold thy son!...John, behold thy mother!* (John 19:26,27). Christ, in His dying moments, was concerned about the future welfare of Mary who had borne Him and whose soul was now pierced with a sword.

Jesus had no earthly possessions to leave His mother, (see 2 Corinthians 8:9). He brought nothing into the world at His birth and He had nothing to leave behind as He left this life. He died as poor as He had lived.

Sin's Explosion

All that He could leave His mother was His love, and He wanted John to love His mother and care for her. What a lesson this is for thoughtless sons and daughters in this cruel age in which we live! Thousands of our elderly parents weep because of being forgotten. Lord, forgive us, for we know not what we do.

Each believer should at this point examine his or her own life to see if his attitudes are in harmony with God's Word concerning family relationships. If not, seek God's ways, obey His commands that your prayers will be unhindered from this day forward.

Chapter 22

Talk Is Cheap When It Comes to Love

Let us come to the Cross. What was happening there? A great fight was going on, a great battle. All the powers of hell were out against Him. But this is what happened, Paul tells us, in Colossians 2:15, *And having spoiled principalities and powers he made a shew of them openly, triumphing over them in it.* They thought they had finished Him. They mustered their last reserves, the fight was on. The Edomites brought out their last reserves, but He conquered them, He smashed them, He put them to an open shame, triumphing over them, He did it alone. No one helped Him. No one was able to assist Him. He, through His lone and solitary death, destroyed him that had the power of death, that is the devil.

—Martyn Lloyd-Jones

Tell me in the light of the Cross, isn't it a scandal that you and I live today as we do?

—*Alan Redpath*

As soon as we cease to bleed, we cease to bless.

—Dr. J. H. Jowett

Sin's Explosion

When Paul went to the Cross, the miracle of conversion and regeneration took place; but later when he got on the Cross, the greater miracle of identification took place.

—Leonard Ravenhill

There is no cheap grace in revival.

—Pratney

Revival comes to scorch before it heals; it comes to condemn ministers and people for their unfaithful witness, for their selfish living, for their neglect of the cross, and to call them to daily renunciation, to an evangelical poverty and to a deep and daily consecration.

—Pratney

I hear of preachers all the time who decided they should not be in the ministry and they have gone to selling insurance or automobiles. I want to tell you that if you are a preacher of the gospel you shouldn't step down to become president of the United States. God has called you to be one of His highest, noble servants and you ought to be faithful to the end. And regardless of how weary and how sometimes lonely the work becomes, all that is necessary to get you through the next day is His "well done."

—Martyn Lloyd-Jones

You say, "Aren't you afraid that people will go to extremes?" No, I am afraid they will not go to any extremes. I am afraid they will not have any tears. I am afraid of the kind of praying with no tears, with no sacrifice, with no confession, and without even the loss of a meal. God have pity on us Christians who have never missed a meal, never lost a night's sleep, never lost a job, never lost a friend for God. No wonder we cannot have revival.

—*John R. Rice*

Who does not remember one story they tell about William Booth? Queen Victoria, that matchless Christian, called him in to inquire, "General Booth, what is the secret of your ministry? How is it that others are so pale, so palid, so powerless, so weak, so pusillanimous, and you are so mighty?"

William Booth looked into the face of his queen, and with tears streaming down his bearded cheeks, said, "Your Majesty, I guess the reason is because God has all there is of me."

—Hyman J. Appleman

If any man will come after me, let him deny himself, and take up his cross daily, and follow me.

—*Luke 9:23*

Salvation is free, but it is not cheap. It cost the Son of God an immeasurable price to redeem humanity and set mankind free from the clutches of Satan and the second death.

Christ's Love Involved Sacrifice

May I begin by pointing out that Christ's love for sinners involved SACRIFICE.

The Lord Jesus so loved you and me that He left Father and home for 33 years. He became a poverty-stricken pauper, if I may use the phrase reverently, in

337

order that we might become children of the King. Second Corinthians 8:9 declares, *For ye know the grace of our Lord Jesus Christ, that though he was rich, yet for your sakes he became poor, that ye through his poverty might be rich.* Oh, what unfathomable love.

What did He relinquish and what was His goal? Psalm 61:11, speaking about the Father and heaven, states that *in thy presence is fulness of joy; at thy right hand there are pleasures for evermore.* Christ, in His high-priestly prayer in John 17, discusses the blessed communion He enjoyed with the Father before Christ's incarnation or coming to earth. Hear Him in verses 5 and 24, *And now, O Father, glorify thou me with thine own self with the glory which I had with thee before the world was. Father, I will that they also, whom thou hast given me, be with me where I am; that they may behold my glory, which thou hast given me: for thou lovedst me before the foundation of the world.*

Though heaven is a glorious place, Christ left it all behind. He tells us why in John 6:38,40,47,51,58. *For I came down from heaven, not to do mine own will, but the will of him that sent me. And this is the will of him that sent me, that every one which seeth the Son, and believeth on him, may have everlasting life: and I will raise him up at the last day. Verily verily, I say unto you, He that believeth on me hath everlasting life. I am the living bread which came down from heaven: if any man eat of this bread, he shall live for ever...This is that bread which came down from heaven...*[and] *he that eateth of this bread shall live for ever.*

In the light of such love, shouldn't we as believers give up a few conveniences to win a lost, dying world to Jesus? The majority of God's people do so little. They occasionally tip God and feel they have executed their financial obligations to the Almighty. Well, those who give sacrificially out of a broken heart for Christ and for the souls of men will be rewarded accordingly at the Judgment Seat of Christ. When that day occurs, and it may be soon, 2 Corinthians 9:6 will become a reality. *He which soweth sparingly* [gives little] *shall reap also sparingly; and he which soweth bountifully* [gives much] *shall reap also bountifully*. It will be worth all our sacrifice when we see Jesus, for He said in Matthew 19:29, *And every one that hath forsaken houses, or brethren, or sisters, or father, or mother, or wife, or children, or lands, for my name's sake, shall receive an hundredfold, and shall inherit everlasting life*. Beloved believer, let's give our best until coronation day so that we shall all hear our Saviour say, "Well done, thou good and faithful servant."

Christ's Love Involved Slander

Christ's love for sinners also involved SLANDER and a voluntary forfeiture of His reputation (see Philippians 2:7). No one in the annals of history was ever hated or profaned more than the sweet Son of God. His enemies dragged His worthy name and character through the depths of degradation. They said:

He casteth out devils though the prince of the devils (Matthew 9:34). *This fellow doth not cast out devils, but by Beelzebub the prince of the devils* (Matthew

12:24). *He hath an unclean spirit* (Mark 3:30). *Some said, He is a good man: others said, Nay; but he deceiveth the people* (John 7:12). *The people answered and said, Thou hast a devil* (John 7:20).

Imagine the audacity of the people as they hurled these vicious accusations at Christ. Let's continue: *The Pharisees therefore said unto him, Thou bearest record of thyself; thy record is not true* (John 8:13). Here they called the Saviour a bold-faced liar. It gets worse in John 8:41 where they said, *We be not born of fornication like you.* Still again, *Thou art a Samaritan, and hast a devil* (8:48). This was a racial slur because Samaritans were hated. In John 10:20 they said, *He hath a devil, and is mad.* He is demented and foams like a mad dog.

These are but a few of the slanderous pronouncements made about the Lord Jesus Christ. Notice the people said that Jesus had a devil, an unclean spirit; that He was a deceiver, a liar; that He was an illegitimate child, a mad dog. Can you believe that they were speaking about Jesus, God in human flesh?

Will those of us who truly follow in His steps receive the same kind of treatment? You had better believe it! Listen to the Saviour in John 15:18,19, *If the world hate you, ye know that it hated me before it hated you. If ye were of the world, the world would love his own: but because ye are not of the world, but I have chosen you out of the world, therefore the world hateth you.*

This same teaching is presented by our Lord in the "Sermon on the Mount." He said, *Blessed are they which are persecuted for righteousness' sake: for theirs is the kingdom of heaven. Blessed are ye when men shall revile you, and persecute you, and shall say all manner of evil against you falsely, for my sake.* [Then what—quit? No!] *Rejoice, and be exceeding glad; for great is your reward in heaven* (Matthew 5:10-12).

Paul said in 1 Corinthians 4:10,13, *We are fools for Christ's sake. We are made as the filth of the world, and are the offscouring of all things unto this day.* Consider the word *offscouring* for a moment. When dishes are washed, the pots often have "goop" on the bottom. One then takes a scouring pad and scrapes the pot clean. The released "goop" is the *offscouring*. UGH! Well dear refined Christian, who is taking a stand for Christ in a wicked world, you are the offscouring, the "goop" off the bottom of the pan in the world's eyes.

Has this been true in your life? If not, why not? God said it would be so if one lived the Christian life. [For] *all that will live godly in Christ Jesus shall suffer persecution* (2 Timothy 3:12). So when heartache and heartbreak occur because of Jesus, bear it. Why? Because James 1:12 states, *Blessed* [or happy] *is the man that endureth temptation* [testing or slander]: *for when he is tried, he shall receive the crown of life.*

Christ's Love Involved Sorrow and Suffering

Christ's love for sinners also involved great SORROW and SUFFERING. We know this to be true from Matthew 26:38 where He cries, *My soul is exceeding sorrowful, even unto death.* This burden for the souls of men often brought tears to Jesus' eyes. One day as He looked down upon Jerusalem from the

Mount of Olives, He saw precious souls milling through the streets in a hopeless condition. He *beheld the city, and wept over it* (Luke 19:41).

On another occasion as He contemplated Calvary's cruel cross, His agony was so great that *his sweat was as it were great drops of blood falling down to the ground* (Luke 22:44). What caused this condition? Medical men inform us that capillaries hold the blood in our bodies. If the capillaries burst, blood will seep through the skin. Jesus prayed so agonizingly over the souls of mankind in the Garden of Gethsemane that His capillaries burst. Immediately His blood seeped through His skin as beads of bloodied perspiration dripped to the ground. Oh, what love!

This love that surpasses all human comprehension is depicted prophetically in Psalm 22. Christ knew this Psalm and understood what was going to happen to Him on Calvary. May your heart be broken as you hear the words of this Psalm:

My God, my God, why hast thou forsaken me? why art thou so far from helping me, and from the words of my roaring? I am a worm, and no man; a reproach of men, and despised of the people. I am poured out like water, and all my bones are out of joint: my heart is like wax; it is melted in the midst of my bowels. My strength is dried up like a potsherd; and my tongue cleaveth to my jaws; and thou hast brought me into the dust of death. For dogs have compassed me: the assembly of the wicked have inclosed me: they have pierced my hands and my feet (Psalm 22:1,6,14-16).

Isaiah, the prophet, also portrays this ignominous scene in chapter 53:1-5. He says, *Who hath believed our report?* [a report so terrifying that the followers of

Messiah Jesus had to turn their faces away in revulsion because the distorted, mangled, mutilated body of their Lord was more than they could endure]...*he hath no form nor comeliness; and when we shall see him, there is no beauty that we should desire him. He is despised and rejected of men; a man of sorrows, and acquainted with grief: and we hid as it were our faces from him; he was despised, and we esteemed him not.* [But why?] *Surely he hath borne our griefs, and carried our sorrows: yet we did esteem him stricken, smitten of God, and afflicted. But he was wounded for our transgressions, he was bruised for our iniquities: the chastisement of our peace was upon him; and with his stripes we are healed.*

Christ suffered horrendously for you. He took your place bearing your sin and its penalty. Yes, *Christ died for our sins* (1 Corinthians 15:3).

Will You Pay the Price of Love?

Have your emotions been stirred? Do you really understand how much Christ loves and wants souls saved? Now it's your turn, Christian. What price are you paying to see souls delivered from a Christless eternity?

In this day of easy-believism, are we also to suffer as Christians? Are we to pay a price in winning lost souls to Jesus? Let's see. *For unto you it is given in the behalf of Christ, not only to believe on him, but also to suffer for his sake* (Philippians 1:29).

It is not enough to believe. One becomes a Christian by believing, but discipleship produces suffering. Believing gets one into heaven, but discipleship

343

awards one with heaven's best crowns to place at the feet of Jesus. Remember, He suffered for us, leaving us an example that we should follow His steps (see 1 Peter 2:21).

Since Christ's suffering was for sinners, ours should be for the same reason. Think of this statement in the light of the millions of Christians who have never won a soul to Christ. Think of the shame that awaits their entrance into heaven (see 1 John 2:28).

Christian, if there are no scars on your brow, there will be no stars in your crown. Are you ready to meet Christ? Will you have souls to present to Him on that day?

Paul was prepared. Listen to an excerpt from his final letter, written the morning he was to die. His life is about to be ended by decapitation—beheading. Soon Paul's head will roll from his body. Is he remorseful, regretful, and sorry? Would he like to relive life without all of the sorrow he experienced as Christ's follower? You be the judge.

Paul wrote, *For I am now ready to be offered, and the time of my departure is at hand. I have fought a good fight, I have finished my course, I have kept the faith: Henceforth there is laid up for me a crown of righteousness, which the Lord, the righteous judge, shall give me at that day: and not to me only, but unto all them also that love his appearing* (2 Timothy 4:6-8). There are no regrets—Paul is going home to be with Jesus forever.

Christian, get a copy of *Foxe's Book of Martyrs*. It will revolutionize your life as you see the price Christians have paid throughout history. They were grateful for salvation by grace, and they gave their all in appreciation and gratitude. Here is a moving example.

In 304 A.D. Timothy and Mara heard a knock at their door. A voice said, "Give us your Scripture portions. We want to burn them." They replied, "Never. We would rather have you burn us than the Bible." Their enemies then took Timothy, put out his eyes, threw him in front of his wife, and said, "Now let him have and read his Bible."

Six weeks passed. The agents returned, saying, "Will you renounce Jesus today?" "Never!" said Timothy and Mara. So the agents took this godly couple and hanged them in front of their little children. Why? Because Timothy and Mara loved Jesus Christ.

Friend, salvation is free, but it is not cheap. Talk is cheap when it comes to love, but true love *endures all things* (1 Corinthians 13:7).

Chapter 23

The Health-and-Wealth Promoters

The fruits of the Spirit were upon Paul, the gifts of the Spirit operated through him. He held citywide revivals while he patched tents to pay expenses! My brother preachers, aren't we a chicken-hearted group by the side of Paul? Sometimes he almost starved! Yet, when the table was full, he fasted. He wished everyone blessing, yet could wish himself accursed. With his revolutionary living and riotous theology, this "spectacle before men," this Christian filled with the Holy Ghost is the redemptive counterpart of the fanatical devotee of the political religion of atheistic Communism.

—Leonard Ravenhill

Paul had no side issues. He had no ambitions—and so had nothing to be jealous about. He had no reputation—and so had nothing to fight about. He had no possessions—and therefore nothing to worry about. He had no "rights"—so therefore he could not suffer wrong. He was already broken—so no one could break him. He was "dead"—so none could kill him. He was less than the least—so who could humble him? He had suffered the loss of all things—so none could defraud him.

—Leonard Ravenhill

347

Sin's Explosion

In such a state of mind and spirit, can we wonder that the apostles "turned the world upside down"? Let the ambitious saint ponder this apostolic attitude to the world. Let the popular, unscarred evangelist living in "Hollywood style" think upon his ways.

—Leonard Ravenhill

Oh, we bankrupt, blind, boasting believers! We are naked and don't know it. We are rich (never had we more equipment), but we are poor (never had we less enduement)! We have need of nothing (and yet we lack almost everything the Apostolic church had). Can He stand "in the midst" while we sport unashamedly in our spiritual nakedness?

Oh, we need the fire! Where is the power of the Holy Ghost that slays sinners and fills our altars? Today we seem much more interested in having churches air conditioned than prayer-conditioned.

—*Leonard Ravenhill*

A modern critic says that we believers have gold for our god and greed for our creed.

—Leonard Ravenhill

Do you really wish for a revival? Will you have one? If God should ask you this moment by an audible voice from heaven, "Do you want a revival?" Would you dare say, "Yes." Are you willing to make the sacrifices? Would your answer be, "Yes"? When shall it begin? Would your answer be, "Let it begin today?—let it begin here. Let it begin in my heart! NOW!"

—*Charles G. Finney*

Health-and-Wealth Promoters

For unto you it is given in the behalf of Christ, not only to believe on him, but also to suffer for his sake.

—Philippians 1:29

The Bittermans, our personal friends, went through a heartbreaking experience in the eyes of multiplied millions. They lost their son to a band of terrorists. What a shock it must have been as they received word from a local newspaper reporter in Lancaster, Pennsylvania, that Chet was dead. Imagine how Chet's wife felt as she heard a shopkeeper in Bogota, Columbia, bang on her gate and cry, "They have found Chet's body in a bus!" What tragic news after waiting and praying for 48 days.

This scene will undoubtedly be repeated often as anti-Christian terrorists—either communists or marxist-motivated murderers—attempt to destroy God's servants. Chet's college ring, returned to his wife a few days prior to his execution, tells the story. It's inscription reads, "To know Him and to make Him known." This young martyr witnessed to his abductors and God promised that His Word would not return unto Him void, but it would accomplish that for which He had sent it (see Isaiah 55:11). God's sovereign plans always work together for good.

In this light, I am reminded of a first-century terrorist named Saul of Tarsus who was instrumental in murdering the first Christian martyr, Stephen. The story is recorded in the Book of Acts, chapters 7 and 8. Stephen, filled with the power of the Holy Spirit, bombasts the crowd with a strong, sin-denouncing sermon. The angered crowd reacts in Acts 7:57 through 8:1:

They cried out with a loud voice, and stopped their ears, and ran upon him with one accord, and cast him out of the city, and stoned him: and the witnesses laid down their clothes at a young man's feet, whose name was Saul. And they stoned Stephen, calling upon God, and saying, Lord Jesus, receive my spirit. And he kneeled down, and cried with a loud voice, Lord, lay not this sin to their charge. And when he had said this, he fell asleep. And Saul was consenting unto his death.

In Acts, chapter 9, we find that Saul of Tarsus met Jesus Christ face-to-face on the Damascus turnpike, and was gloriously transformed. Undoubtedly, Stephen's departing words, *Lord, lay not this sin to their charge*, impressed themselves indelibly in this executioner's mind, hounding him to Jesus. Thus, Stephen's death probably produced the greatest apostle of all times—the beloved grace preacher, Paul. Because God's Word always accomplishes its mission, there will come a day in the future—even if it takes months or years—when Christ's glory will manifest itself through Chet Bitterman's homegoing. Only eternity will reveal the multiplied results of this martyr's death.

Health and Wealth for All?

Now in the light of Chet's martyrdom, I want to deal with an important scriptural issue, "prosperity truth." Some ministers make statements such as, "It is not God's will that anyone be sick. No Christian need ever suffer, furthermore, all believers should have a superabundance of material goods." Such teachings sound attractive as their promoters pull isolated texts out of context. However, multiplied numbers of Christians are left in a state of despondency because they remain sick or poor.

May I speak to every child of God who is currently experiencing deep trial and agony of soul. May I comfort the sick and impoverished. You are *not* out of the will of God. It is not sin or unbelief in your life that keeps you from being healed or becoming wealthy. Let's allow the God of the Scriptures to speak for himself. *Yea, let God be true and every man a liar* (Romans 3:4).

First, Jesus never taught health and wealth for all. The Bible teaches that Christ was born in a borrowed stable, was laid in a borrowed manger and, 33 years later, ended up in the borrowed grave prepared for Joseph of Arimathaea (see Mark 15:43). He was so poor that when *a certain scribe came, and said unto him, Master, I will follow thee whithersoever thou goest.* [Jesus replied,] *The foxes have holes, and the birds of the air have nests; but the Son of Man hath not where to lay his head* (Matthew 8:19,20).

Think of it! Every creature had a place to sleep at night except Jesus, the Lord of Glory. Why did our Lord—the God of the universe—the One who created heaven and earth—become a poverty-stricken pauper, if I may use the term reverently? The answer to this overwhelming question is best expressed in 2 Corinthians 8:9, *Ye know the grace of our Lord Jesus Christ, that, though he was rich, yet for your sakes he became poor, that ye through his poverty might be rich.*

Oh, if Jesus had only understood prosperity truth—He might have been born in a palace, been reared in a mansion, eaten at the Waldorf Astoria, and been buried in a mausoleum. No, He became poor, physically, so that you and I might become rich, spiritually. Yes, only spiritually. Allow me to prove my position convincingly and scripturally.

Suffering—The Hallmark of Godliness

Troubled, heartbroken child of God, you are not being ignored by the Heavenly Father because of a lack of faith, instead, suffering is often the hallmark of godliness. Paul could say in 2 Timothy 3:10-12, *But thou hast fully known my doctrine, manner of life, purpose, faith, longsuffering, charity, patience, persecutions, afflictions which came unto me at Antioch, at Iconium, at Lystra; what persecutions I endured: but out of them all the Lord delivered me.* He quickly adds, *Yea, and all that will live godly in Christ Jesus shall suffer persecution.*

Don't fret, then, beloved, when testing comes. It is the will of God for your life. God has never promised "moonlight and roses" for His children. That is a man-made teaching. The Holy Spirit says, *For unto you it is given in the behalf of Christ, not only to believe on him, but also to suffer for His sake* (Philippians 1:29). When the promised trials and tribulations hit—don't give up—don't quit! You are not a bumbling backslider who does not have the faith of a grain of mustard seed and cannot remove mountains.

Instead, you are in the *center* of His will! So rejoice in the midst of the adversary's attacks, for crowns and rewards are being earned for all eternity! That's why 1 Peter 1:7 declares, *that the trial of your faith, being much more precious than of gold that perisheth, though it be tried with fire, might be found unto praise and honor and glory at the appearing of Jesus Christ.* James also has this hour in mind when he says in chapter 1, verse 12, *Blessed is the man that endureth temptation: for when he is tried, he shall receive the crown of life, which the Lord has promised to them that love him.*

Regardless of the circumstances, then, whether sickness, hunger, poverty, or even martyrdom, remember that God loves you and is working out His glory through you. Paul constantly taught that the Christian life is one which brings repercussions. Still, he reassured his converts that in the midst of Satan's attacks they could be victorious. He did *not* say they could live without trials, heartaches, sickness and poverty. Rather, he promised that the Lord would be with them when these tragedies occurred.

Romans 8:35-39 states, *Who shall separate us from the love of Christ? shall tribulation, or distress, or persecution, or famine, or nakedness, or peril, or sword? As it is written, For thy sake we are killed all the day long; we are accounted as sheep for the slaughter. Nay, in all these things we are more than conquerors through him that loved us. For I am persuaded, that neither death, nor life, nor angels, nor principalities, nor powers, nor things present, nor things to come, nor height, nor depth, nor any other creature, shall be able to separate us from the love of God, which is in Christ Jesus our Lord.*

Wow! What a blow this is to "prosperity truth"! Do all of God's children suffer? Can faith put an end to heartache and poverty? If so, then the greatest saints of all ages were spiritual flops! Here is more proof.

The New Testament writers, with the exception of John, laid down their lives for the Saviour. Matthew died from the wounds of a halberd. Mark was dragged through the streets by a team of wild horses until death ensued. Luke was hanged. John was thrown into boiling oil. Though he lived, he was disfigured for life. Peter and Jude were crucified, and James was smashed to death with a club.

Paul, last but not least, suffered more than the others combined. He could say in 1 Corinthians 4:10-13,16, *We are fools for Christ's sake, but ye are wise in Christ; we are weak, but ye are strong; ye are honourable, but we are despised. Even unto this present hour we both hunger, and thirst, and are naked, and are buffeted, and have no certain dwellingplace; And labour, working with our own hands: being reviled, we bless; being persecuted, we suffer it: Being defamed, we intreat: we are made as the filth of the world, and are the offscouring of all things unto this day. I beseech you* [plead with you, beg of you], *be ye followers of me.*

In 1 Corinthians 15:31, Paul says, *I die daily.* And in 2 Corinthians 4:8-10 he continues, *We are perplexed, but not in despair; Persecuted, but not forsaken; cast down, but not destroyed; Always bearing about in the body the dying of the Lord Jesus.*

Again, in 2 Corinthians 11:23-28, Paul cries out, *In labours more abundant, in stripes above measure, in prisons more frequent, in deaths oft. Of the Jews five times received I forty stripes save one. Thrice was I beaten with rods, once was I stoned, thrice I suffered shipwreck, a night and a day I have been in the deep; In journeyings often, in perils of waters, in perils of robbers, in perils by mine own countrymen, in perils by the heathen, in perils in the city, in perils in the wilderness, in perils in the sea, in perils among false brethren; In weariness and painfulness, in watchings often, in hunger and thirst, in fastings often, in cold and nakedness. Beside those things that are without, that which cometh upon me daily, the care of all the churches.*

They scourged Paul with the forerunner of the Roman cat-o-nine-tails. Three times they used clubs on his body and once crushed his head with rocks. Thinking he was dead, they discarded his body at the garbage dump of Lystra (see Acts 14:19).

Yes, discipleship producing crowns and rewards at the Judgment Seat of Christ is costly. Those who do not sacrifice here will have nothing in that day. They shall stand in Christ's presence ashamed (see 1 John 2:28). They shall suffer loss of all rewards (see 1 Corinthians 3:15). One who is a disciple, a follower of Christ throughout this earthly pilgrimage, has no regrets as eternity approaches.

Listen to Paul again in 2 Timothy 4:6-8. He is about to have his life ended by decapitation, his head will soon roll from his body as the sword severs it. Is he remorseful, regretful, and sorry? Would he like to relive his life without all of the sorrow experienced as Christ's follower? Should he have practiced "prosperity truth"? You be the judge!

For I am now ready to be offered, and the time of my departure is at hand. I have fought a good fight, I have finished my course. I have kept the faith: Henceforth there is laid up for me a crown of righteousness, which the Lord, the righteous judge shall give me at that day: and not to me only, but unto all them also that love his appearing. "There are no regrets. I am going home to be with Jesus forever," said Paul.

Believer, don't seek to live a life of ease in Zion. If there are no scars, there will be no crowns. Don't let the present day teachers of "the health-and-wealth" gospel rob you of eternal rewards. Remember Matthew 5:10 promises, *Blessed are they which are persecuted for righteousness' sake: for theirs is the kingdom of heaven.*

Chapter 24

"Just Name It and Claim It" Prosperity Truth

Brother, practice is over! The game has begun. Basic training is past. Combat is here. Study hall is ended. The final examination has started. Rehearsal is over. The curtain is pulled. Stones of Lystra are being gathered for us as well as the Apostle Paul.

—Leonard Ravenhill

This morning, there are many who came to me, earnestly urging me not to preach in the afternoon because several people had threatened to do terrible things to me. Because this report was spread around, many of the "better sort of people" came to see the threats fulfilled. I believe this added more than a thousand to the ordinary congregation.

—*John Wesley*

Most of my friends advise me to leave Epworth if I should ever get from hence. I confess I am not of that mind because I may yet do good there; and tis like a coward to desert my post because the enemy fires thick upon me. They have only wounded me yet and I believe

357

can't kill me. I hope to be home by Christmas. God help my poor family.

—John Wesley

We can have riots without revival. But in the light of the Bible and church history, where can we have revival without riots?

—Leonard Ravenhill

The Apostle Paul's first question upon arriving in a city was "Where's your jail?" He knew his preaching usually put him there.

—Jack Van Impe

Pentecost meant pain, yet we live for pleasure. Pentecost meant burden, yet we love ease. Pentecost meant prison, yet most of us would do anything rather than for Christ's dear sake get into trouble.

—Leonard Ravenhill

If I had a thousand heads I would rather have them all cut off, than to revoke.

—Luther at Diet of Worms

Yea, and all that will live godly in Christ Jesus shall suffer persecution.

—2 Timothy 3:12

Michelle has cancer. Her leg must be amputated. Solemn words for a little 8-year-old girl and her parents. In the midst of sorrow, this courageous little sweetheart and her family bravely faced the horrendous ordeal and the discouragement which followed.

Sad was the day when little Michelle, a bald, discolored skeleton from chemotherapy, tried to live with her difficulties and went swimming. She overheard an unkind human being say, "Why do they allow freaks to swim here?" This little girl—with a big, crushed heart—determined to make the best of life regardless of ungracious individuals.

Soon the brave little lady entered the Handicapped National Skiing Competition at Winter Park, Colorado, and became a winner! Her "big moment" came in 1977 when Wayne Newton presented her the "Victor Award."

He said, "Let me ask you a question, Michelle. What did you tell the other kids about your leg?"

"Well," she began, "sometimes I would say I was on a river trip and I fell off the boat and an alligator bit it off—and I got so scared my hair fell out." The room was filled with a warm, natural laughter because a little girl could speak so lightly about her cancer and its effects through chemotherapy.

Then Wayne Newton said, "We think extraordinary courage is what you have shown in your fight against one of life's toughest opponents, and that qualifies you to win this miniature 'Victor Award' you're holding. We hope you will enjoy it always because you're an incredible lady."

I know you will agree that Michelle is all Wayne Newton said she is. But beyond this courage, her faith and the faith of her parents, was undoubtedly the sustaining power of God during such an hour of trial. The question I propose is, "How does this story and the suffering of so many of God's choicest saints fit into the modern teaching called "prosperity truth"?

This theory, spliced together from isolated Bible texts, teaches that none of God's children need ever be sick, discouraged, depressed, or poor. Rather, it is the will of God that all believers experience health and wealth. Beloved I want to prove from the Word of God that "prosperity truth" is a man-made teaching—completely out of harmony with the Bible. I want all Christians presently undergoing the deep trials of poverty, sickness, and impending death, to listen carefully.

Why Christians Suffer

You are not in this condition because of a lack of faith in your life, or because you have not claimed man-made promises. There are many reasons why Christians suffer. We want to examine God's Book for the answers, keeping the texts in their contextual setting. When one takes a text out of context, it becomes a pretext—or a farce!

A. W. Tozer, former leader of the Christian Missionary Alliance, said, "A field where tearless men have done us untold harm is in prayer for the sick. There have always been reverent, serious men who felt it their sacred duty to pray for the sick that they might be healed in the will of God. It was said of Spurgeon that his prayers raised up more sick persons than the ministrations of any doctor in London. But when tearless promoters took up the doctrine, it was turned into a lucrative business. Smooth, persuasive men used superior salesmanship methods to make impressive fortunes out of their campaigns. Their big ranches prove how successful they have been in separating the sick and suffering from their money. And all this in the Name of the Man of sorrows who had not where to lay His head!" How sad.

Edith Schaeffer, wife of the great theologian, Dr. Francis Schaeffer, stated, "We are sometimes given such wrong ideas that it is no wonder we are mixed up. Are Christians meant to be happy all the time? Are we meant to be feeling fulfilled constantly? If Christians are meant to be always happy (if all their ailments are to be healed if they have enough faith; if all their troubles are to disappear as soon as they pray; if they are meant to be completely fulfilled all the time) and still are unhappy at the moment, the conclusion must be that they are not Christians."

Do believers suffer? *Is* it God's will when they do? *Can* faith banish all perplexing problems? *Is* it God's will that every Christian have health and wealth? Apparently not. I say this *dogmatically* and *emphatically* in the light of the Scriptures!

Job suffered horrendously. First, the Sabeans slaughtered all of his servants. Then, lightening destroyed his sheep. Next, the Chaldeans killed his camels and their keepers. Suddenly, a tornado hit, killing all of his children. Job must have wondered about the "prosperity doctrine" that all believers should have health and wealth. Actually, he knew better. His genuine faith in God manifested itself— not as he claimed deliverance, but as he cried out, *Naked came I out of my mother's womb, and naked shall I return thither: the Lord gave, and the Lord hath taken away; blessed be the name of the Lord. In all this Job sinned not, nor charged God foolishly* (Job 1:21,22). Now that's *REAL* faith—the kind that says with Job, *Though he slay me, yet will I trust in him* (Job 13:15).

Jeremiah was another of God's servants who knew the bitter pangs of affliction. Chapter 38, verse 6 declares, *Then took they Jeremiah, and cast him into the dungeon of Malchiah, the son of Hammelech, that was in the court of the prison: and they let down Jeremiah with cords. And in the dungeon there was no water, but mire: so Jeremiah sunk in the mire.*

Do you think that Jeremiah lived a "charmed life" without affliction simply because he was a prophet? Do you think that the Lord had a canopy of protection around him simply because he proclaimed God's message? The answer is no, and the same is true for all God's servants. *For unto you it is given in the behalf of Christ, not only to believe on him, but also to suffer for his sake* (Philippians 1:29).

When Jeremiah victoriously shouted, *Great is thy faithfulness* (Lamentations 3:23), it was not because his pockets jingled or because his release from a vermin-infested, stinky underground dungeon was imminent. No, it was because he remembered the goodness of God in past days. Hear him in Lamentations 3:21-23, *This I recall to my mind, therefore have I hope. It is of the Lord's mercies that we are not consumed, because his compassions fail not. They are new every morning: great is thy faithfulness.* Could *YOU* praise God in the dungeon? *Real* faith is not found in claiming deliverance, but in enduring the will of God in adversity!

Stephen, the first martyr of the Christian church, also knew the reality of suffering for Jesus' sake. Acts 7:59,60 reports, *They stoned Stephen, calling upon God, and saying, Lord Jesus, receive my spirit. And he kneeled down, and cried with a loud voice, Lord, lay not this sin to their charge. And when he had said this, he fell asleep.* Beloved, was Stephen's faith not sufficient to have those stones turned into pebbles which would have no effect? Were the prayers of God's people for this saint inefficient for some reason? Stephen felt pain and experienced injuries like others. These particular stones snuffed out his heartbeat and breathing, and Stephen died like anyone else. Why…when he was so full of the Holy Ghost? (see vs. 55).

His victory was not in having his bodily needs met, but in the fact that his faith and love for others made his dying words an everlasting memorial to the grace of God. He said, *Lay not this sin to their charge.* You see, once again, that God's children do suffer. That's why we must pray according to God's prescribed standard in 1 John 5:14. This text declares, *And this is the confidence that we have in him, that, if we ask any thing ACCORDING TO HIS WILL, he heareth us* (emphasis mine). *AMEN!*

"Prosperity Truth"

The Apostle Paul never taught "prosperity truth"—that all can be healthy and wealthy in Jesus. In discussing the sacrificial love of the Macedonians, he said in 2 Corinthians 8:2, *How that in a great*

TRIAL OF AFFLICTION the abundance of their joy and their DEEP POVERTY abounded unto the riches of their liberality (emphasis mine). In other words, these dear Christians in Greece—while steeped in the depths of poverty—outdid themselves in collecting an offering for their brothers in Jerusalem. Paul did not teach them the principal of "faith to possess mansions," but godly faith to share the little that one has.

Oh, Paul knew nothing of this twentieth century, man-made teaching entitled, "prosperity truth." He could say in Romans 8:17,18, *We suffer with him* [Christ], *that we shall also be glorified together. For I reckon that the sufferings of this present time are not worthy to be compared with the glory which shall be revealed in us.* In Ephesians 6:20, he calls himself "an ambassador in bonds" because he served God while imprisoned. Could not his great faith get him out of his mess? Man-made teachings answer yes— but God says, "No, this is not My will."

Paul again contradicts the teaching of health and wealth for all saints in 1 Corinthians 4:11-13. He says, *Even unto this present hour we both hunger, and thirst, and are naked, and are buffeted, and have no certain dwellingplace; And labour, working with our own hands: being reviled, we bless; being persecuted, we suffer it: Being defamed, we intreat: we are made as the filth of the world, and are the offscouring of all things unto this day.*

Christian, do you think you have more faith, live closer to the Lord, know more of the power of the Holy Spirit, and have greater answers to prayer because you live a life that has more comfort, less illness, less persecution, less criticism, or less attacks of Satan in one form or another? Something is wrong with your thinking, then, for *all that live godly in Christ Jesus shall suffer persecution* (2 Timothy 3:12).

In Philippians 3:10, Paul cries, *That I may know him, and the power of his resurrection, and the fellowship of his sufferings, being made conformable unto his death.* Imagine! Paul wanted to fellowship in the *sufferings* of Christ! No deliverance message there.

These sufferings are further described in 2 Corinthians 1:5,8,9, *For as the sufferings of Christ abound in us, so our consolation also aboundeth by Christ. For we would not, brethren, have you ignorant of our trouble which came to us in Asia, that we were pressed out of measure, above strength, insomuch that we despaired even of life: But we had the sentence of death in ourselves, that we should not trust in ourselves, but in God which raiseth the dead.*

Dear Christian, are you discouraged, depressed, and perhaps even praying for your own destruction? This has been the experience of many children of God under attack. Even the great Apostle Paul said in the text just quoted that he "despaired even of life." Don't give up, but *pray without ceasing* (1 Thessalonians 5:17). There is victory in Jesus! Like Paul, thank God for your battle wounds and scars—they will bring rewards at the Judgment Seat of Christ. When the battle is over, you will wear a crown! James 1:12 tells us, *Blessed is the man that endureth temptation: for when he is tried, he shall receive the crown of life, which the Lord hath promised to them that love him.*

Chapter 25

Me, Be Grateful?

First, Judas had an attitude that permitted griping. Listen to me! Few things in your life will damn your effectiveness for God as having a spirit, an attitude, a personality that permits griping. Christian, griping is a wicked, godless, filthy, damning sin. And God help the child of God who wants to win souls, who wants to have God's power in his life, who wants to be effective, who wants to see revival, who is concerned about this nation or his community, who permits the wicked, godless, filthy sin of griping.

—Martyn Lloyd-Jones

A merry heart doeth good like a medicine: but a broken spirit drieth the bones.

—*Proverbs 17:22*

And we know that all things work together for good to them that love God, to them who are the called according to his purpose.

—Romans 8:28

Sin's Explosion

I was passing through a deep trial and brooding. My wife came into my study dressed in black saying, "God is dead and I wear black for His funeral." I said, "Nonsense, Woman, God lives." She answered, "Well then, act like God lives."

—*Martin Luther*

Take satanic oppression to Calvary.

—Jack Van Impe

Submit yourselves therefore to God, Resist the devil, and he will flee from you.

—*James 4:7*

What does worry do? It does not empty tomorrow of its sorrow, but it empties today of its strength. It does not make one escape evil—it makes one unfit to cope with evil when it comes.

—Ian McClaren

Be careful for nothing; but in every thing by prayer and supplication with thanksgiving let your requests be made known unto God.

—*Philippians 4:6,7*

In every problem, faith sees an opportunity.

—Jack Van Impe

I stood before a block of marble and said, I see an angel in that slab of stone and with hammer and chisel I shall liberate him.

—*Michaelangelo*

Me, Be Grateful?

I rejoice, because as I lay dying, I am too feeble to work, to read my Bible or even move my lips in prayer—all I can do is lie still in God's arms and trust and there is no fear.

—J. Hudson Taylor

I will bless the Lord at all times: his praise shall continually be in my mouth.

—*Psalms 34:1*

Whatever you plant, depression or praise, will grow.

—Author unknown

I can do all things through Christ which strengtheneth me.

—*Philippians 4:13*

Be content with such things as ye have.

—*Hebrews 13:5*

There are many ways that we express our thanks. We say, "Thank you," "Many thanks," "Much obliged," and "Thanks a lot." Expressing one's gratitude for another's kindness is nothing more or less than good manners.

However, when it comes to thanking God for His goodness, most of us become ingrates. Sad! One man even said to me, "I work forty hours a week; why should I thank God?"

Sin's Explosion

I like what a newspaper columnist recently said. "On this day, take a few minutes to think about what you have to be thankful for. How's your health? Not so good? Well, thank God you've lived this long. A lot of people haven't.

"You're hurting? Thousands, maybe millions, are hurting more. (Have you ever visited a Veteran's Hospital? or a rehabilitation clinic for crippled children?) If you awakened this morning and were able to hear the birds sing, use your vocal chords to utter human sounds, walk to the breakfast table on two good legs, and read the newspaper with two good eyes, praise the Lord. A lot of people couldn't.

"How's your pocketbook? Well, most of the world is a lot poorer. No pensions. No welfare. No food stamps. No Social Security. In fact, one-third of the people in the world will go to bed hungry tonight.

"Are you lonely? The way to have a friend is to be one. If nobody calls you, call someone. Go out of your way to do something nice for somebody. It's a sure cure for the blues.

"Are you concerned about your country's future? Hooray! Our system has been saved by such concern. Your country may not be a rose garden, but it also is not a patch of weeds. In America, freedom rings. You can still worship at the church of your choice, cast a secret ballot, and even criticize your government without fearing a knock on the head or a knock on the door at midnight. And if you want to live under a different system, you are free to go. There are no walls or fences—nothing to keep you here."

Contentment Is a Command

Oh, be thankful. Did you know that contentment is a command from God? He says in Hebrews 13:5, *Be content with such things as ye have*. Contentment is indicative of our spiritual temperature, and it also indicates a thankful spirit.

John Wesley records a conversation with a porter at Oxford College which changed his life. The man called at Wesley's room late one evening and said that he wished to talk with Mr. Wesley. After talking for quite some time, Mr. Wesley, in a spirit of pleasantry, said to the porter, "Go home and get another coat."

The man replied, "This is the only coat I have in the world, and I thank God for it."

Then demanded Wesley, "Go home and get your supper."

The man again replied, "I have no money or food, but I have had a good cold glass of water today. And I thank God for it."

John Wesley again cried, "Go home and rest."

The porter answered, "I have no home, but thank God that I have dry stones upon which I can recline at night."

John Wesley, the founder of Methodism, then said, "You thank God that you have nothing to wear, nothing to eat, and no bed in which to sleep. Is there any other reason you are grateful?"

"Oh, yes," said the porter, "I thank God that He has given me life and health and a heart to love and serve Him."

Sin's Explosion

Is is any wonder that John Wesley declared that his conversation with this pauper had revealed to him something to which he had been a total stranger?

Where do you stand today, dear friend? Oh, be thankful, for the offering of thanksgiving to God is the duty of all His children, whether circumstances are good or bad, right or wrong, happy or heartbreaking.

Why? He is God, and He is in control. The Bible says, *Offer unto God thanksgiving* (Psalm 50:14). [Give] *thanks always for all things* (Ephesians 5:20). *Continue in prayer...with thanksgiving* (Colossians 4:2). *In every thing give thanks* (1 Thessalonians 5:18). Yes, *Thanksgiving...* [to] *our God for ever and ever* (Revelation 7:12).

Thankfulness, as a duty then, is prominent in the Bible. It should have a big place in our lives, for thankfulness is the declarative mood of gratitude, a great incentive to faith, a glorifier of God, and a subduer of the lower nature.

Be Thankful in All Things

At this point, I can almost hear someone saying, "I can agree that praise to God is suitable when blessings abound, but should one literally thank God for everything?" Is it possible to praise God when the road is tough, when circumstances are unbearable, when the night is dark, when situations are disagreeable, when the cup of woe is bitter, when the black wings of disease flutter over the baby's cradle, when the bill collector is at the door, when our neighbors mistreat us and our friends despise and forsake us? Yes, even then, we should say, "Thank You, Lord."

Paul wrote the majority of the verses just quoted and he praised God for everything. Speaking of his sufferings as an apostle, he said in 1 Corinthians 4:9-13, *For we are made a spectacle unto the world, and to angels, and to men. We are fools for Christ's sake, but ye are wise in Christ; we are weak, but ye are strong; ye are honourable, but we are despised. Even unto this present hour we both hunger, and thirst, and are naked, and are buffeted* [beaten] *and have no certain dwelling place* [no home like others]; *And labor, working with our own hands: being reviled, we bless; being persecuted, we suffer* [allow] *it: Being defamed, we intreat: we are made as the filth of the world, and are the offscouring of all things unto this day.*

What do you have to say about all this heartache, Paul? *In every thing give thanks; for this is the will of God in Christ Jesus concerning you* (1 Thessalonians 5:18).

In 2 Corinthians 4:8-10, Paul again mentioned the hatred he encountered as a good soldier of the faith. He declared, *We are troubled on every side, yet not distressed; we are perplexed, but not in despair; Persecuted, but not forsaken; cast down, but not destroyed; Always bearing about in the body the dying of the Lord Jesus.* What about this abuse, Paul? *And we know that all things work together for good to them that love God, to them who are the called according to his purpose* (Romans 8:28).

Be ye thankful (Colossians 3:15) seemed to be Paul's motto. When he was in peril of his life in

Sin's Explosion

Damascus, suspected by his fellow believers in Jerusalem, persecuted in Antioch, stoned in Lystra, assaulted in Iconium, beaten and imprisoned in Philippi, attacked by a lewd and envious crowd in Thessalonica, pursued by callous enmity in Berea, despised in Athens, blasphemed in Corinth, exposed to the fierce wrath of the Ephesians, bound with chains and sent as a prisoner to Rome, Paul still praised God.

Yes, at all times, in all places, in all things he made known his requests unto God with thanksgiving. Though he was *in perils of waters, in perils of robbers, in perils by* [his] *own countrymen, in perils by the heathen, in perils in the city, in perils in the wilderness, in perils in the sea, in perils among false brethren; In weariness and painfulness, in watchings often, in hunger and thirst, in fastings often, in cold and nakedness* (2 Corinthians 11:26-27), STILL Paul always abounded in thanksgiving.

Though he was in prison without his freedom, in winter without an overcoat, in court without a friend, in poverty without a donor, in exile without a home, yet he was ever singing his hymn of gratitude to his God.

How different we are from Paul—and how indifferent to God's command, "Be ye thankful." Most of us have a place to sleep, clothing to wear, food to eat, and a vehicle to drive. Yet we grumble endlessly.

I wish I could take you to Egypt today to observe the Coptic Christians at work. Because of their faith in Jesus Christ, they are unable to obtain employment in this predominantly Muslim land. Hence, they sift through the garbage and discarded junk of the land for food in order to exist. Their occupation is passed on from generation to generation, and there is no hope for improvement because of their beliefs.

Nevertheless, in the midst of their poverty, they have great love for their Lord Jesus. If they would renounce the Savior for Mohammed, their lot in life would change drastically. But they will not do that. Instead, they eke out an existence on garbage and castaways because they love God. Philippians 4:11 and 13 is their source of strength. *I have learned, in whatsoever state* [condition] *I am, therewith to be content.* [For] *I can do all things through Christ which strengtheneth me.*

This is the spirit of revival.

Chapter 26

I'll Take the Fruit

No erudition, no purity of diction, no width of mental outlook, no flowers of eloquence, no grace of person can atone for lack of fire.

—E. M. Bounds

Apostolic preaching is not marked by its beautiful diction, or literary polish, or cleverness of expression, but operates "in demonstration of the Spirit and of power."

—*Arthur Wallis*

When I think of the power that the Apostle Paul had, of the power that Peter—just an ignorant, unlearned fisherman—had on Pentecost, of the power of Charles G. Finney, of the power of Billy Sunday, and of the power of Dwight L. Moody; when I read about the revivals in the United States in the years gone by when under the power of the Holy Spirit the preachers of God stood in the pulpit and declared in no uncertain terms the Word of God unflinchingly and called men to repentance; I feel like crying out: That is what I need so much!

—Joe Henry Hankins

Sin's Explosion

Charles G. Finney prayed for it, and God, according to Finney's own testimony, baptized him in the power from on high. Dwight L. Moody was walking down the street in New York City, just a common ordinary shoe clerk, and God, in answer to his cry, so poured out the Holy Spirit on him that he had to be taken to a nearby room. Some wanted to call for a doctor, but he said, "No! No! No!" The power swept in such waves over his soul that he had to cry to God to stop, that he could not stand any more. Do not tell me that the Holy Spirit has gone out of business!

—Joe Henry Hankins

Look at these apostles. Look at them before Pentecost, weak, helpless. Look at them after Pentecost, filled with a blazing power. See the courage with which Peter, who denied his Lord, is now fearlessly facing the hostile crowd and the authorities that have power to put him to death. Look at John Wesley, before May 24, 1738, a complete failure in the ministry. But look at him afterwards. The same man with the same abilities, the same power, the same everything, how do you explain the change? You cannot explain it in terms of Wesley. What was it? Oh, it was the Spirit of God that came upon him.

—Martyn Lloyd-Jones

The kind of revival we need is an old-fashioned, Holy Ghost, heaven-sent revival from Almighty God that will break the stubborn, hard hearts of God's people; that will humble their proud spirits; that will bring them down in sackcloth and ashes, confessing their sins and crying to God for mercy and cleansing. Then again they will arise

in the power of His might to shake this old world for
Christ.

—*Joe Henry Hankins*

At none of the meetings was there an "invitation."
Whitefield merely preached and then waited for the
Spirit to move. There were no counselors, no decision
cards. When people were converted they leaped up to
tell about it or made it known later.

—America's Great Revivals

Power from on high is the supreme need of today.

—*Charles G. Finney*

We need Joshuas to lead the Lord's people into the
Promised Land of Spirit-empowered living.

—Jack Van Impe

It was said that after the thousands of people who
attended the funeral and passed by the bier of the late
General Booth, the casket was closed and the people
were preparing to take his body out of the cathedral to the
cemetery for burial, the cries and the weeping and the
lamentation of a man were so loud people couldn't at first
discern what he was saying. Finally when some of the
pallbearers walked around the coffin they noticed a man
on his knees sobbing out a phrase repetitiously, a man
who had been saved under the ministry of General
Booth. He had been a derelict on the streets of London
and his life had been touched and his soul had been
saved by this firebrand for God. And do you know what
this man was praying? He was sobbing out over and over
again. "Do it again, O Lord! Do it again, O Lord!"

—*Martyn Lloyd-Jones*

Sin's Explosion

But the fruit of the Spirtit is love, joy, peace, longsuffering, gentleness, goodness, faith, meekness, temperance: against such there is no law.

—Galatians 5:22,23

The Holy Spirit is often neglected within great segments of Christendom. This is sad. Why? He is God, just as the Father and the Son are God (see Acts 5:3,4). He is also the member of the Godhead who wrote the Bible. Second Timothy 3:16 states, *All scripture is given by inspiration of God.* Who is this God? Second Peter 1:21 answers the question, *Holy men of God spake as they were moved by the Holy Ghost.*

Further proof of the Holy Spirit's deity is found in His titles and attributes. He is called the Spirit of Grace, Holiness, Judgment, Knowledge, Life, Love, Might, Promise, Prophecy, Revelation, Supplication, Truth, Understanding, and Wisdom. He is described as omnipotent (or all-powerful) as to Christ's resurrection, because Christ was quickened or made alive by the Spirit (see 1 Peter 3:18).

The Holy Spirit is also omniscient (knows all things) because 1 Corinthians 2:10 states, *The Spirit searcheth all things, yea, the deep things of God.* He is also omnipresent, or everywhere at all times. The psalmist cries out in chapter 139:7-10, *Whither shall I go from thy spirit? or whither shall I flee from thy presence? If I ascend up into heaven, thou art there: if I make my bed in hell, behold, thou art there. If I take the wings of the morning, and dwell in the uttermost parts of the sea: Even there shall thy hand lead me, and thy right hand shall hold me.* Clearly, the reference is directly to the Holy Spirit in the contextual setting.

The Spirit's Personality

In addition to being God, the Holy Spirit is definitely a person, distinct from the Father and the Son. He is not merely an energy or influence, but possesses personal attributes as do the Father and the Son. He can speak (see Acts 13:2), strive with sinners (see Genesis 6:3), and can be resisted (see Acts 7:51). He can also be vexed (see Isaiah 63:10) and tested (see Acts 5:9). He has feelings, because Ephesians 4:30 warns, *And grieve not the holy Spirit of God, whereby ye are sealed unto the day of redemption.* The evidence is abundant, then, that the Holy Spirit does what other persons do.

The Spirit's Ministry

During the Age of Grace in which we live, the Holy Spirit's ministry includes: (1) illuminating sinners (see 1 Corinthians 2:11-14); (2) regenerating sinners (see John 3:5); (3) restraining sinners (see 2 Thessalonians 2:7,8); (4) striving with sinners (see Genesis 6:3); and (5) sealing the saints (see Ephesians 4:30). He also engages in numerous other ministrations. Please order my full-length book or tape, *The Baptism of the Holy Spirit* for a complete study on this subject. My desire in the remainder of this chapter is to discuss the Spirit's baptism and filling at salvation and for service.

First, I want to make unquestionably clear the fact that all—ALL who receive Christ as personal Saviour also receive the Holy Spirit and are born into the family of God and are baptized into the body of Christ the moment the salvation experience occurs. This is true because *except a man be born of water and of the Spirit, he cannot enter into the kingdom of God* (John 3:5). First Corinthians 12:13 adds, *For by one Spirit are we all baptized into one body*. This baptism (of the Spirit, not water) occurs simultaneously with the new birth experience. Because of this baptism, all believers receive the Holy Spirit. In fact, they cannot be saved without Him. That's why Romans 8:9 says, *Now if any man have not the Spirit of Christ, he is none of* [Christ's].

So, this Holy Spirit dwells in every believer. However, He does not necessarily control each believer. Hence, there is a "filling of the Spirit" which every believer, after salvation, may enjoy many times. There is one baptism, but many fillings. That is why the literal Greek of Ephesians 5:18 states, *Be being filled with the Spirit*.

Now the filling and the baptism are two distinct things. The baptism is the placing into the body of Christ at salvation, and the filling is one's yielding to the indwelling Spirit's control. Let's delve deeper into this subject.

Not only does every believer receive the baptism at salvation, but he also receives one or more gifts as well. Much is heard today about the Charismatic Movement. May I shock you and boldly say that every Christian is a Charismatic! You see, the word, "charismatic"—or in the Greek, *charisma*—means a "gift from the Holy Spirit." Thus, when the Spirit baptizes the new believer into the body of Christ at salvation, He also bestows a gift, or His *charisma*, upon him.

Romans 12, 1 Corinthians 12, and Ephesians 4 are the "charismatic" or "gift" chapters of the Bible. Romans 12 speaks about the Body into which all God's children are placed at salvation. Verses 4-8 state, *For we have many members in one body, and all members have not the same office: So we, being many, are one body in Christ, and every one members one of another. Having then gifts differing* [yes, differing— not all the same gift, but differing ones] *according to the grace that is given to us, whether prophecy, let us prophesy according to the proportion of faith; Or ministry, let us wait on our ministering: or he that teacheth, on teaching; Or he that exhorteth, on exhortation: he that giveth, let him do it with simplicity* [or liberality]; *he that ruleth, with diligence; he that sheweth mercy, with cheerfulness.*

Romans 12:3 tells us, *God hath dealt to every man the measure of faith.* Some have one of the gifts mentioned above, while others must find theirs in 1 Corinthians 12:8-11, *For to one is given by the Spirit the word of wisdom; to another the word of knowledge by the same Spirit; To another faith by the same Spirit; to another the gifts of healing by the same Spirit; To another the working of miracles; to another prophecy; to another discerning of spirits; to another diverse kinds of tongues; to another the interpretation of tongues: but all these* [hear it again: all these] *worketh that one and selfsame Spirit, dividing to every man* [how many? every man] *severally as he* [the Holy Spirit] *will.* It is not the gift one seeks that is important, but rather the gift that the Holy Spirit wills to give by grace. Please stay with the Book, not man's ideas.

Different Gifts for All Believers

God does not will that all members of His Body should have the same gift. When one has three eyes or seven fingers he is deformed. So it is with the body of Christ when there is an improper balance of gifts. That's why Paul says in 1 Corinthians 12:15-18, *If the foot shall say, Because I am not the hand, I am not of the body; is it therefore not of the body? And if the ear shall say, Because I am not the eye, I am not of the body; is it therefore not of the body? If the whole body were an eye, where were the hearing? If the whole were hearing, where were the smelling? But now hath God set the members every one of them in the body, as it hath pleased him.*

Every part of the body is needed, and every member in Christ's Body has a gift that fits into the program as needed. In fact, a total of 23 separate gifts are listed in the "gift" chapters mentioned earlier. We again find in 1 Corinthians 12:28, *And God hath set some in the church, first apostles, secondarily prophets, thirdly teachers, after that miracles, then gifts of healings, helps, governments, diversities of tongues.*

The point I want to make now is that every believer has at least one gift and each believer's gift differs. Verses 29-31: *Are all apostles?* [The answers is obvi-

ously no.] *are all prophets?* [No.] *are all teachers?*
[No.] *are all workers of miracles?* [No.] *Have all the
gifts of healing?* [No.] *do all speak with tongues?*
[No.] *do all interpret?* [No.] *But covet earnestly the
best gifts.*

Let's progress now to the teaching concerning the
filling of the Spirit. As stated previously, the baptism
and the filling are two distinct things. Though all are
baptized by the Spirit, the majority of believers are
not usually filled. Also, though there is only one
baptism, there are many fillings. Ephesians 5:18
states, *Be filled with the Spirit.* The literal Greek
declares, *Be being filled*, which implies a continuous
process. Every believer needs it as much as his gas-
guzzling automobile needs gasoline in order to run
efficiently. The baptism produces the gifts, but the
filling enables one to minister the gifts spiritually.

Though all believers have gifts, not all are spiritual. Thousands today who claim gifts are carnal
because they are not being filled daily by the Spirit.
Let me prove this from 1 Corinthians 13:1-3, *Though I
speak with the tongues of men and of angels* [gift],
and have not charity [love—the fruit of the Spirit], *I
am become as a sounding brass, or a tinkling cymbal.
And though I have the gift of prophecy, and understand all mysteries and though I have all faith* [gift],
*so that I could remove mountains, and have not char-
ity* [fruit], *I am nothing. And though I bestow all my
goods to feed the poor* [the gift of helps] *and though I
give my body to be burned, and have not charity*
[fruit], *it profiteth me nothing.*

Five gifts are mentioned in these three verses:
tongues, prophecy, knowledge, faith, and helps. All

five are gifts of either the past or present. They are all part of *the manifestation of the Spirit...given to every man* (1 Corinthians 12:7). However, they can all be ministered in a state of carnality. One is not spiritual because of tongues, knowledge, faith, or helps. Why? Because it takes the fruit of the Spirit to minister the gifts spiritually. The gift itself is for service, and the filling so that the service might be spiritual.

Gifts, then, really prove nothing since all believers have them, and since they may all be ministered in a backslidden condition. As a matter of fact, all the gifts can be duplicated by Satan! Don't take my word for it. Look at the statement of the Lord Jesus Christ in Matthew 7:22, *Many will say to me in that day, Lord, Lord, have we not prophesied in thy name? and in thy name have cast out devils? and in thy name done many wonderful works?* These individuals manifested the gifts of prophecy, discernment of spirits, miracles, and helps (or works). Nevertheless, verse 23 reveals that Christ *never knew* them. Now, since "never" means "never," it is obvious that they manifested the gifts without being saved. They did not possess the fruit of the Spirit, but rather were "workers of iniquity." So, let's seek the fruit of the Spirit which produces godliness.

No believer has ever reached the place where he does not need to walk by means of the Spirit, for if we walk in the Spirit, we *shall not fulfill the lust of the flesh* (Galatians 5:16). A full inward victory over the flesh is gained only by the working of the Spirit in response to a specific dependence upon Him.

The nine words describing this fruit are: love, joy, peace, longsuffering, gentleness, goodness, faith, meekness, and temperance (see Galatians 5:22,23). These represent superhuman qualities which the flesh could never produce. Only God, the Holy Spirit, is able to make mortal beings act this way. No human can duplicate—or devil counterfeit—the fruit of the Spirit. It is the only way to be like Jesus. Someone has well said that Galatians 5:22,23 constitute the shortest biography of Christ ever written.

The Fruit of the Spirit

Only the fullness of the Spirit can make one like Jesus. Notice that the term, "fruit," is singular, meaning that all nine graces form the fruit. The Holy Spirit does not produce just a few of these, but usually all nine when one is Spirit-filled. Let's consider each one individually.

1) LOVE: This is not the romanticized or sexual love of the street or of society's rebels. It is the divine love that is shed abroad in our hearts by the Holy Spirit (see Romans 5:5). It makes one love the lowly, the unlovely, and the unclean. It makes one love members of another race or denomination. It does not look down upon those whose gifts differ. In Corinth, this love was missing and the gifts became a source of competition. This is where Satan can deceive us. He can imitate the gifts in and through us, but he cannot imitate or produce the fruit of the Spirit.

Do not misunderstand. I am not against gifts, but I repeat that gifts alone prove nothing. The real evidence is found in the fruit one bears as he ministers the gifts. Oh, that we might be filled with all the fullness of God (see Ephesians 3:19). This Holy Spirit-produced love makes us love others, *Beloved, let us love one another, for love is of God* (1 John 4:7).

Do you have the real evidence of the Spirit's filling? It is described in 1 Corinthians 13:4-7, [Love] *suffereth long, and is kind;* [love] *envieth not* [is not jealous]; [love] *vaunteth not itself* [boasting about one's gifts], *is not puffed up. Doth not behave itself unseemly, seeketh not her own, is not easily provoked, thinketh no evil; Rejoiceth not in iniquity, but rejoiceth in the truth; Beareth all things, believeth all things, hopeth all things, endureth all things.*

The world is waiting to see this evidence. Get filled and show it to unregenerate mankind!

This is the love that Jack Van Impe needed—the love of the Spirit that makes brothers in Christ reach out to one another regardless of denominational tags or ethnic backgrounds. It is the love that keeps us from ridiculing, vilifying, and maligning one another. It is the love that keeps us from mislabeling one another. This is why I will never (with God's help) mock a brother whose views differ from my own.

In bygone days, I delighted in "putting down" other children of God because of their views. Never again! I may not always agree, but I will respect and love a brother who differs on non-essential issues. Beloved, please pray that I will continually seek a new infilling daily so that my ministry will always manifest the nine-fold fruit of the Spirit. May I also say that if any brother in Christ ever reads a piece of my literature which makes fun of or attempts to hurt a member of God's family in another group, please know that it was the former Jack Van Impe who wrote it. The new one loves you if you are His. We are members of one Body, one family, and are therefore brothers and sisters in Christ—and I love you.

2) JOY: This grace is not the superficial happiness that springs from sports or television, for happiness depends upon happenings. Instead, it is the joy of the Lord which is one's strength (see Nehemiah 8:10). It is a contentment in times of suffering, sorrow, and even death. It is *joy unspeakable and full of glory* (1 Peter 1:8).

3) PEACE: This is not the peace with God that accompanies salvation (see Romans 5:1), but *the peace of God which passeth all understanding* (Philippians 4:7). It fills the hearts and minds of those who are Spirit dominated, and produces a sublime calm in spite of every disturbance, heartbreaking circumstance, or adverse condition. As a result, God is glorified before an unsaved world.

4) LONGSUFFERING: This quality can only be produced by the Holy Spirit within a believer. It is the opposite of impatience. It cannot be produced by members of Adam's race, but is wrought within the Christian by God himself. Exodus 34:6 states, *The Lord God* [is] *merciful and gracious, longsuffering, and abundant in goodness and truth.* This is exactly why the ungodly receive countless opportunities to be saved, *The Lord is...longsuffering to us-ward, not willing that any should perish, but that all should come to repentance* (2 Peter 3:9).

Sin's Explosion

This same attitude can be the believer's portion, for God strengthens us *with all might, according to his glorious power, unto all patience and longsuffering with joyfulness* (Colossians 1:11). Thus, we are to walk *with all lowliness and meekness, with long-suffering, forbearing one another in love; Endeavouring to keep the unity of the Spirit in the bond of peace* (Ephesians 4:2,3). Yes, we are to *be patient toward all men* (1 Thessalonians 5:14). How are you doing? Do you have the real evidence of the Spirit's fullness?

5) GENTLENESS: Again, this is a fruit from God, for *the wisdom that is from above is first pure, then peaceable, gentle, and easy to be entreated* (James 3:17). Paul could also say, *We were gentle among you* (1 Thessalonians 2:7). Bickering, backbiting, fighting, and fussing church members forget that *the servant of the Lord must not strive; but be gentle unto all men* (2 Timothy 2:24). Do you have the fruit? Remember, it cannot be obtained by human effort or by imitation, but only as a direct filling by the Holy Spirit.

6) GOODNESS: This grace is produced at salvation and made to bloom in one's life as the Spirit fills a believer. Jesus said, *None is good* (Luke 18:19). Paul said, *There is none that doeth good, no, not one* (Romans 3:12). Men talk about doing good, but it is only egotism seeking praise. The Spirit within, however, produces real goodness toward others.

7) FAITH: The term in this listing is actually, "faithfulness." Lamentations 3:23, speaking about God states, *Great is thy faithfulness*. This same faithfulness in a Christian may become a daily reality.

One does not have to be up and down spiritually. God's faithfulness, wrought in a believer by the Spirit, can make him faithful daily!

8) MEEKNESS: This is the most difficult fruit to possess, for the moment we think we have it, we've lost it. Again, the flesh cannot generate meekness and humility because such is only puffed-up flesh. Instead, it takes the filling of the Spirit to *put on...meekness* (Colossians 3:12).

9) TEMPERANCE: This term, meaning, "self-control," speaks for itself. Praise God, the Holy Spirit produces it in those who have His fullness.

We have seen that God demands a high and holy standard of life for His children, and that He has also provided the means to produce it. *Walk in the Spirit, and ye shall not fulfill the lust of the flesh* (Galatians 5:16). So, le 's begin seeking the fruit instead of the gifts. Remember, it is wrong to seek gifts which we desire when the Holy Spirit divides, or gives gifts, to every man as He wills (see 1 Corinthians 12:11). On the other hand, we should seek the nine-point fruit of the blessed Spirit, for this He wills for all believers!

The fruit can only be realized by those:

1. Who *grieve not the Holy Spirit of God* (by willfully sinning, Ephesians 4:30).

2. Who *quench not the Spirit* (by failing to obey God's commandments concerning service, 1 Thessalonians 5:19).

3. And who *walk in the Spirit* (a continual attempt to adhere to God's will, Galatians 5:11).

In simple terms, one must turn from all known sin to a daily reliance upon the Holy Spirit, praying for a fresh infilling if he is to evidence the fullness and fruit of the Spirit. Then, and only then, will he love all God's people. Then, and only then, will he minister on the basis of Galatians 6:1,2, *Brethren, if a man be overtaken in a fault, ye which are spiritual, restore such an one in the spirit of meekness; considering thyself, lest thou also be tempted. Bear ye one another's burdens, and so fulfil the law of Christ.*

The Spirit-filled life is a state of perpetual revival—therefore *be filled with the Spirit* (Ephesians 5:18).

Chapter 27

Ask If You Mean It

I preached yesterday to more than ten thousand hearers. I was so buffeted by feelings of inadequacy, both before and after, that was I not forcibly detained, I would have fled from every human face.

—Charles Wesley

Now here is an interesting thing. Jesus was thirty years old. He had never worked a miracle until that time. The second chapter of John tells how soon after He was baptized and filled with the Spirit, He turned the water into wine (grape juice) at a wedding. And the scripture says, This beginning of miracles did Jesus in Cana of Galilee (John 2:11). Jesus never worked a miracle until He was thirty years old. He was the Son of God. He did not work any miracles until the miracle-working power of the Holy Ghost came upon Him.

—*John R. Rice*

If Christ waited to be anointed before He went to preach, no young man ought to preach until he, too, has been anointed by the Holy Ghost.

—F. B. Meyer

You will never organize a revival. It takes the Holy Spirit.

—*Martyn Lloyd-Jones*

Sin's Explosion

The Church that is man-managed instead of God-governed is doomed to failure. A ministry that is college-trained but not Spirit-filled, works no miracles.

—Samuel Chadwick

Without any expectation of it, without ever having the thought in my mind that there was any such thing for me, without any recollection that I had ever heard the thing mentioned by any person in the world, the Holy Spirit descended on me in a manner that seemed to go through me, body and soul. I could feel the impression like a wave of electricity, going through and through me. Indeed, I could not express it any other way. It seemed like the very breath of God. I can recall distinctly that it seemed to fan me like immense wings.

No words can express the wonderful love that was shed abroad in my heart. I wept aloud with joy and love. These waves came over me and over me and over me, one after the other until I recollect I cried out, "I shall die if these waves continue to pass over me." I said, "Lord I cannot bear it any more." Yet I had no fear of death.

—Finney, in his autobiography, pp.22

After Moody's baptism in the Holy Spirit, he began powerful evangelistic meetings with Ira D. Sankey, whom he had met the year before. "The sermons were not different; I did not present any new truths; and yet hundreds were converted. I would not now be placed back where I was before that blessed experience if you could give me all the world!"

—Erdman, Deeper Experiences
of Famous Christians, pp. 82,83

Now we come to the appeal, and try to persuade them to come forward. No, not at all. Before he had finished preaching they were crying out, and saying, "What shall we do?" There was no need to test the meeting. The Holy Ghost had done it. People were so deeply convicted of sin, so humbled and broken and alarmed and terrified, that they interrupted the sermon and cried out, saying, "Men and brethren, what shall we do?" They are in agony of soul, suffering this profound conviction of sin.

That is the story of every revival. There is always that kind of interruption, almost a disorder, what somebody called a divine disorder. And then, that in turn leads to repentance.

—Martyn Lloyd-Jones

I had never won a soul as a preacher. I laid on my daddy's grave for 24 hours or more, praying for the filling of the Spirit. It happened. I have never had a barren altar since.

—Jack Hyles

You shall receive power after that the Holy Ghost is come upon you.

—Acts 1:8

Believers are powerless and ineffective in their daily lives because they do not partake of the vast storehouse of power that is available to them in the Person of the Holy Spirit. As a result, they depend upon personality traits and psychological manipulations rather than the power of God. They forget that God says in Zechariah 4:6, *Not by* [human] *might, nor by* [human] *power, but by my spirit.*

Man, with all his reliance on tricks, gimmicks, and manifold activities, could accomplish so much more if God, the Holy Spirit, originated, motivated, and activated the program. He alone supplies the power needed by powerless human beings. He alone is the match to ignite the fire, the fuel to propel the motor. A person cannot move without His assistance.

Acts 1:8 states, *Ye shall receive power, after that the Holy Ghost is come upon you.* Do you have this power? Or are you still serving God in the energy of the flesh? Just as there is a difference in cultivating a field with a shovel or with a tractor, so there is a mighty difference in one's service when empowered by the all-powerful Holy Spirit.

Holy Spirit Power for Believers

This power is released in a Christian as the indwelling Holy Spirit is allowed to take full control. Do not misunderstand—every saved person has this Holy Spirit indwelling him—[We] *have been all made to drink into one Spirit* (1 Corinthians 12:13).

All means ALL. In fact, it is correct to say that it is impossible to be a child of God if one does not have the Holy Spirit, for *if any man have not the Spirit of Christ, he is none of his* (Romans 8:9). Romans 5:5 says, *The love of God is shed abroad in our hearts by the Holy Ghost which is given unto us.* Who? A select few? No! *The manifestation of the Spirit without having Him, and this manifestation is given to every man who says, Jesus is the Lord* (vs. 3).

While it is true that every believer has the Holy Spirit (and has all of Him, for He does not enter in percentage portions), this does not guarantee that He has all of us. Therefore, subsequent to salvation, every believer needs the filling of the Spirit.

Ephesians 5:18,19 says, *Be filled with the Spirit; Speaking to yourselves in psalms and hymns and spiritual songs, singing and making melody in your heart to the Lord.* One evidence of the filling, then, is a heart overflowing with spiritual songs.

Another evidence is Holy Spirit power for witnessing. *Ye shall receive power, after that the Holy Ghost is come upon you* [the result]: *and ye shall be witnesses unto me* (Acts 1:8). Seek the power the apostles had to witness as they bore ridicule, hatred, persecution, and death for the Lord Jesus Christ.

May I go one step further? I care not what you call your experience with the Holy Spirit. However, do not pray for "the fullness of the Holy Ghost" unless you are willing to become hated and even slaughtered for the name of Jesus. This is where the power of the Holy Spirit leads the sold-out, dedicated, Spirit-filled Christian.

Let's look at the Book of Acts for a moment and see. Peter, after being filled with the Holy Spirit in Acts 2:4, becomes a power-laden giant for God. Earlier in his life—in fact, only seven weeks earlier—he sat by a fire denying the Lord (see Matthew 26). At that point in his life, he was a powerless witness. After he allowed the Holy Spirit to take full control and possession of his body, he became a one-man army for the Saviour.

Please notice that the texts quoted mention "boldness" and "power" as the results of the filling of the Spirit. These two attributes, which the indwelling Spirit generates in the believer when He is allowed to have control, cannot be easily duplicated in the flesh. Boldness and power in the face of persecution and death can only be produced by the blessed Spirit of God.

The Boldness of Peter

Consider the boldness of the Apostle Peter. Acts 4 states, *Then Peter, filled with the Holy Ghost, said unto them, Ye rulers of the people, and elders of Israel...Be it known unto you all, and to all the people of Israel, that by the name of Jesus Christ of Nazareth whom ye crucified, whom God raised from the dead, even by him doth this man stand here before you whole. This* [Christ] *is the stone which was set at nought of your builders, which is become the head of the corner: Neither is there salvation in any other: for there is none other name under heaven given among men, whereby we must be saved* (vss. 8,10-12).

Verse 13 states that these people saw the BOLD-NESS of Peter and John. Visualize the faces—filled with antagonism—the high priest and his relatives and a great multitude of those who had gathered together as Peter denounces their sin publicly and declares that this Christ they killed is the only way of salvation! It takes Holy Spirit boldness to be uncompromising.

Are you seeking the fullness of the Holy Ghost for the same reason, or because it is the popular thing to do?

This same crowd hated Peter's message and threatened Peter and John in verses 18-20, *And they called them, and commanded them not to speak at all nor teach in the name of Jesus. But Peter and John answered and said unto them, Whether it be right in the sight of God to hearken unto you more than unto God, judge ye. For we cannot but speak the things which we have seen and heard.*

That is boldness, my brother! Did they quit? No! Acts 4:33 states, *With great power gave the apostles witness of the resurrection of the Lord Jesus: and great grace was upon them all.*

In Acts 5:40-42 they are beaten for the sweet name of Jesus. And guess what? They departed from the presence of the council, rejoicing that they were counted worthy to suffer shame for His name. Did it stop them? *And daily in the temple, and in every house, they ceased not to teach and preach Jesus Christ.* The only thing that stopped these Spirit-filled warriors was death.

The Power of Paul

In Acts 9:17, Paul too was filled with the Spirit. He was baptized by the Spirit at salvation, as all believers are (see 1 Corinthians 12:13), and then filled as all believers should be (see Ephesians 5:18). This filling prepared him for the Lord's plan, *I will shew him how great things he must suffer for my name's sake* (Acts 9:16).

Sin's Explosion

Has anyone ever suffered as much as Jesus or Paul? This battle-scarred apostle enumerates his sufferings in 2 Corinthians 11:23-27:

In labours more abundant, in stripes above measure, in prisons more frequent, in deaths oft. Of the Jews five times received I forty stripes save one. Thrice was I beaten with rods, once was I stoned, thrice I suffered shipwreck, a night and a day I have been in the deep; In journeyings often, in perils of waters, in perils of robbers, in perils by mine own countrymen, in perils by the heathen, in perils in the city, in perils in the wilderness, in perils in the sea, in perils among false brethren; In weariness and painfulness, in watchings often, in hunger and thirst, in fastings often, in cold and nakedness.

Why was he so hated? Because *he went into the synagogue, and spake boldly for the space of three months, disputing and persuading the things concerning the kingdom of God* (Acts 19:8); because his preaching caused an uproar in the city (see Acts20:1); and because he called sin and sinners by name.

In Acts 13:9,10 we see Paul setting his eyes on Elymas the sorcerer and saying, *Thou child of the devil, thou enemy of all righteousness, wilt thou not cease to pervert the right ways of the Lord?* A Holy Spirit-filled life denounces sin in an uncompromising way. It also often brings death because they beheaded Saint Paul.

Stephen also experienced the same in Acts 7:55 when he, *being full of the Holy Ghost*, BOLDLY exposed sin PUBLICLY—and was murdered.

Friend, do you want to be filled with the Spirit? Think twice before asking Him to take full control of your life. It may cost you everything you have. However, it will be worth it all when we see Jesus. He said in Matthew 5:10-12, *Blessed are they which are persecuted for righteousness' sake: for theirs is the kingdom of heaven. Blessed are ye, when men shall revile you, and persecute you, and shall say all manner of evil against you falsely, for my sake. Rejoice, and be exceeding glad: for great is your reward in heaven: for so persecuted they the prophets which were before you.*

Chapter 28

Get Revived—
He's Coming

I have no hesitation in asserting that there are large numbers of people who have been so over concerned with the question of prophecy that they themselves have become dry and useless. And there are churches of which that is true.

—Martyn Lloyd-Jones

If those who run from prophecy conference to prophecy conference never live holy lives and never win souls, they have failed to understand that prophecy must become a purifying hope. Otherwise, it becomes a series of mere intellectual facts producing argumentative personalities who know more about the number of hairs in the Antichrist's beard than they do about Jesus.

—*Jack Van Impe*

Until this last century, no Christians thought their task was to just "take care of your own lives and run up your bills for the Antichrist."

—Pratney

Sin's Explosion

Many today spend multiplied hours speculating on Daniel's image, the identity of Antichrist, and the name of the beast through a decoding of the 666 mystery—and never take time to win a soul to Christ. What a shame.

—Jack Van Impe

And every man that hath this hope in him purifieth himself, even as he is pure.

—1 John 3:3

I am shocked. Through 40 years of ministry, I have informed millions that the signs of the times indicate that Christ's Second Coming is at the door. Yet, never have I witnessed such an avalanche of events indicating that we may be but months, weeks, or even days away from our homegoing.

In writing the book *Revelation Revealed*, I often came across the expression, *Behold, I come quickly.* In searching for the exact meaning of this phrase, I discovered that in the original Greek, it means, "When one sees the beginning of the prophesied events and the rapid succession of signs following speedily, Christ will come suddenly."

Beloved, I am convinced that such an hour has arrived! This is my dogmatic conviction because of the many predictions Christ made in Matthew, chapter 24. For example, the Saviour stated, *Take heed that no man deceive you. For many shall come in my name, saying, I am Christ; and shall deceive many. And ye shall hear of wars and rumors of wars...For nation shall rise against nation, and kingdom against kingdom: and there shall be famines, and pestilences, and earthquakes, in divers places. All these are the beginning of sorrows.*

Then shall they deliver you up to be afflicted, and shall kill you: and ye shall be hated of all nations for my name's sake. And then shall many be offended, and shall betray one another, and shall hate one another. And many false prophets shall rise, and shall deceive many. And because iniquity shall abound, the love of many shall wax cold (vss. 4-12).

Christ continued in Matthew 24:29,30, *Immediately after the tribulation of those days shall the sun be darkened, and the moon shall not give her light, and the stars shall fall from heaven, and the powers of the heavens shall be shaken: And then shall appear the sign of the Son of man in heaven.*

In concluding this section, the Lord added in verse 33, *When ye shall see all these things, know that it is near, even at the doors.* Please circle the word "all" in this verse, for it is the key that unlocks the entire chapter! We have always had signs occurring during every era. However, this is the first time in world history that we have witnessed the explosion of ALL SIGNS simultaneously.

In this chapter, I will mention just a few of the many signs currently being observed. May these shocking reports help you to see that all the events prophesied by the Lord Jesus Christ are presently in progress, proving that the trumpet blast calling Christians home *in the twinkling of an eye* (2 Corinthians 15:52), must assuredly sound soon.

False Christs

In Matthew 24:3, Jesus was asked, *When shall these things be? and what shall be the sign of thy coming* [to earth], *and of the end of the world* [or Age of Grace]? He replied in verse 5, *Many shall come in my name, saying, I am Christ; and shall deceive many.* Has it happened? Since the year 1900, over 1,100 false Christs have appeared on the scene, the latest being Jim Jones, San Francisco; Maharaj Ji, India; and Dr. Sun Myung Moon, Korea, not to mention scores of lesser-known, self-proclaimed messiahs.

Eventually, a false Christ—one who is probably alive even at this moment—will proclaim himself as the true Christ and become accepted on an international scale. The Bible predicts such an hour in 2 Thessalonians 2:4, when the Antichrist, *who opposeth and exalteth himself above all that is called God, or that is worshipped...sitteth in the temple of God, shewing himself that he is God.*

This internationally defied dictator will inaugurate a world peace program which holds the world spellbound for 42 months, or 3 1/2 years. Then, in the middle of the seven-year period of Tribulation, he breaks all of his pledges and destroys his contractual obligations with Israel (see Daniel 9:27).

At this time, Russia begins a world war as she invades Israel (see Ezekiel 38). This war involves all nations (see Zechariah 14). This is God's outline from the Bible.

First, the international dictator establishes global peace, and, when the world believes that Utopia has arrived, the bottom falls out of the hopes and aspirations. *For when they shall say, Peace and safety; then sudden destruction cometh upon them* (1 Thessalonians 5:3). A conference held to reduce nuclear weaponry may be the beginning of the end. This thought leads to the next sign Christ mentioned.

Wars and Rumors of Wars

Ye shall hear of wars and rumors of wars: see that ye be not troubled: for all these things must come to pass, but the end is not yet. For nation shall rise against nation, and kingdom against kingdom (Matthew 24:6).

From this proclamation one sees that the world can expect nothing but rivalry and battles until the Antichrist produces the false peace of the Tribulation era. Thirty to forty limited wars have been fought since the end of the second World War, and presently one out of every four nations on earth is engaged in conflict. In just one, Iran vs. Iraq, nearly one million have died.

The News and Observer in Raleigh, North Carolina, reports, "Five years of fighting between Iran and Iraq have resulted in a toll of war dead that may be approaching a million, according to intelligence estimates." This is minor! Soon, we will experience the greatest global confrontation in the annals of history, for we are marching toward Armageddon at this very moment.

Lord Shear, reporting on the meeting of the Stockholm International Peace Research Institute said, "Thirty-five nations will have developed nuclear bombs before the eighties end and war will become inevitable."

A nuclear war is so certain that doomsday trucks have been readied for nuclear attack. A recent Washington Associated Press report stated, "The Pentagon, as part of an effort to improve wartime command links, has built and tested a number of doomsday trucks that could be used by the president and generals to fight a protracted nuclear war, federal documents show.

"Although details are secret, the program is built on the premise that a president, after fleeing to an airborne command post during a nuclear attack, may not have any major communication bases left on the ground after the first salvos.

"One answer, the Pentagon believes, would be an 18-wheel tractor trailer, hardened against the effects of nuclear blast and radiation and equipped with a variety of radio and satellite communications gear. Such a truck could be transported by air or stored in areas of the country that could be expected to escape attack.

"It is unclear exactly how many of the doomsday trucks may have been built."

Parade Magazine reported, "Incidentally, a recent computer study by Dr. Stan Openshaw of Newcastle University in England reveals that somewhere between 43.9 million and 44.2 million Britons—80 percent of the country's total population—would be dead or dying within two weeks after an enemy nuclear bombing."

The latest CIA and British Intelligence reports concerning the Soviet Union are also very grim. They state that the development of new weapons systems located throughout the Soviet Union, along with expenditures of enormous sums for underground civil defense shelters, can only mean that Russia is preparing for war. Ezekiel 38 and 39 picture such Russian hordes from the north swarming to the Middle East.

The Red Horse of the Apocalypse is about to appear. Revelation 6:4 states, *There went out another horse that was red: and power was given to him that sat thereon, to take peace from the earth, that they should kill one another: and there was given unto him a great sword.* The signs abound—come quickly, Lord Jesus.

Famines

Christ added in Matthew 24:7, *And there shall be famines, and pestilences.*

Presently, two billion of the world's inhabitants are going to bed hungry each night. Thousands are dying painful deaths, while scores of others are too numb from hunger to realize what is happening. Ethiopia is an example. Paul Erlich, a biochemist at Stanford University, says, "It is already too late to prevent famines that will kill millions. Already one-half billion are starving and another billion are malnourished. There is no possible solution in the near future because it is too late to produce enough food, so mass starvation is under way."

Soon the voice of Revelation 6:6 will sound, *A measure of wheat for a penny....* A measure in Bible times was a quart, and a penny was a day's wages. Imagine, a loaf of bread for a day's labor! It's coming—and SOON!

Presently a movement is rapidly coming into existence called Globalism. It is composed of three smaller movements:

1. The Trilateral Commission
2. The Council on Foreign Relations
3. The New Age Movement

Its goals are:

1. A one-world government
2. A new one-world religion
3. A new world economic system
4. A new race of humans

The *Hour of Prophecy* reported, "The Globalist think tank, the Club of Rome, adheres to the Malthusian theory that the world's natural resources cannot sustain a population greater than 2.5 billion. They believe that if the population continues to expand, we will either all starve or die in a nuclear disaster. So, the Club of Rome, which meets at the Smithsonian Institute in Washington, D.C., has taken on the task of rolling back the world's population by two billion by the year 2000. That's just 12 years away and the world's population now is around 4.5 billion people. It seems a formidable task to get rid of two billion people in 12 years. Some of the methods accepted so far are:

1. Promotion of homosexuality in the public school system (non-reproductive sex).
2. Promotion of birth control.
3. Promotion of abortion.
4. Promotion of genocide in poverty-stricken Third World nations (this is accomplished by funding Marxist revolutions in which many innocent civilians are slaughtered).
5. Promotion, through the public school system, of the concepts of euthanasia for the aged and

mentally ill. Soon this will include the mentally retarded and congenitally malformed.

6. Promotion of the concept of the acceptability of suicide. Demise pills for the elderly or non-productive persons (non-persons) of society are being suggested.

7. Production of planned famine in selected areas.

"Famine is already devastating large parts of Africa. Very little is being done to provide food for these people. Much of our surplus grain is going into Russia's strategic reserve so that they may soon wage war and not be hungry." It's all part of the plan. Could men have created the AIDS virus purposely to fulfill a death producing program? Read on.

Pestilence

Pestilence is also on the rampage. The swine flu scare, Legionnaire's disease, and other maladies were but the beginning. Presently, the insect world is multiplying at an unbelievable rate. Entomologists estimate that the number has now climbed to one quintillion among five million different species. In fact, if one could weigh all insects together, their combined weight would be twelve times that of the entire human race.

A new and revolting form of pestilence is AIDS. The following headline and report from Washington is frightening:

"AIDS a Threat to Everyone in U.S., Researcher Says"

Sin's Explosion

"In chilling testimony before a Senate subcommittee Thursday, a top Harvard medical researcher said that AIDS is a 'serious threat to every single human being in this country' and that at least four million Americans are infected with the deadly virus.

"AIDS is 'spreading beyond what we expected' and is 'a much, much bigger problem than we thought we had,' said Dr. William A. Haseltine of the Harvard Medical School as he appealed for more government money for research into the disease.

"'Neither a vaccine nor an effective treatment is on the immediate horizon,' said Dr. James Mason, acting assistant secretary of health, even though government spending during the next fiscal year could total more than $200 million, almost double the $109 million this year.

"'We can expect that unless immediate and effective measures are taken, virtually all intravenous drug users in this country and around the world will be infected within the next few years,' Haseltine said in his prepared testimony.

"To illustrate what that means even to heterosexuals who don't use drugs, he cited a study showing that U.S. soldiers in West Germany are being infected with AIDS by Berlin prostitutes who have acquired the disease from their intravenous drug use.

"'Those GIs will sexually transmit the virus to their wives and girl friends, and we will face military manpower problems as infected soldiers start showing the debilitating symptoms of the disease, a process that sometimes takes years,' Haseltine said.

"While it is not known how many of the four million or more infected Americans, some 75,000 of them women, will actually develop AIDS, Haseltine predicted that at least half of them will come down with a 'life-threatening disease' and that 'all will get sick.'"

Undoubtedly the pestilence that Jesus predicted will soon rear its head in monstrous proportions, and will be felt by every country on earth. This, along with what comes out of the bottomless pit in Revelation 9:2 (causing the plague of verse 3) is just around the corner. Listen to the prediction: *There came out of the smoke locusts upon the earth: and unto them was given power, as the scorpions of the earth have power*. The purpose is to destroy and kill. Oh, it's wonderful to be saved, awaiting the hour of deliverance via the Rapture.

Earthquakes

Jesus also said,[There shall be] *earthquakes, in divers places* (Matthew 24:7).

Men foolishly say, "We've always had earthquakes. How can this be a sign?" Get ready, Mr. Skeptic! The Lord made this prediction around 30 A.D. From the year He made the statement until 1959, a total of 24 major earthquakes were recorded. Since 1960, however, more than 30 major quakes have jostled the earth. Think of it—24 major quakes in 1,959 years, and over 30 in less than 28 years. How quickly could the hour of Tribulation soon engulf the world!

Signs in Space

Verses 27-30 of Matthew 24 tells us, *For as the lightning cometh out of the east, and shineth even unto the west; so shall also the coming of the Son of man be. For wheresoever the carcase is, there will the eagles be gathered together. Immediately after the tribulation of those days shall the sun be darkened, and the moon shall not give her light, and the stars shall fall from heaven, and the power of the heavens shall be shaken: And then shall appear the sign of the Son of man in heaven.*

Luke adds to this account in chapter 12:25,26, *And there shall be signs in the sun, and in the moon, and in the stars; and upon the earth distress of nations, with perplexity; the sea and the waves roaring; Men's hearts failing them for fear, and for looking after those things which are coming on the earth: for the powers of heaven shall be shaken.*

Now watch it. These signs point to the close of the Tribulation Hour because they signal the return of the King to earth. Verse 27 says, *Then shall they see the Son of man coming in a cloud with power and great glory.* This is the coming of Christ to set up His glorious millennial reign (see Revelation 20:6).

As stated previously, these space signs, which are to take place at the conclusion of the Tribulation Hour, or almost seven years after the believers' departure via the Rapture, are already showing partial fulfillment. Humans walking, driving, and planting a flag on the moon certainly make one realize that the signs are for twentieth century citizens. Had one made such a prediction at the turn of the century, he would have become a candidate for a mental institute. Today, space activity has become so commonplace that no one even talks about the first step Neil Armstrong took on the moon in 1969.

If one thinks he has observed frightening signs in the twentieth century, let him study the predictions for the future. Through these he will certainly come to the conclusion that Christ's astounding prophetic statements about space are beginning to fill the skies in an alarming way.

Aerospace writer Edwin G. Pipp recently stated that the next war could be fought entirely in space. He reports, "Military experts laughed at the mention of space warfare only two years ago, but today it is neither a laughing matter nor the figment of comic book, movie serial, or science fiction imaginings. In fact, inquiries by the *Detroit News* have led to the conclusion that the United States and Russia are now spending millions of dollars on equipment that could be used in future battles between spacecraft hundreds of miles above the earth."

Articles such as these help one realize that Satan and his demonic hosts could use the world's inventions for the war of wars described in Revelation 12:7, which states, *And there was war in heaven.* What a text in the light of recent negotiations regarding the "Star Wars" defense program and arms reductions.

To the argumentative skeptic who ridiculously states, "Oh, we have always had signs—nothing has changed. It's the same as it was in Grandma's day," I say, "Get your head out of the sand, Mr. Ostrich, and fix your eyes on the heavenlies. The space age is with us, and Christ's prophecies are occurring with such alarming rapidity that only a hardened heart could doubt it."

Sin's Explosion

To all of the startling signs already discussed, one could fill pages dealing with such current headlines as:

"Spread of Satanic Cults Should Be Watched"

"Increased Cocaine Use Spreading to Teens, Expert Says"

"Technology Won't Serve Verification Problems"

"Experts Fear Race of 'Man-Beasts' in Organ-Swap Horror"

"Prison Population Hits Record High"

"The Common Feature of New World Currencies for a New World Order"

What do all these alarming facts signify? Jesus said, *When ye shall see ALL these things, know that it is near, even at the doors* (Matthew 24:33, emphasis mine).

Are you ready? Are you winning others and preparing them for Christ's return? Let's live by the Holy Spirit's warning in Romans 13:11,12, *And that, knowing the time, that now it is high time to awake out of sleep: for now is our salvation nearer than when we believed. The night is far spent, the day is at hand: let us therefore cast off the works of darkness, and let us put on the armour of light.*

If ever believers needed to be living in a constant state of revival, it is now.

Chapter 29

666 and World Revival

Men may try to destroy a prophet's body, but they cannot destroy the prophet.

—Leonard Ravenhill

Look closely at Paul! that cadaverous countenance, that scarred body, that stooped figure of a man, chastened by hunger, kept down by fasting and ploughed with the lictor's lash; that little body, brutally stoned at Lystra, and starved in many another place; that skin, pickled for thirty-six hours in the Mediterranean Sea! Add to this list danger upon danger; multiply it with loneliness; count in the one hundred and ninety-five stripes, three shipwrecks, three beatings with rods, a stoning, a prison record, and "deaths" so many that the count is lost. And yet if one could add it all up, it must be written off as nothing, because Paul himself thus consigned it. Listen to him: "Our light affliction, which is but for a moment." That's contempt of suffering, if you like!

—*Leonard Ravenhill*

No hat will I have but that of a martyr, reddened with my own blood.

—Savonarola, when rejecting a cardinal's hat

Sin's Explosion

Pico della Mirandola said, "The mere sound of Savonarola's voice was as a clap of doom; a cold shiver ran through the marrow of his bones; the hairs of his head stood on end as he listened." His sermons caused "such terror and alarm, such sobbing and tears that people passed through the streets without speaking, more dead than alive" as he prophesied coming judgment on the church and the country. He continued to preach fearlessly for righteousness until a fierce reaction and opposition resulted in his ultimate arrest, torture, and hanging.

—*Pratney*

Most joyfully will I confirm with my blood that truth which I have written and preached.

—John Huss on the stake

The only saving faith is that which casts itself on God for life or death.

—*Martin Luther*

Zwingli, from Switzerland, had a weak voice, short sight, and, to put it kindly, lacked the gifts of a popular orator. Yet, his preaching set Switzerland afire (one hearer felt as if he were "lifted up by the hair and suspended in space!"). Contracts were put out on Zwingli's life and he was eventually killed, cut into four pieces, and tossed into a fire.

—Pratney

"Now I leave off to speak any more to creatures, and turn my speech to Thee, O Lord. Now I begin my intercourse with God which shall never be broken off. Farewell, father and mother, friends and relations! Farewell, meat and drink! Farewell, the world and all delights! Farewell, sun, moon, and stars! Welcome God and Father! Welcome sweet Lord Jesus, Mediator of the New Covenant! Welcome Blessed Spirit of Grace, God of all Consolation! Welcome Glory! Welcome Eternal Life! Welcome Death!" Dr. Matthew MacKail stood below the gallows and as his martyr cousin writhed in the tautened ropes, he clasped the helpless jerking legs together and clung to them that death might come the easier and sooner. And so, with Christ was Hugh MacKail *"with his sweet boyish smile." "And that will be my welcome,"* he said, *"because 'the Spirit and the Bride say, Come.'"*

—*The martyrdom of Hugh MacKail,*
A Covenanter who died for his testimony

Because thou hast kept the word of my patience, I also will keep thee from the hour of temptation, which shall come upon all the world, to try them that dwell upon the earth.

—*Revelation 3:10*

Chapter seven of the Book of Revelation may be divided into two portions dealing with two groups. Verses 1 through 8 discuss the 144,000 Israelites and verses 9 through 17 concerns the multitudinous Gentiles. This chapter portrays God as compassionate, merciful and loving, and this is right for *God is love* (1 John 4:8). In fact, *God so loved the world, that he gave his only begotten Son, that whosoever believeth in him should not perish, but have everlasting life. For God sent not his Son into the world to condemn the world; but that the world through him might be saved* (John 3:16,17).

Mankind's wickedness, rebellion, and sin produce judgment. *For the wages of sin is death* (Romans 6:23), *and they that plow iniquity, and sow wickedness, reap the same* (Job 4:8). The judgments described in the preceding chapters of the Book of Revelation were unleashed because of the hardness of men's hearts. They rebelled, and continued to rebel, for thousands of years. At last, God decided that global judgment must fall—beginning in chapter six.

The love of God, however, is so great that, at this point, He declares a "time out." He still loves the human race, and longs to save mankind. He desires for men everywhere to open their minds and hearts, and come unto Him. The result is this chapter—dealing with the mercy of God in the midst of Tribulation. He creates a lull before the storm in order to call men to salvation and revival.

The 144,000 Israelites

And after these things I saw four angels standing on the four corners of the earth, holding the four winds of the earth, that the wind should not blow on the earth, nor on the sea, nor on any tree (Revelation 7:1).

The fact that the angels are standing on the four corners of the earth does not signify that the earth is square. God knows the world He made is round. *He sitteth upon the circle of the earth* (Isaiah 40:22). This

statement was in the Bible when Christopher Colum-
bus believed it and was making a fool of himself by
claiming that the world was round. The God who
made it and sits upon the circle of it knows it is not
square. Therefore, the term *the four corners of the
earth* is but a Bible expression depicting North,
South, East, and West—the four points of the compass. The four angels, standing at these four positions
administering judgment, are commanded to relent so
that there might be a time of great revival as the
servants of God are sealed in their foreheads.

*And I saw another angel ascending from the east,
having the seal of the living God: and he cried with a
loud voice to the four angels, to whom it was given to
hurt the earth and the sea,*

*Saying, Hurt not the earth, neither the sea, nor the
trees, till we have sealed the servants of our God in
their foreheads* (vss. 2,3).

The wicked get their seal—666—under the super-
deceiver, the great imitator, the Antichrist (see chapter 13, verses 17 and 18). The genuine believers
receive their seal from the angel of God at this point in
time.

*And I heard the number of them which were sealed:
and there were sealed an hundred and forty and four
thousand of all the tribes of the children of Israel. Of
the tribe of Juda were sealed twelve thousand. Of the
tribe of Reuben were sealed twelve thousand. Of the
tribe of Gad were sealed twelve thousand. Of the tribe
of Aser were sealed twelve thousand. Of the tribe of
Nephthalim were sealed twelve thousand. Of the tribe
of Manasses were sealed twelve thousand. Of the tribe
of Simeon were sealed twelve thousand. Of the tribe of*

*Levi were sealed twelve thousand. Of the tribe of
Issachar were sealed twelve thousand. Of the tribe of
Zabulon were sealed twelve thousand. Of the tribe of
Joseph were sealed twelve thousand. Of the tribe of
Benjamin were sealed twelve thousand* (vss. 4-8).

This group cannot be the Church, for the Church is
already in heaven (chapter 4, verse 1). Also, the
Church is not Jewish but composed of all races,
people, and tongues. Again, this group does not
picture the Seventh Day Adventists or the Jehovah's
Witnesses. Both have claimed this in their theological
writings. The Seventh Day Adventists say that the
144,000 are faithful Sabbath Day observers. The
Jehovah's Witnesses teach that the 144,000 are the
overcomers of the flock. Both are drastically wrong.

The 144,000 are not Englishmen, or Americans
either, as the advocates of British Israelism teach.
They make the Israelites become forerunners of the
Anglo Saxons. Come on now, Herbert Armstrong and
Garner Ted. Surely you cannot be that foolish. These
are Jewish tribes with Jewish names. Do the names
Juda, Reuben, Gad, Aser, Nephthalim, Manasses,
Simeon, Levi, Issachar, Zabulon, Joseph, and Ben-
jamin sound British? Had they been Heathcliff, Sir
Winston, or Sherlock Holmes you might have had
reason to propone such nonsense. Under the circum-
stances, however, you had better allow Jews with
Jewish names to head up Jewish tribes in a Jewish
nation—Israel.

Presently, the Jews are not certain of their tribal
heritage. The omniscient, all-knowing God untangles
this condition at the appointed time. Actually, no one
really knows what his stock is. As a result of migra-

tions, most people are a hodgepodge of differing nationalities. Perhaps it is best not to know or trace one's ancestry. We might be embarrassed to discover out roots! One might learn that he is a descendant of Attila the Hun. Persons planning to study their family tree should beware. They might find some of their relatives hanging by the neck while the evolutionists find theirs hanging by the tail!

The 144,000 Jewish evangelists are anointed by the Spirit. Joel 2:28,29 describe the situation as these Spirit-filled preachers proclaim the gospel of the kingdom: *And it shall come to pass afterward, that I will pour out my spirit upon all flesh; and your sons and your daughters shall prophesy, your old men shall dream dreams, your young men shall see visions: And also upon the servants and upon the handmaids in those days will I pour out my spirit.*

There is a great deal of confusion concerning the presence of the Holy Spirit during the Tribulation Hour. This has resulted from a faulty understanding and interpretation of 2 Thessalonians 2:7: *For the mystery of iniquity doth already work: only he who now letteth will let, until he be taken out of the way.* The term *letteth* is the Old English word for "hinders." The picture being painted here is the rise of Antichrist. Second Thessalonians 2:6 states, *Ye know what withholdeth that he* [the Antichrist] *might be revealed in his time.* Then verse seven, already quoted, makes it clear that the hinderer—the Holy Spirit—continues to hinder the Antichrist's rise until the Holy Spirit is taken out of the way.

This is another reason millions believe in the pre-tribulation Rapture. The hinderer lives in the hearts of

423

His people. *But ye are not in the flesh, but in the Spirit, if so be that the Spirit of God dwell in you. Now if any man have not the Spirit of Christ, he is none of his* (Romans 8:9). Also, 1 Corinthians 3:16, *Know ye not that ye are the temple of God, and that the Spirit of God dwelleth in you?* Because of this truth, God's Spirit cannot be taken unless those in whom He lives are taken. Hallelujah!

One should note, however, that the Spirit's removal speaks of His restraining power only. The Holy Spirit of God is the third member of the Trinity. As God, He is omniscient (all-knowing), omnipotent (all-powerful), and omnipresent (everywhere at all times). Therefore, the Holy Spirit himself cannot be removed from the earth because He, as God, is in all places simultaneously and constantly.

David states in Psalm 139:7-10, *Whither shall I go from thy spirit? or whither shall I flee from thy presence? If I ascend up into heaven, thou art there: if I make my bed in hell, behold, thou art there. If I take the wings of the morning, and dwell in the uttermost parts of the sea; Even there shall thy hand lead me, and thy right hand shall hold me.* Since the Holy Spirit is everywhere at all times, only His restraining influence against sin is removed during the Tribulation Hour.

Presently, Christians are the salt of the earth and the light of the world (see Matthew 5:13-16). The evacuation of Christians, in whose hearts the Holy Spirit lives, is the way—the only way—His restraining influence on sin is removed, ridding the world of salt and light (see Matthew 5:13,14). Christians are God's preservative forces, as well as the dispellers of darkness. Imagine what happens when the Spirit's restraining influence (the Church) is removed via the rapture of the Church. Quite literally, all hell will break loose upon earth. Still, even during this time, the Spirit's continuing personal presence on earth produces one of the greatest revivals in the history of mankind.

The message of the 144,000 centers on the person and work of the Lord Jesus Christ. This was the emphasis of the Old Testament preachers. *To [Jesus] give all the prophets witness, that through his name whosoever believeth in him shall receive remission of sins* (Acts 10:43).

In addition to preaching the message of the shed blood of Jesus, the 144,000 proclaim the advent of the King, *And this gospel* [or good news] *of the kingdom shall be preached in all the world for a witness unto all nations; and then shall the end come* (Matthew 24:14). This is not the message of His first coming—the Rapture (see chapter 4, verse 1) but the revelation or revealing of Christ as King (see chapter 19, verse 16).

In order to get a picture of the complete message the kingdom messengers proclaim, one must study the life of John the Baptist. John's message was: (1) **repentance** for he said, *Repent ye: for the kingdom of heaven is at hand* (Matthew 3:2). (2) **the blood** for [he] *saith, Behold the Lamb of God, which taketh away the sin of the world* (John 1:29). This message of repentance and the blood was to prepare the hearts of the people for the third part of his message—the coming of the King. Christ was rejected in the days of

Sin's Explosion

John the Baptist but will be accepted when the 144,000 Jews preach the identical message.

At this time, a worldwide revival ensues for one of the elders asks, *What are these which are arrayed in white robes? and whence came they? And I said unto him, Sir, thou knowest. And he said to me, These are they which came out of great tribulation, and have washed their robes, and made them white in the blood of the Lamb* (7:13,14). Let's study this God-sent, Holy Spirit-empowered revival step by step.

The Multitudinous Gentiles

After this I beheld, and, lo, a great multitude, which no man could number, of all nations, and kindreds, and people, and tongues, stood before the throne, and before the Lamb, clothed with white robes, and palms in their hands (vs. 9).

John states, *After this...* After what? After the 144,000 Jewish evangelists are sealed by the Spirit of God. God's message is always to the Jew first, then to the Gentile. *For I am not ashamed of the gospel of Christ: for it is the power of God unto salvation to every one that believeth; to the Jew first, and also to the Greek* (Romans 1:16). Now that the Jews have heard, John sees a great multitude which no man could count for every race and nationality standing before the throne. Their white robes prove that they have trusted in the message of the blood and are clothed in the righteousness of Christ. The waving of the palms in their hands signifies victory. They have overcome the world, the flesh, and the devil. They are joyous because they have survived the first six seals of judgment. Their joy leads to praise.

And [they] *cried with a loud voice, saying, Salvation to our God which sitteth upon the throne, and unto the Lamb* (vs. 10).

This multitude recognizes the source of their salvation and victory. They cannot be kept silent. Who can when the grace of God does its mighty work of salvation in one's heart! Immediately the angels join with them in praise to the Father and to the Son.

And all the angels stood round about the throne, and about the elders and the four beasts, and fell before the throne on their faces, and worshipped God, saying, Amen: Blessing, and glory, and wisdom, and thanksgiving, and honour, and power, and might, be unto our God for ever and ever. Amen. (vss. 11,12).

What a glorious scene as the angels surrounding the throne and God's people (represented by the elders) fall on their faces in worship, praise, and adoration!

Their seven-fold praise session centers around, blessing, glory, wisdom, thanksgiving, honour, power, and might, to God forever and forever! No wonder they say amen! We add, "Amen and Amen!" Next, one of the elders asks a question.

And one of the elders answered, saying unto me, What are these which are arrayed in white robes? and whence came they? (vs. 13).

The answer?

And I said unto him, Sir, thou knowest. And he said to me, These are they which came out of great tribula-

tion, and have washed their robes, and made them white in the blood of the Lamb (vs. 14).

This is another proof that the Church is in heaven, not upon earth. Why? John does not recognize this group. He knows the raptured Church in heaven (see chapter 4, verse 1), but not the ones on earth in this text. These are Tribulation saints who have *washed their robes, and made them white in the blood of the Lamb.* Please hear God once again. *These are they which came out of great tribulation.* That settles it, and explains why John—who recognized the Church in heaven—is in the fog concerning these individuals. They are new brothers and sisters in Christ, though presently unknown to John. They have been saved in a different period of time—a time when he and the Church were in heaven. The Church was not on earth to make their acquaintance.

The next scene is exciting. Each group saved during different dispensations of time has different duties to perform. The Church is the bride of Christ and enjoys the 1,000-year honeymoon upon earth (see chapter 20, verse 4). They reign as rulers, kings, and priests (see 1 Peter 2:9 and Revelation 1:6). The 144,000 serve as bodyguards of the Lamb and His Bride (see chapter 14, verse 4).

The Gentiles saved during the revival of the Tribulation will be temple servants, waiting on Christ and His Bride. They serve in the glorious temple (described in Ezekiel 40 through 48) which is set up immediately after Russia—under the names of God, Magog, Meshech, Tubal, and Rosh—is destroyed (see Ezekiel 38 and 39). Everything is so near. Russia may march soon. Antichrist will be smashed. The

Lord will return with His Bride. The millennial temple will be erected and the Gentiles will serve.

Therefore are they before the throne of God, and serve him day and night in his temple: and he that sitteth on the throne shall dwell among them (vs. 15).

Because God is dwelling among them, the deprivations they suffered under the Antichrist are now abolished. Under the reign of the world dictator, there was little food and one had to take the mark of the beast, 666, to obtain sustenance. These believers, who refused the number, had to eke out an existence day by day. Now with the Lord in their midst, the picture changes.

They shall hunger no more, neither thirst any more, neither shall the sun light on them, nor any heat (vs. 16).

Verse 16 refers to the scorching effects of the sun during the Tribulation Hour. [As] *the fourth angel poured out his vial upon the sun; and power was given unto him to scorch men with fire* (Revelation 16:8). In addition, the word *heat* has reference to the fires of persecution as found in 1 Peter 1:7. Such trials are finished forever.

From this point onward, the people of God from all dispensations enjoy the presence of God. Their days of suffering, heartache, and abuse by an ungodly world are finished. Tears are wiped away as every remembrance of past sorrow is obliterated from their minds.

For the Lamb which is in the midst of the throne shall feed them, and shall lead them unto living fountains of waters: and God shall wipe away all tears from their eyes (vs. 17).

Sin's Explosion

For a verse-by-verse study of the Book of Revelation, order my book *Revelation Revealed*.

Chapter 30

Trading Ashes for Crowns

There are degrees of reward in Heaven and the judgment seat of Christ is going to be a place of rewards. And if you have been a soul winner, if you have been doing the main thing, if you have been bringing souls to Jesus Christ, when you come to the judgment seat of Christ you are going to hear Him say, "Well done, thou good and faithful servant."

I do not care whether it is the bus ministry, a five-minute broadcast, a telecast, the primary purpose of all the organizing of a local assembly of God's believers, the end result, the primary work, the chief work, is that souls might be won to Christ. And I would rather this morning have a W.D. degree than any degree that I know anything about: "Well done, thou good and faithful servant."

—Martyn Lloyd-Jones

Oh, that believers would become eternity-conscious! If we could live every moment of every day under the eye of God, if we did every act in the light of the judgment seat, if we sold every article in the light of the judgment seat, if we tithed all our possessions in the light of the judgment seat, if we preachers prepared every sermon with one eye on damned humanity and the other on the judgment seat—then we would have a Holy Ghost revival that would shake this earth and that, in no time at all, would liberate millions of precious souls.

—Leonard Ravenhill

Soul winners will be men who have learned what it is to die to self, to human aims and personal ambitions; men who are willing to be "fools for Christ's sake" who will bear reproach and falsehood, who will labor and suffer and whose desire will be, not to gain earth's accolades, but to win the Master's approbation when they appear before His awesome judgment seat. They will be men who will preach with broken hearts and tear-filled eyes, and upon whose ministries God will grant an extraordinary effusion of the Holy Spirit.

—Pratney

How shall I feel at the judgment seat, if multitudes of missed opportunities pass before me in full review, and all my excuses prove to be disguises of my cowardice and pride?

—Dr. W. E. Sangster

Brethren, in the light of the "bema seat," we had better live six months with a volcanic heart, denouncing sin in places high and low and turning the nation from the power of Satan unto God (as John the Baptist did) rather than die loaded with ecclesiastical honours and theological degrees and be the laughing stock of hell and of spiritual nonentities.

—Leonard Ravenhill

Scars produce crowns.

—*Jack Van Impe*

**Face to face with Christ my Saviour,
Face to face, what shall it be?**

—**Mrs. Frank A. Breck**

So then every one of us shall give account of himself to God.

—*Romans 14:12*

Someday, perhaps very soon, every Christian must meet God for an investigative judgment of his entire life. This moment will be a time of jubilant victory for some. Jesus said, *He that receiveth a prophet in the name of a prophet shall receive a prophet's reward; and he that receiveth a righteous man in the name of a righteous man shall receive a righteous man's reward* (Matthew 10:41). Paul adds, *If any man's work abide which he hath built thereupon, he shall receive a reward* (1 Corinthians 3:14).

On the other hand, this moment will be a time of weeping for others. Paul, dealing with this hour of judgment, states in 2 Corinthians 5:11, *Knowing therefore the terror of the Lord, we persuade men.* Terror? Yes, terror! How often Christians hilariously shout, "Praise the Lord, Jesus is coming soon!" Though His return will be the most joyous event of the ages for some, it will also be a time of intense and immense sorrow for others. First John 2:28 declares, *And now, little children, abide in him; that, when he shall appear, we may have confidence, and not be ASHAMED before him at his coming.*

Notice carefully that when Christ returns, **all** believers are summoned into His presence—both the confident and the ashamed. The confident appear before the tribunal with "good works" whereas the ashamed have naught but "bad works" (see 2 Corinthians 5:10). This fact is exceedingly important because multitudes today think that one sin can keep a child of God out of heaven. The text plainly states that the "ashamed" meet Christ at His appearing.

At the sound of the trumpet, when the dead in Christ rise first and living believers join them to meet Christ in the clouds (see 1 Thessalonians 4:17), the "ashamed" also enter heaven. However, the *abundant* entrance is reserved for those who earned it upon earth (see 2 Peter 1:11). This text *proves* that the wayward go home to meet Christ though *ashamed*. Since one can only bear shame for error and wrongdoing, then it is dogmatically clear that the wrongdoers meet Christ at His appearing or return. I grant you that they are embarrassed and lose all of their rewards, but they are nevertheless present at the roll call of the ages, and *saved so as by fire* (1 Corinthians 3:25) or "by the skin of their teeth," to use a modern day expression.

What produces their embarrassment and humiliation as believers?

Neglected Opportunities

Multitudes of God's people *could do so much more for Christ if they would,* but the *flesh* stands in the way. When they do serve, it is often with selfish motives. Their hue and cry is, "What will *I* get out of this? What is in it for *me*?" The result? Modern Christianity has become big business. Religious performers today charge exorbitant rates. Some receive $1,000 to $2,500 for a performance. What a judgment of terror awaits these mercenary "gospel entertainers." Though saved by fire, their works will dissolve into incinerated ashes. The wood, hay, and stubble will disintegrate because they had their reward. About face, Christian!

Then again, there are those who have little or no time for spiritual exercises. They seldom read God's Holy Word, seldom attend God's house, seldom give their tithes, and never win souls. This is sin! James 4:17 states, *Therefore to him that knoweth to do good, and doeth it not, to him it is sin.* These sins of omission—failing to do God's will—also produce remorse in that day.

Friend, if I am describing **you**, it is not too late to change. As long as one has the breath of life, he can decide to do the will of God. Confess your sins, seek again your first love of Christ, rekindle the flames of devotion to the Lord Jesus immediately. Then use your opportunities to serve Him wisely. One who obeys God will not be sorry. The faithful will be rewarded a hundred fold at the Bema Seat. Scholars calculate this to be a 10,000 percent yield!

No wonder Paul said in 2 Corinthians 9:6, *He which soweth sparingly* [meagerly] *shall reap also sparingly; and he which soweth bountifully* [abundantly] *shall reap also bountifully.* One cannot outgive God at 10,000 percent interest! Galatians 6:7, often quoted to the unsaved, but directed to Christians concerning giving, states, *Be not deceived; God is not mocked* [or fooled]*: for whatsoever a man soweth, that shall he also reap.*

Christian, your heavenly mansion will only be as beautiful as you build it now. Jesus said in John 14:2, *In my Father's house are many mansions.* The literal rendering should state, "In my Father's house are numerous and differing kinds of dwelling places." Not all mansions will be identical. Building blocks for one's eternal home are being sent ahead from earth. Jesus said, *Lay not up for yourselves treasures upon earth, where moth and rust doth corrupt, and where thieves break through and steal: But lay up for yourselves treasures in heaven* (Matthew 6:19,20).

If one's earthly treasure is piled up in stocks and bonds and banks, he has his reward. On the other hand, if the treasure is sent ahead, it awaits the believer with added and fantastic dividends. Take your choice, Christian. You can have it here for 70 years, die, and leave it for the ungodly to spend; or you may send it ahead for eternal blessings. Hang on and lose it, or let go and retain it forever. **It is up to you!** (Those who supported our ministry can rejoice in the knowledge of the rewards they will have in heaven because they helped us reach tens of thousands who made decisions for Christ through our television programs and world radio broadcasts in the languages of the people.)

May I share a heart-moving experience with you? When Rexella and I were in Hershey, Pennsylvania, a man sitting in a wheelchair asked to speak to us. When we reached the area where he sat, he began to weep, saying, "I am an invalid, as you can see. I have multiple sclerosis and osteo-arthritis. The pain is more than I can humanly bear. In fact, my pain medication costs me one hundred dollars per month. Nevertheless, I have made a decision after much prayer. I want to give you one hundred dollars and do without this month's medicine. I know the pain will be excruciating, but it is the least I can do for Christ who suffered such agony for me. Please take the money and use it for His glory." Rexella and I, both in tears, replied, "We cannot accept this gift." Again weeping audibly, the man said, "Would you deprive me of a blessing? Take it for the glory of God and the salvation of souls."

How many thousands who have a superabundance of material blessings—stocks, bonds, bank accounts, and other possessions—do nothing but "tip" God occasionally. Do you still think there will be no difference at the time rewards are given? Do you honestly believe that it will be the same for all? *Be not deceived; God is not mocked: for whatsoever a man soweth, that shall he also reap* (Galatians 6:7). We are all going home soon—either confident or ashamed. Will it be a time of victory or anguish, triumph or tears for YOU? It is not too late to make a new start.

Neglected Holiness

There will also be tears in heaven because of neglected holiness. There is no doubt about it. God demands that His people live holy lives. *For God hath not called us to uncleanness, but unto holiness* (1 Thessalonians 4:7). *Who hath saved us, and called us with an holy calling...* (2 Timothy 1:9). *Follow peace with all men, and holiness* (Hebrews 12:14). *Be ye holy; for I am holy* (1 Peter 1:16). This means that we are not to fashion ourselves *according to the former lusts* (1 Peter 1:14), instead we are to *abstain from fleshly lusts* (1 Peter 2:11) *and to put on Christ and not make any provision for the flesh to fulfill the lusts thereof* (Romans 13:14).

How different from the lowly standards held by many carnal church members who constantly play "musical chairs" with the pagans of this world. These indifferent backsliders run with the world. Are they saved? God alone really knows! One thing is certain—if they are Christ's, their double standards will be investigated. *For we must all appear before the judgment seat of Christ; that every one may receive the things done in his body, according to that he hath done, whether it be GOOD or BAD* (2 Corinthians 5:10, emphasis mine).

Oh, what weeping, what wailing, what travail, what heartache and heartbreak as they meet Jesus face-to-face. Their entrance into God's presence will not be "abundant" (see 2 Peter 1:11). They shall be tremendously "ashamed" (see 1 John 2:28). The "terror of the Lord" will be meted out in judgment (see 2 Corinthians 5:11) and they will suffer the loss of all rewards (see 1 Corinthians 3:15). No wonder the lukewarm are weeping. They suffer the loss of all things except their salvation.

This loss extends beyond the loss of rewards for a meaningless life. It includes losing, through foolish living, rewards previously earned during years of spiritual service! Yes, God has a system of addition and subtraction, pluses and minuses, in His book-keeping system. Therefore, one's accumulation of "good works" can be swiftly destroyed through disobedience.

You do not believe these statements? **Here is proof:** *Look to yourselves, that we lose not those things which we have wrought* [or earned], *but that we receive a full reward* (2 John 8). God is saying, in effect, "Be careful how you live, where you go, how you serve, if you want a full reward."

Again, *hold that fast which thou hast, that no man take thy crown* (Revelation 3:11). In simpler terminology, God is saying, "Hang on to your earned crown and do not let anyone entice you, mislead you, drag you down, or destroy the good works you have accumulated or you will suffer loss." Paul, led by the Holy Spirit, also declares in 1 Corinthians 9:27, *But I keep under my body, and bring it into subjection: lest that by any means, when I have preached to others, I myself should be a castaway* [a reject for rewards]. He could not mean the loss of salvation by this term because we have already seen that the "ashamed" are present at heaven's roll call, though saved by fire. Instead, Paul is saying, "Look, I am a red-blooded man with desires similar to others. However, I simply will not allow my flesh to control me. Instead, I constantly battle and batter my fleshly appetites into subjection. Yes, I keep my bodily appetites under control lest I lose everything I have ever earned."

Now if this was true for Paul, it is equally true for all. In fact, Paul's service record is unparalleled in the history of Christendom. No one suffered as he did except the Lord Jesus himself. Listen to the list of "good works" Paul accumulated in 2 Corinthians 11:23-27:

In labours more abundant, in stripes above measure, in prisons more frequent, in deaths oft. Of the Jews five times received I forty stripes save one. Thrice was I beaten with rods, once was I stoned, thrice I suffered shipwreck, a night and a day I have been in the deep; In journeyings often, in perils of water, in perils of robbers, in perils by mine own countrymen, in perils by the heathen, in perils in the city, in perils in the wilderness, in perils in the sea, in perils among false brethren; In weariness and painfulness, in watchings often, in hunger and thirst, in fastings often, in cold and nakedness.

Wow! What a servant of God—beaten, battered, stoned, crushed, robbed, persecuted, hated, and starved. Surely this portfolio of earned works would bring Paul heaven's greatest "Oscar." It would if he remained faithful! Remember, he said as quoted earlier, "If I did not keep my body under and bring it into subjection, I myself would be a castaway, disapproved, and rejected for heaven's 'Emmy Awards.' Therefore, I fight the good fight of faith—fight the world, the flesh, and the devil—so that my Saviour will say to me in that day, 'Well done, thou good and faithful servant.'"

How about YOU, Christian? If the Judgment Seat took place within the next 24 hours, would you lose some or all of your rewards? Millions are going home ashamed, embarrassed, or red-faced!

Tears in Heaven

The result will be intermittent weeping for 1,007 years. This is proven by studying the chronological outline of the Book of Revelation. Chapter 1, verse 19, states, *Write the things which thou hast seen, and the things which are, and the things which shall be hereafter*. One immediately notices the three tenses of the English language—past, present, and future. Chapter 1 is the past, Chapter 2 and 3 contain the present, and Chapters 4 through 22 reveal the future.

We are presently awaiting the homegoing of believers—the Rapture—which is described in Revelation 4:1 when God says, *Come up hither*. The seven years of Tribulation follow in Chapter 6 through 18. Christ returns to earth as King of kings and Lord of lords in Chapter 19, verses 11-16, rules the earth for 1,000 years (see chapter 20:4-6), and judges the world after His millennial reign (see chapter 20:11-15). Then, finally and forever, God wipes away all tears from the eyes of His children (see chapter 21:4). Thus, from the Rapture call in Revelation 4:1 to the wiping away of tears in Revelation 21:4, there is intermittent and spasmodic weeping for 1,007 years!

Is your foolish episode with the world that important to you? Will it be worth it all when we see Jesus? Turn from the path of sin to the path of service, and prepare for a glorious, triumphant entrance into the presence of the King!

Other Books by Jack Van Impe

Heart Disease in Christ's Body
Shocking! Explosive! Documented! A ringing defense of historic, biblical Fundamentalism and a call for love and cooperation among all members of the body of Christ. $7

11:59...and Counting!
What does the future hold for you and your loved ones? The questions that plague humanity are answered in this detailed account of mankind's march toward the Tribulation, Armageddon, and the hour of Christ's return. $7

Israel's Final Holocaust
Over 218,000 in print! One of the most helpful explanations of Israel's role in end-time Bible prophecies ever published. What will the final holocaust be...and how will it affect you? $5

ALCOHOL: The Beloved Enemy
Liquor and the Bible. Filled with wisdom and reasoning, this important book thoroughly covers the alcohol question. Includes historic background, current research, and statistics that may shock you. Bible help for a major problem. $5

Revelation Revealed
Re-released! Yes, you *can* understand what many consider to be the most complex book in the Bible. Dr. Van Impe's verse-by-verse teaching reveals the meaning of this prophetic treasure. $5

Great Salvation Themes
Do you have unsaved loved ones...and don't know quite how to reach them? This book includes inspired messages by Dr. Van Impe that have been used to win thousands of souls through radio, TV, and city-wide crusades. $5

The Baptism of the Holy Spirit
Dr. Van Impe's easy-to-understand study of who the Holy Spirit is, what He does, and why His baptism is for every believer. Includes what the Bible says about the personality, attributes, gifts, fruit, and power of the Holy Spirit. $2

God! I'm Suffering, Are You Listening?

Why do good people go through seemingly senseless suffering? Dr. Van Impe explains from a biblical perspective why even Christians suffer and the best way to make the most of misfortune. $2

The Happy Home: Child Rearing

Many parents are confused about how to raise their children to love and serve God. Dr. Van Impe provides sound Bible principles, as well as practical advice for raising children to be happy Christian adults. $2

America, Israel, Russia, and World War III

What will the end of the world be? Is a nuclear holocaust inevitable? Dr. Van Impe explains how Bible prophecy is being fulfilled, and the roles America, Israel, and Russia will play in the Battle of Armageddon. $2

Escape the Second Death

Five powerful salvation messages especially directed to the unsaved. A great witnessing tool. Explains the Bible way to be born again. (Excerpted from *Great Salvation Themes* .) $2

Exorcism and the Spirit World

What every Christian should know about Satan, demons, and demonic activity. Reveals the dangers of association with the occult, describes Satan worship, and tells how to defeat demon forces through the delivering power of the Holy Spirit. $2

The True Gospel

The only "good news" is that Christ died for our sins, was buried, and rose again. There is no other good news. Dr. Van Impe also covers Christ's last seven sayings upon the cross, and the importance of His resurrection. $2

Everything you always wanted to know about Prophecy

But didn't know who to ask! Dr. Van Impe answers questions on the Rapture, the Judgment seat of Christ, the Tribulation, and more. Headlines and international events interpreted in the light of Christ's soon return. This booklet will challenge you to live a life of holiness and service. $2

Can America Survive?
NEW EDITION! This dynamic book deals with where we've come from as a nation, where we are now, and what the future holds. Thoughtful, biblical answers for more than 30 compelling questions facing every concerned Christian today! $2

The Judgment Seat of Christ
Sheds light on the misunderstood subject of God's judgment. Covers the five judgments of the Bible, including the judgment of works, and a special section on the believer's crowns to be awarded on Judgment Day. $2

This Is Christianity
Millions who claim to be Christians—including church members—are not because they have never been born again. The message of this book will help you understand this vital subject and know what it means to be a follower of Christ. $2

The Cost of Discipleship and Revival
To be a true follower of Jesus Christ, the Bible says you must take up your cross and die to self. But just what kind of price do you have to pay? Find the answer, plus keys to revival, in the pages of this enlightening book. $2

What Must I Do to Be Lost?
Are you trusting in the traditions of men, your church, your good works? All the doctrines of the church will not get you into heaven. There is only one way to be saved—find out how in the pages of this book. $2

Religious Reprobates and Saved Sinners
A timely message by Dr. Van Impe that distinguishes "religion" from genuine salvation. If you've ever wondered how to separate the wolves from the sheep, you must read this frank, tell-it-like-it-is booklet! $2

AIDS: 150 Million 1991
Now in print! Contains the unedited transcript of the TV special, documenting the dangers of this deadly disease. A shocking exposé! $2

JACK VAN IMPE MINISTRIES
ORDER FORM

QTY	DESCRIPTION	PRICE EACH	TOTAL
	SIN'S EXPLOSION	$7	
	HEART DISEASE IN CHRIST'S BODY	$7	
	11:59... AND COUNTING!	$7	
	ISRAEL'S FINAL HOLOCAUST	$5	
	ALCOHOL: THE BELOVED ENEMY	$5	
	REVELATION REVEALED	$5	
	GREAT SALVATION THEMES	$5	
	THE BAPTISM OF THE HOLY SPIRIT	$2	
	GOD! I'M SUFFERING, ARE YOU LISTENING?	$2	
	THE HAPPY HOME: CHILD REARING	$2	
	AMERICA, ISRAEL, RUSSIA, AND WORLD WAR III	$2	
	ESCAPE THE SECOND DEATH	$2	
	EXORCISM AND THE SPIRIT WORLD	$2	
	THE TRUE GOSPEL	$2	

SUBTOTAL A

*ORDER FORM CONTINUED NEXT PAGE.

QTY	DESCRIPTION	PRICE EACH	TOTAL
	EVERYTHING YOU ALWAYS WANTED TO KNOW ABOUT PROPHECY	$2	
	CAN AMERICA SURVIVE?	$2	
	THE JUDGMENT SEAT OF CHRIST	$2	
	THIS IS CHRISTIANITY	$2	
	THE COST OF DISCIPLESHIP AND REVIVAL	$2	
	WHAT MUST I DO TO BE LOST?	$2	
	RELIGIOUS REPROBATES AND SAVED SINNERS	$2	
	AIDS: 150 MILLION 1991	$2	

SUBTOTAL B

SUBTOTAL A

TOTAL AMOUNT ENCLOSED

NAME _____

ADDRESS _____

CITY _____STATE _____ZIP _____

Please tear out Order Form and send to:
   Jack Van Impe Ministries
   Box J • Royal Oak, Michigan 48068
   In Canada: Box 1717, Postal Station A
   Windsor, Ontario N9A 6Y1

JACK VAN IMPE MINISTRIES
ORDER FORM

QTY	DESCRIPTION	PRICE EACH	TOTAL
	SIN'S EXPLOSION	$7	
	HEART DISEASE IN CHRIST'S BODY	$7	
	11:59... AND COUNTING!	$7	
	ISRAEL'S FINAL HOLOCAUST	$5	
	ALCOHOL: THE BELOVED ENEMY	$5	
	REVELATION REVEALED	$5	
	GREAT SALVATION THEMES	$5	
	THE BAPTISM OF THE HOLY SPIRIT	$2	
	GOD! I'M SUFFERING, ARE YOU LISTENING?	$2	
	THE HAPPY HOME: CHILD REARING	$2	
	AMERICA, ISRAEL, RUSSIA, AND WORLD WAR III	$2	
	ESCAPE THE SECOND DEATH	$2	
	EXORCISM AND THE SPIRIT WORLD	$2	
	THE TRUE GOSPEL	$2	

SUBTOTAL A

*ORDER FORM CONTINUED NEXT PAGE.

QTY	DESCRIPTION	PRICE EACH	TOTAL
	EVERYTHING YOU ALWAYS WANTED TO KNOW ABOUT PROPHECY	$2	
	CAN AMERICA SURVIVE?	$2	
	THE JUDGMENT SEAT OF CHRIST	$2	
	THIS IS CHRISTIANITY	$2	
	THE COST OF DISCIPLESHIP AND REVIVAL	$2	
	WHAT MUST I DO TO BE LOST?	$2	
	RELIGIOUS REPROBATES AND SAVED SINNERS	$2	
	AIDS: 150 MILLION 1991	$2	

SUBTOTAL B

SUBTOTAL A

TOTAL AMOUNT ENCLOSED

NAME _____

ADDRESS _____

CITY _____STATE _____ZIP _____

Please tear out Order Form and send to:
Jack Van Impe Ministries
Box J • Royal Oak, Michigan 48068
In Canada: Box 1717, Postal Station A
Windsor, Ontario N9A 6Y1